CHAPTERS ON CHAUCER

LONDON: GEOFFREY CUMBERLEGE
OXFORD UNIVERSITY PRESS

CHAPTERS ON CHAUCER

By

KEMP MALONE

BALTIMORE
THE JOHNS HOPKINS PRESS
1951

PRINTED IN THE UNITED STATES OF AMERICA
BY J. H. FURST COMPANY, BALTIMORE, MARYLAND

To

MY MOTHER

AND THE MEMORY OF

MY FATHER

PREFACE

All eleven chapters of this book first took shape as lectures. The first five, and the last three, were originally prepared for undergraduate audiences at the University of California (1949) and the University of London (1948) respectively. The two *Troilus* chapters grew out of a study of openings and endings which I made some years ago for my Chaucer seminary. Chapter VIII is an expanded or rather a completed version of a much shorter paper read, by invitation, at a meeting of a learned society and later published in a learned journal (*ELH* 13.38-45). Parts of Chapters V and X have also appeared, in somewhat altered form, in learned journals: *PAPS* 94. 317-320 and *ES* 31. 209-215. I wish to thank the editors for letting me keep these passages in the present volume. My thanks also to W. H. Clemen for permission to quote a passage from his book *Der junge Chaucer*, and to the following publishers for leave to quote passages from publications of theirs:

The Clarendon Press: *The Evolution of England*, by J. A. Williamson
Columbia Univ. Press: *Chaucer's World*, by Edith Rickert
Harvard Univ. Press: *Chaucer and his Poetry*, by G. L. Kittredge
Henry Holt and Co.: *The Best of the Canterbury Tales* (ed. J. M. Manly) and *Some New Light on Chaucer*, by J. M. Manly
Houghton Mifflin Co.: *The Poetry of Chaucer*, by R. K. Root

The book as a whole is meant for readers who have some acquaintance with Chaucer's writings but are not professional Chaucerians, though I think that much of what I have to say will prove of interest to specialists as well. My chapters owe a great deal, of course, to earlier students of Chaucer, on whose labors we present-day workers in the field must build. I should not be bringing out this book, however, if I did not believe it to have freshness of approach and interpretative values of its own.

K. M.

TABLE OF CONTENTS

CHAPTER I

GEOFFREY CHAUCER AND THE FOURTEENTH
CENTURY

THE ENGLISH had a flourishing and extensive literature in the so-called Dark Ages, although most of
that literature has not come down to us — only a very
small part of it has withstood the tooth of time. Our
earliest surviving verse goes back to the sixth century,
and in the course of the seventh, eighth, ninth, tenth, and
eleventh centuries a large number of poems and prose
pieces were written, many of them admirable specimens
of literary art, and at least one of them, *Beowulf*, a work
of outstanding genius, one of the chief glories of English
literature as a whole.

If such was the achievement of the Dark Ages in
England, one might legitimately expect even greater things
in the twelfth and thirteenth centuries, for these were the
centuries in which medieval civilization reached its height
and produced masterpieces unexcelled before or since. It
was in the twelfth and thirteenth centuries that Gothic
architecture took shape and flourished in western Europe.
It was then that most of the masterpieces of medieval
literature were composed, masterpieces like the *Divine
Comedy* of Dante, the Icelandic sagas, the *Gesta Danorum*
of Saxo Grammaticus, and the *Tristan* of Gottfried von
Strassburg. The famous French epic, the *Song of Roland*,
dates from the beginning of the twelfth century, and in
that century and the next French literature got its start
and grew great. But its older sister, English literature,

1

during the same period underwent a disastrous decline, almost to the point of extinction, and not until the fourteenth century, when the great days of the Middle Ages were over, do we again find vigorous and significant literary activity in English. The literary history of England in the Middle Ages is unique. No other country of Europe rose so high in the period before 1100; no other country of Europe sank so low in the period after 1100.

It was, of course, the Norman Conquest which brought about this tremendous, this catastrophic decline in English literary culture. The worst fate that can befall any nation is dominance by men of an alien tongue. In the nature of the case the speech of the rulers becomes the chief vehicle of culture, the medium in which the civilizing forces of the time are given expression, and the hapless subjects, few of whom ever succeed in mastering a language not their own, are cut off from the main stream of civilization and stand condemned, not only to physical serfdom but also to spiritual degradation. Such was the fate which loomed before the English nation when Harold fell at Hastings.

And yet, in the second half of the fourteenth century, after 300 years during which French remained the language of the upper classes in England, we find English culture not only still alive but come into its own again. This survival and ultimate triumph in the face of conditions so adverse is one of the miracles of history. Or, rather, it bears eloquent witness to the strength of the English nationalism which King Alfred and his successors had built up. Here as always the fortress and citadel of the national culture was the national language, that English speech which not only set off the conquered from their French masters by an ever present outward sign, but also served as the great vehicle of the national spirit, and the chief barrier against the constant progress of the

French conquest, which, not stopping with political domination and economic exploitation, tended to wipe out all traces of English culture and to make the English people into low-grade Frenchmen.

Thanks to its rich literary heritage, handed down from the days of freedom, the English language was able to maintain itself as a written as well as a spoken tongue. English monks and priests kept on writing in their native speech, clinging stubbornly to a tradition not at all characteristic of the medieval Church in general but highly characteristic of the Church of England, and this in virtue of a practice centuries old and promoted by King Alfred himself, the father of English prose. Literature in England, prose and verse alike, continued to be cultivated to some degree in the darkest years of the French domination, and clergy joined hands with laity in maintaining the inherited verse forms alongside the rimes and meters which in other Germanic lands (Iceland excepted) had won a complete victory. The old alliterative measure was not given up, indeed, until Tudor times, and has left its mark on our poetical tradition and practice to the present day. The great literary revival of the fourteenth century proves the vitality of English literary tradition.

Here we cannot make any study of this great literary revival as a whole. We must confine ourselves to its chief figure, Geoffrey Chaucer. This is the easier to do because Chaucer stands somewhat apart from the native literary movement which produced *Piers Plowman, Gawain and the Green Knight,* and other masterpieces of his day. These compositions were done in the old alliterative measure and carry on, directly, the literary tradition of Old English times. Chaucer knew alliterative verse; he refers to it in his writings. But he did not choose to follow it. Likewise he made no use of the old poetical vocabulary, the poetic diction inherited from Old English and still current in the metrical romances and alliterative poems of the fourteenth century. In meter and diction Chaucer was an innovator, so far as English was concerned. Let me hasten to add that he did not invent meters or words, so far as we know, although in a number of cases he seems to have been the first to use a given meter, or a given word, in English poetry. He took his meters from the international stock, and many of his words came from the same source. For Chaucer was a citizen of the world.

Geoffrey Chaucer was born and brought up in London, and at an early age he became a member of the royal court. He kept these court connections all his life. He was a servant of the king, and of various princes, in many capacities. Such service in those days was not so highly specialized as it now is, and we search in vain for a modern label which will fit Chaucer's work. He was a diplomat, sent on missions to France and Italy. He was a civil servant, collecting customs duties and doing many other jobs that the king needed to have done. He was a soldier, fighting for the king in the French wars. All his life his associations were with the court, with the people who ruled England. He made his living not by writing but by serving the king at home and abroad. His work and his associations made him at home almost everywhere in western Europe. He knew at least three languages besides English: Latin, French, and Italian. He was widely read in Latin, French, and Italian literature. When he wrote verse, it was easy and natural for him to use the meters then fashionable in western Europe generally, meters nearly all handed down from Greece and Rome, and embellished by a system of rimes that had first become familiar in the Latin hymns of the Church and had gradually been taken up in all the vernaculars: not only in French, Spanish, and Italian but also in German, Scandinavian, and English verse.

Chaucer's diction, like his meters, came in part from the world of international affairs and of international culture in which he habitually moved. Chaucer knew lots of long words of foreign origin and if such words were current in the English of his day he did not hesitate to use them in his verse. His willingness to do so may not seem very startling to the modern reader, but up to the fourteenth century English poets had steered pretty clear of foreign words, on the whole. A few such words had crept into use, but the poetic vocabulary had remained overwhelmingly native. Poetry is always much slower than prose to take alien elements, and this was very strikingly the case with traditional English poetry, which depended largely on a special poetic vocabulary for its effects.

Chaucer's practice in this matter may be described as follows. He rejected altogether the old words that had survived in poetic usage but were no longer used in actual speech. He kept rhetorical diction (that is, the " high style " taught in the treatises on rhetoric, a heritage from classical antiquity) wherever it seemed to him appropriate or effective. Otherwise he used a colloquial style, sometimes more or less varied to fit the speaker. His characters, including himself, talk in the ordinary everyday speech of fourteenth-century England, though they talk much better than such people ever do in real life. Chaucer's language is simply the language spoken in his home town, London, by cultivated people, in the fourteenth century. It abounds in clichés, set phrases, stereotyped expressions, or the like, but few of these are locutions found only in literature and freighted with centuries of poetic association; they are nearly all current coins of speech. Even such a figure as *ful lyk a fiers leoun*, obviously literary in origin, belonged to common speech, and tags like *as to my doom* ' in my opinion ' were expressions of every day.

In his themes, again, and in the way he treated them,

Chaucer was international-minded. He started out with subjects and methods of treatment fashionable in the western Europe of his day. He made no effort to revive the glories of the English literary past. In fact, he probably knew little or nothing about these glories. He wrote for his own day. I may add that he made no effort to imitate the Latin classics either, not to mention the Greek classics, with which he was not familiar. Chaucer lived when the so-called Italian Renaissance was beginning, and he knew fourteenth-century Italy, but the Renaissance as a movement had little or no influence on him. He remained a full-fledged medieval. He seems to have written, in his youth, a good many lyrics, but few of these have come down to us and nearly all his important work lies in the field of narrative poetry. He told stories in verse.

Chaucer got most of his stories from books, and told them again in his own way, following his sources closely sometimes and very freely indeed at other times. So far as we know, he never invented a story, though we have not been able to find the exact sources of some of his poems. Certain tales that he told give every indication of having had oral sources. This holds particularly of the smutty stories. For instance, the miller's tale and the reeve's tale, Chaucer's two stories of university life, are exceedingly smutty and we have found no written sources for them; Chaucer may have picked them up on visits to Oxford and Cambridge, or in conversation with Oxford and Cambridge men.

Chaucer's practice of using stories already in circulation, instead of inventing new ones, was regular in his time, and continued to be regular for a long time to come. Shakespeare, as everybody knows, did the same thing. Our modern insistence on originality would have seemed a mad idea to our forefathers. Obviously (they would have said) the best stories are the old stories, the stories that have stood the test of time, the stories that are already familiar to the reading public. If your readers know the story you are telling they will enjoy your version of it much better than they would enjoy something quite new and strange to them. For one thing, knowing what to expect, the strain on their nervous systems would be much less, and they would have much less trouble seeing the point you were making.

This principle is familiar to us all in jokes. If you have never heard a joke before, you often have to use your wits and, even so, you may fail to get the point. This is embarrassing both to you and to the one who is telling the joke. How much better it works out if you have heard the joke before! Then you laugh at the proper time and the joker enjoys your appreciation and is impressed by your intelligence. In much the same way most people enjoy hearing again a piece of music which they have heard many times before, and very few people enjoy music which is new and strange to them. They must become familiar with it before they can like it.

Medieval stories usually followed familiar patterns, and the hearers or readers knew in advance what they were going to get. Yet novelty was not wanting. Each author had his own style, his own way of handling the familiar matter, and these individual differences gave to each composition its particular flavor. Things are not really so very different today, in spite of our emphasis on originality. We change the names and situations about a bit, but most plots fall into a few familiar types: love stories, adventure stories, detective stories and the like; and the discerning reader can often predict the course of events in general if not in detail.

Most of our space in this book will be given to Chaucer's two masterpieces, *Troilus and Criseyde* and *The Canterbury Tales*. Some of his other poems will also be taken up. But before we begin our study of Chaucer's poetry we had better have a look at Chaucer's world. The fourteenth century in England was a period of transition. The feudal system of lords and serfs was changing, not without violence, into a society in which all men were free, though far from equal. The old lords of the manor still dominated the countryside, but in the towns a so-called middle class had arisen which was growing steadily in riches and power. Representatives of these townsmen, and of the country gentry, were admitted to the sessions of parliament to hear what decisions had been made and, through a spokesman (whence the term " speaker " still in use), to give their consent to a grant of money to the king. They also had the right of petition. The parliament proper was made up of the lords spiritual and temporal (that is, bishops, abbots, and nobles). These debated the questions brought before the meeting, and seats were provided for them, but the commoners had to stand and listen in silence. They had meetings of their own beforehand, of course, to decide what instructions to give to their " speaker," and eventually these meetings became the sessions of the House of Commons. Chaucer himself once (in 1386) served in the Commons; he represented the shire of Kent. By that time the Commons had won for themselves a good deal of power, chiefly because of the weakness of the king and the troubles of the realm.

Such troubles were nothing new, of course. Throughout medieval times, and later still, the maintenance of law and order was indeed a precarious and uncertain business. Much depended on the character of the king. Under a weak ruler like Stephen, anarchy reigned. Under a strong ruler like Henry II, order of a kind might be reëstablished. Chaucer wrote in a period when the English scepter was in feeble hands: Edward III had fallen into an early dotage, and his successor Richard II proved unfit to govern. The ravages of the Black Death, and the evils that always go with warfare, made the domestic misrule even harder to bear. So many ablebodied men had died of the plague or been killed or maimed in the French wars that the supply of workmen fell grievously short of the demand, goods of all kinds, even food, became scarce, and prices rose to match. Parliament passed laws to keep wages down but succeeded only in infuriating the lower classes, who at length took arms and rose in revolt against their oppressors, demanding nothing less than the abolition of serfdom, and its replacement by a system of fixed rentals. King Richard, then a mere boy, rode out to meet the rebels, listened to what they said, pardoned them for their rebellion, and promised them that the services they owed their lords would be commuted into a payment of rent. They took him at his word and dispersed peaceably. But their loyalty proved their undoing. The king did not keep his promise, the leaders of the peasants were hunted down, and the rising failed. Well might the poor serfs say, " we are men, made in God's image, and they treat us like beasts." It took a hundred years more of unremitting effort to rid England altogether of serfdom, and it was not until late in the nineteenth century that agricultural laborers won the right to vote.

In Chaucer's day the peasants were not the only ones to resort to violence. The townsmen too had their grievances and used force to redress them. The soldiers back from the French wars had had plenty of practice abroad in preying on the civilian population, and many of them kept this up after their homecoming, with their fellow-countrymen for prey. But the barons, as always, were the worst offenders against law and order. They had won their holdings by force of arms in the Norman Conquest of the eleventh century, and three centuries later they were still an unruly lot. Indeed, they grew worse rather

than better as time went on, until in the fifteenth century
orderly government gave place to a state of things not far
removed from anarchy. A recent historian thus describes
the baronage of the fourteenth and fifteenth centuries (J.
A. Williamson, *Evolution of England*, p. 150):

The baronage . . . may be allowed one virtue, that of readiness to
stake their lives in battle or conspiracy. Their courage was high
indeed, but all their other qualities were low, and thus the use to
which they put their virtue rendered it something near a vice. Of
mercy, justice, public spirit, religious zeal, faithfulness, the instances
are few and far between. The ideals of chivalry were more talked
about than ever, . . . and ever more rarely practised. . . . The romance
of chivalry gilded a reality of crime, . . . Intellects were vigorous;
souls slept.

As the state grew more and more incapable of performing its proper function in society, the maintenance of law
and order, so the Church grew more and more incapable
of performing *her* true function, the cure of souls. Medieval culture, both secular and religious, was breaking
down. Chaucer himself bears abundant witness to the
worldliness and corruption so widespread among the clergy
in those days. We shall take up in due course his own
treatment of this subject. Here it will be enough to say
that his words are borne out by an overwhelming mass of
evidence drawn from many trustworthy sources.

The evil ways into which so many churchmen had fallen
moved the pious to indignation, and in England a great
reformer arose, John Wiclif. He was a high official of
Oxford University, and the religious movement which he
set going might well be called the first Oxford movement.
It was to be followed, in the eighteenth century, by an
even greater and far more successful movement of religious
reform, led by another Oxford man, John Wesley. The
third Oxford movement, the one which now goes by that
name, started about a hundred years after the second and

had several leaders, the most famous of whom, John Henry Newman, finally left the Church of England and became a Roman Catholic. The Oxford movement of Chaucer's day began as a protest against the worldliness and immorality of the clergy. Wiclif, the leader of the movement, believed that the root of the evils that beset the Church was love of worldly goods. To quote,

Jesus Christ was poor in his life, that he had no house of his own by worldly title to rest his head therein, as he himself saith in the gospel. And St Peter was so poor that he had neither silver nor gold to give a poor crooked man, as Peter witnesseth in the book of Apostles' deeds. St Paul was so poor of worldly goods that he worked with his hands for his livelihood and his fellows', and suffered much persecution, and waking of great thought for all churches in Christendom, as he himself witnesseth in many places of holy writ. And St Bernard writeth to the Pope, that in this worldly array, and plenty of lands and gold and silver, he is successor of Constantine the Emperor, and not of Jesus Christ and his disciples. And Jesus confirming this testament said to his apostles after his rising from death to life, " My Father sent me and I send you," that is, to labor and persecution, and poverty and hunger and martyrdom in this world, and not to worldly pomp such as the clergy now practise. By this it seemeth that all these worldly clergy having secular lordship, with array of worldly vanity, are hugely cursed of God and man, for they do against the rightful testament of Christ and his apostles. (modernized from the Middle English text in F. Mossé, *Moyen-Anglais* I 313 f.).

We shall see later that Chaucer felt much as Wiclif did about this matter. But Wiclif, true reformer that he was, took the consequences of his position without hesitation. If he had had his will, he would have made a clean sweep of all the possessions of the Church, and he would have reduced to holy poverty all men in holy orders, from the Pope down. Chaucer, on the contrary, had no remedies to propose. He praised the poor clerics, and satirized the rich ones, and let it go at that. He took the world as he found it, and set down what he saw in a spirit critical enough but far removed from the righteous indignation of the reformer. Chaucer was first of all an artist, and he wrote accordingly, using what went on about him as grist to his artistic mill. Not that his writings lack edifying, didactic elements. His reading public expected of him works that gave *sentence* as well as *solas*, instruction as well as enjoyment, and, like Shakespeare, he saw to it that his public got what it wanted. But his chief interest lay in his art, not in his message. He was a story-teller, not a propagandist; a poet, not a preacher.

The great schism in the western church, which began in 1378 and lasted for more than 70 years, had less effect on the fortunes of Wiclif and his movement than one might have expected. The spectacle of two popes, each claiming to be the vicar of Christ and each consigning the other to eternal damnation, was not edifying, but for political reasons England gave her support to Urban VI and his successors. In the minds of the English rulers, and indeed of most Englishmen who took any interest in European politics, opposition to France was the decisive consideration, and this attitude of theirs led them quite naturally (one might almost say automatically) to stand with Urban and to oppose his French-supported rival Clement. Wiclif himself took no such stand, it is true. He thought in religious terms, and had only scorn for the rival popes, who as he saw it were fighting each other for worldly power. If he could have brought his patron, John of Gaunt, to share his views the Protestant Reformation might have begun in fourteenth-century England, instead of in sixteenth-century Germany. But John of Gaunt was a politician, not a reformer. He found Wiclif useful in the dispute with Pope Gregory XI over the tribute which King John had obligated England to pay to the popes but which the popes had long been unable to collect. Here Wiclif's views about clerical poverty, and his belief that the Church should not concern herself with worldly matters, made him just the man to represent the Crown in opposing the papal claims. But when he called *both* the rival popes of the great schism anti-Christ he showed himself to be hopelessly unpolitical, and other utterances of his that smacked of what would later be called Protestantism lost him the backing of John of Gaunt and at last even of his university, which stood behind him as long as safety permitted. He spent his last years in a country parsonage, training " poor priests " (that is, priests vowed to poverty) to carry on his work. These priests, the so-called Lollards, spread Wiclif's gospel of righteousness and unworldliness all over England, but savage persecution, including many burnings at the stake for heresy, kept their numbers low. Wiclif himself died and was buried peacefully enough, before the persecution had reached its height, but later, at the behest of Pope Martin V, his body was dug up and burned. Thus he joined the company of his martyred followers.

Though Wiclif in his theology anticipated the Protestantism of the sixteenth century, in his philosophical thinking he clung to the realism dominant in the thirteenth century. That is to say, he taught the reality of universals, whereas his colleague at Oxford, the Franciscan friar William of Occam, upheld and led to triumph the nominalist view of things, according to which universals are mere names and only the particular has reality. If we must base our reasoning on the particulars of which our five senses give us experience, we can learn to know much but we must be content to take much on faith: for instance, the truths of revealed religion. This philosophically grounded opposition of faith and reason prepared the way for the rise of experimental science. On the religious side, it smoothed the path to mysticism. For the intellectual life too, then, the age of Chaucer was an age of transition.

Nowadays learned Englishmen like Wiclif and William of Occam would write in English. Since they lived in the fourteenth century, however, they wrote in Latin. In so doing they were merely conforming to custom. Throughout the Middle Ages, and well into modern times, Latin was the official tongue of western Christendom. In this tongue the services of the Church were held, and works of learning were written, books designed for international circulation. The various vernaculars (English, French, German, etc.) were of course the natural vehicles, each in its own country, for the literature of entertainment, as also for works written for the instruction of the unschooled masses. Wiclif, for instance, wrote many sermons in English. The average parish priest was hardly competent to compose a sermon of his own, but he could read to the congregation a sermon composed by somebody else, and this was what he usually did if he preached at all. Large collections of English sermons had been available since the tenth century, for the use of preachers. Many of these sermons were masterpieces of literary prose, and if the priest who used them had any oratorical gifts he could count on attentive hearers. Medieval congregations liked to hear sermons. The sermon was the only part of the service they could understand, as everything else was in Latin, and the Latin words, if they could be heard at all, could not be identified by even a skilled Latinist, so indistinct or obscured was the pronunciation.

But most parish priests were none too good as preachers, and their parishioners had to depend upon visiting ecclesiastics for really stirring sermons. The bishop might be expected to preach when he came, but even bishops are often dull, and it was friar and pardoner who specialized in sermons guaranteed to rouse the congregation. Chaucer includes such a sermon in his *Canterbury Tales*. He departs from realism when he has his pardoner preach in iambic pentameter rimed couplets, but the sermon remains an excellent one of its kind. It begins thus:

C 463   In Flaundres whylom was a companye
        Of yonge folk, that haunteden folye,
        As ryot, hasard, stewes, and tavernes,
        Wheras, with harpes, lutes, and giternes,
        They daunce and pley at dees both day and night,
        And ete also and drinken over hir might.

The preacher starts off, as you see, with a story. Since this is a sermon, the story may be expected to have a moral. Such a story, used for moral instruction, is technically known as an *exemplum*. It gets its name from the fact that it serves as an example, an illustration, of the moral point which the preacher is trying to drive home. The pardoner's exemplum is unusual in that it makes two thirds of the sermon, leaving only a third of the whole for truly homiletic matter. In other words, the pardoner devotes most of his time in the pulpit to story-telling. But his congregation hardly objected to that.

The scene of the tale is set abroad, in rich, luxurious Flanders. This exotic setting, in itself enough to whet the appetite, is combined with a picture of youthful licentiousness calculated to stir the senses and fire the imagination of everybody in the congregation with any blood left in his veins. We get a catalog of the wicked doings of this company of young folk who were practising folly in Flanders. They were engaged in riotous living and gambling in whore-houses and taverns, where, to the accompaniment of lascivious music, they would dance and play at dice both day and night, gorging themselves all the while with fine food and strong drink. What a picture to paint for this country congregation! How they would revel in it, and lick their chops! But the pardoner, after a few more details, drops the story and preaches for quite a stretch against the sins of gluttony, gambling, and profanity. When he gets back to his exemplum, his company of young folk reappear as three rioters, whose drunken folly and avarice bring them to violent deaths. Then comes the moral of the story, which the pardoner drives home in eloquent words:

C 895   O cursed sinne, ful of cursednesse!
        O traytours homicyde, o wikkednesse!
        O glotonye, luxurie, and hasardrye!
        Thou blasphemour of Crist with vileinye
        And othes grete, of usage and of pryde!
        Allas! mankinde, how may it betyde,
        That to thy creatour, which that thee wroghte,
        And with his precious herte blood thee boghte,
        Thou art so fals and so unkinde, allas!

After a sermon so full of thrills one would expect the congregation to be swept off their feet. The pardoner was a scoundrel, and the gains he extracted from his hearers were ill-gotten, but the parishioners, when they gave him their nobles, sterlings, silver brooches, spoons, rings, or wool, surely thought he had given them their money's worth, and looked forward with eagerness to his next visit. Chaucer's world, like our own, loved to be humbugged.

In a university religious service the sermon, too, would be in Latin. Indeed, the students were required to speak Latin among themselves, even in their bedrooms. Needless to add, the professors lectured in Latin, and the examinations (which were normally oral, not written) were conducted in Latin. We know very little about the grammar-schools, where pupils were prepared for the university, but we may safely presume that the masters tried their best to make the schoolboys talk Latin and that in the upper forms some proficiency in Latin conversation was actually achieved. We know from Ælfric's *Colloquy* that English schoolboys practised Latin conversation in the tenth century, and if things got no better by the fourteenth they surely got no worse in this particular.

Children in the lower forms of the grammar-school of course had to construe their Latin in the vernacular, as they were mere beginners. According to the *Polychronicon* of Ranulf Higden (written about 1342), the vernacular used for construing was French:

Children in school, against the usage and manner of all other nations, are compelled for to leave their own language and for to construe their lessons and their things [i. e. Latin prayers] in French, and have [had to do so] since the Normans came first to England. Also, gentlemen's children are taught for to speak French from time that they are rocked in their cradles and can speak and play with a child's brooch [i. e. trinket]. (modernized from Trevisa).

John Trevisa, in his translation of Higden, interpolates here the following passage (which I give in modernized form):

This manner was much used tofore the first murrain [i. e. plague] and is since some deal changed. For John Cornwall, a master of grammar, changed the lore [i. e. art of teaching] in grammar-school and construction from French into English; and Richard Pencrych learned that manner of teaching [Latin] from him, and other men [learned] from Pencrych; so that now, the year of our Lord 1385, the ninth [year] of the second king Richard . . ., in all the grammar-schools of England children leave French and construe and learn in English, and have thereby advantage on one side and disadvantage on another; their advantage is that they learn their grammar in less time than children were wont to do; disadvantage is that now children of grammar-school know no more French than their left heel knows [French], and that is harm for them, if they shall pass the sea and travel in strange lands, and in many cases [i. e. occasions] also. Also gentlemen have now much left [i. e. given up] for to teach their children French.

Be it noted that what the children learned in school was Latin, not French or English. The teaching of English and other modern tongues did not establish itself in the school system until the nineteenth century. English as the language of instruction, however, as we have just seen, came back into the grammar-schools in the fourteenth century, after 300 years during which it had been displaced by French. At the same time English regained its old position in the life of the country generally, from the royal court down. Once more we have found the age of Chaucer an age of transition.

CHAPTER II

THE BOOK OF THE DUCHESS

IN ANY STUDY of Chaucer's poetic art one must ever bear in mind that he was a courtier, and that he found his audiences in palaces, not in halls of learning nor yet on the market-place. Chaucer wrote not only for his own day but also for his own public of lords and ladies, kings and queens. For the first time in 300 years the royal court welcomed an English poet and listened to his verse.

Courtly poetry in English had flourished for centuries in the good old days before the Norman Conquest, but after that catastrophe it died out for want of hearers: the old aristocracy had perished by the sword and the new rulers spoke only French and had no literary interests of any kind. William's two royal sons were no better than the Conqueror himself in this or any other respect, though Henry's queens both won record (accurate or no) for their patronage of scholars. Under Stephen anarchy kept literature down. With the change of dynasty in 1154 the royal court again became a literary center, but the new king, Henry II, though he was not a Norman, was very much a Frenchman, and his patronage, and that of his queen, were bestowed accordingly. Things got no better for another 200 years.

In remote parts of the country English speech and English song won back a foothold with the aristocracy earlier than in Westminster, but the English current in such provincial centers differed markedly from that of London, and the courtly poems composed in these local

20 CHAPTERS ON CHAUCER

dialects seem to have had a local circulation only. Thus, that masterpiece of courtly poetry, *Sir Gawain and the Green Knight*, survives in a single manuscript. If Chaucer had tried to read it, he would have tried in vain, one must suspect, although the *Gawain* poet was a contemporary of his. Certainly he would have needed a glossary not to be had in those days, though modern editors have provided us with one, luckily for our comfort.

One of the worst effects of the Norman Conquest was the loss of the linguistic unity which had grown up in Old English times. By the end of the tenth century a standard literary English had developed and was in use all over England. The regional dialects lived on, of course, but came to be thought unsuitable for literary purposes. The King's English was the only kind of English deemed worthy of written record. If the nation had had a happier fate, this standard speech would have gone from triumph to triumph, and the poets of medieval England, whether of the north, the south, or the midlands, would have composed their verses in a tongue known to all. But the Normans undermined the foundations of this unity, not only by introducing French, but also by using it (alongside Latin) for all the practical purposes which the King's English had formerly served. In consequence, the old standard speech fell out of use, and nothing was left but the regional dialects, which held their own in the mouths of men. A standard literary speech is one of the fine flowers of civilization. Its existence in the tenth and eleventh centuries bears witness to the high state of culture in the England of that period. Its loss under Norman rule marks the cultural decline which the Norman Conquest brought about.

It was to be Chaucer's fortune to give literary prestige to his own dialect of English, the London speech which he used in all his writings and which, largely through him, soon became the standard medium of literary expression for all Englishmen. Other powerful influences were at work to the same end, it is true, but Chaucer's contribution, if not decisive, remains substantial and deserves our whole-hearted recognition. By this achievement he and his fellows gave to their country once again the linguistic unity which the Normans had taken from her. Thanks to this unity, all Britain in due course was won for English civilization, and English literary culture gained the tool without which its future glories could never have been realized. In helping to shape this tool to our use Chaucer made his most significant contribution to the Anglo-Saxon world.

We have seen that English courtly poetry died out after the Norman Conquest and that when Chaucer turned to poetical composition he found no native courtly tradition to draw upon. In France, however, a tradition of courtly poetry still lived, though it had seen its best days.[1] The major French work in this kind was the *Roman de la Rose,* an allegorical love-vision in which the rose represents the lover's ideal. Chaucer seems to have begun his poetical career by translating this poem into English. We do not

---

[1] The English courtly poetry of pre-Norman times belongs to heroic literary tradition. The poems are relatively short. They fall into two types, comparable to the epic and the panegyric of the ancients, though with significant differences. See my discussion in *A Literary History of England* (ed. Baugh, New York, 1948), pp. 45-59. The French courtly poetry upon which Chaucer drew belongs to a tradition later than the English one in origin and vogue: the romantic literary tradition of the twelfth and succeeding centuries. The poems deal with lovers and their ladies. The treatment of the love theme is highly conventionalized. Modern taste prefers the heroic to the romantic tradition of courtly poetry, but Chaucer had the genius to make the romantic stereotypes come alive. See further below.

Interestingly enough, the earliest French courtly poem which can be connected with the English court, David's lost poem on King Henry I, reminds one by its subject-matter of English courtly poetry. The poet may well have used an English poem as his model. We know that Marie de France, much later in the twelfth century, translated her *Fables* from an English original, now unhappily lost.

know whether he translated it all; only a fragment of his translation proper survives. But in nearly all his poems we find echoes of the *Roman de la Rose* time and again. Chaucer must have known the poem very well indeed, if not actually by heart. It was a treasure-house upon which he drew freely all his life.

Chaucer's first original poem of any length, the *Book of the Duchess*, was cast in the highly conventional form of a love-vision, but is in fact an elegy on the death (in 1369) of the Duchess Blanche, first wife of Chaucer's patron, John of Gaunt. The poem reveals at every turn Chaucer's dependence on French models — and his independence of them. Modern philologists have shown in detail that Chaucer, in composing his poem, used not only the *Roman de la Rose* but also poems by William of Machaut, Oton de Grandson, and John Froissart. Besides, he made some use of classical poets, chiefly Ovid. He drew on these sources to suit himself, sometimes translating a line or a passage literally, sometimes making changes in word or thought or both. He owed to his French sources not merely much of the wording of his poem but also its structural pattern and its theme of courtly love. Yet the *Book of the Duchess* differs profoundly from anything ever before composed in the courtly-love *genre*. Chaucer poured new wine into an old bottle, and while he was doing it he made the bottle over. We can better weigh his achievement when we have looked at the poem more narrowly.

The *Book of the Duchess* is a poem of 1334 lines, done in rimed iambic tetrameter couplets except for a couple of short passages which we shall consider later on. The poet purports to be telling the story of a personal experience of his, and he speaks in the first person throughout. He begins by saying that he cannot sleep and is a prey to melancholy. He has been in this state for eight years, and sees no hope of getting well, for only one physician can heal him. He does not tell us who this physician is, but everyone familiar with courtly love will know at once that Chaucer is talking about his lady, who, by denying him her favors, keeps him hopelessly love-sick. Chaucer is suffering from the pangs of unrequited love. His sleeplessness and melancholy are conventional symptoms of this sad state, and his prospects of recovery are slim indeed, since after eight years of devotion he has not been able to move his lady to take pity on him.

In not revealing the lady's name Chaucer was complying with one of the requirements of courtly-love etiquette, the requirement of secrecy. But his behavior as a lover would have been more courtly still if he had said nothing at all about her. Here he started out with the best intentions. After telling us of his sleeplessness and melancholy he goes on to say,

> 30 But men myght axe me why soo
> I may not sleepe, and what me is.
> But natheles, who aske this
> Leseth his asking trewely.
> Myselven can not telle why
> 35 The sothe.

By insisting that he himself does not know what is the matter with him, and why he cannot sleep, he seems to be covering his tracks reasonably well. But then he proceeds to uncover them:

> 35   But trewly, as I gesse,
> I holde hit be a siknesse
> That I have suffred this eight yeer,
> And yet my boote is never the ner;
> For there is physicien but oon
> 40 That may me hele.

After this confession there can be no possible doubt that Chaucer is love-sick. The cat is out of the bag, and the only thing left to do is drop the subject. That is exactly what Chaucer does:

> 40   But that is don.
>   Passe we over untill eft;
>   That wil not be, mot nede be left;
> 43   Our first mater is good to kepe.

Here ends what may be called the opening of the poem. Chaucer makes it sound very personal and intimate indeed, but he got the idea from one of his sources, the *Paradys d'Amours* of Froissart. His first 15 lines, in fact, are little more than a translation from Froissart. And the idea was not original with Froissart either. Medieval science taught that mental suffering might give rise to dreams, and in the courtly-love poetry of Chaucer's day a state of sleeplessness and melancholy made a conventional prelude to a love-vision. Chaucer's love-sickness, therefore, is not to be taken as genuine.[2] It is a conventional device, which leads up neatly enough, as we shall see, to the next phase of the action. It also gives a courtly atmosphere from the start, and introduces the speaker in a part which arouses sympathy and at the same time has a humorous aspect, for there is something ridiculous about an unsuccessful lover, particularly if he has danced attendance on the lady for eight years. Chaucer was not the man to miss a humorous effect, and his love-sickness here and elsewhere serves, among other things, to make us smile.

After telling of his chronic sleeplessness and melancholy, the poet goes on to say that the other night, when he saw he could not sleep, he sat up in bed and had someone give him a book to read. He thought that was a better way to kill time than playing chess or backgammon. In the book he found a tale that moved him to wonder. " This was the

[2] For a contrary view, see Margaret Galway, " Chaucer's Hopeless Love," *MLN* 60. 431-439. She identifies the lady as Joan of Kent, wife of the Black Prince and mother of King Richard II.

tale," he said, and proceeded to tell it. It was the story of
Ceyx and Alcyone, familiar to medieval readers in the
Metamorphoses of Ovid. Chaucer's French contemporary
Machaut had told this tale in his *Fonteinne Amoureuse,*
and Chaucer, in telling it once more, followed Machaut
rather than Ovid for the most part. Chaucer's version may
be summarized thus (lines 62-214) :

There was a king named Ceyx, who had a wife named Alcyone, " the
best that might bear life." It befell that Ceyx went on a voyage.
A storm sank his ship and he and all his men were drowned. When
he did not come back home his wife sorrowed much. At last she felt
she must have some word of him, and she prayed to Juno for help,
begging her for sleep and a dream which would tell her whether her
husband was alive or dead. The goddess answered her prayer,
putting her into a deep sleep and sending a messenger to the cave
of Morpheus, the god of sleep, with instructions to have Morpheus
enter into the dead body of Ceyx and make it speak to Alcyone
in a dream, revealing to her what had happened. The messenger
did his duty, and Morpheus followed the instructions he got. When
Alcyone learned the truth, she waked, saw nothing, cried " allas! "
and died three days later.

After telling this tale Chaucer apologizes for cutting
down Alcyone's last words to a mere " allas," explaining
that it would take too much time to tell more. He wants
to go back to his first topic, the sleeplessness which led
him to tell the tale of Ceyx and Alcyone.

221   For thus moche dar I seye wel,
       I had be dolven everydel,
       And ded, ryght thurgh defaute of slep,
       Yif I ne had red and take kep
       Of this tale next before. . . .
231   Whan I had red this tale wel,
       And overloked hyt everydel,
       Me thoughte wonder yf hit were so;
       For I had never herd speke, or tho,
       Of noo goddes that koude make
       Men to slepe, ne for to wake;

For I ne knew never god but oon.
And in my game I sayde anoon —
And yet me lyst ryght evel to pleye —
" Rather then that y shulde deye
Thorgh defaute of slepinge thus,
I wolde yive thilke Morpheus, . . .
246   I wil yive him the alderbeste
Yifte that ever he abod hys lyve.
And here on warde, ryght now, as blyve,
Yif he wol make me slepe a lyte,
Of down of pure dowves white
I wil yive him a fether-bed, . . .
254   And many a pilowe, . . .
261   this shal he have,
Yf I wiste where were hys cave,
Yf he kan make me slepe sone,
As did the goddesse quene Alcione. . . ."
270   I hadde unneth that word ysayd
Ryght thus as I have told hyt yow,
That sodeynly, I nyste how,
Such a luste anoon me took
To slepe, that ryght upon my book
Y fil asleepe, and therwith even
Me mette so ynly swete a sweven,
So wonderful, that never yit
Y trowe no man had the wyt
To konne wel my sweven rede; . . .
290   Loo, thus hyt was, thys was my sweven.

Here the poet says he would have been dead and buried for sheer want of sleep if he had not read and pondered this tale. Through it he learned, for the first time, about the gods of sleep. The thing seemed a miracle to him if it were so, and, though he was not a man given to playfulness, he amused himself by saying that he would make gifts to Morpheus better than that god had ever looked for in all his life, starting right now with a feather-bed and all that went with it, if Morpheus would only make him go to sleep at once, as Juno made Alcyone. The words had hardly left his mouth when he went to sleep right on his book, and then and there he dreamt a dream so wonderful that no man ever lived clever enough to interpret it rightly. The rest of the poem, except for the last few lines, is the story of the dream.

In the foregoing I have tried to keep Chaucer's tone as well as his thought. The lightness of his touch and the simplicity of his wording cannot be reproduced but they can at least be suggested. Neither the prayer for sleep nor the gift of the feather-bed is original with Chaucer; he got the one from Froissart, the other from Machaut. But he ties the two traits to each other and to the story of Ceyx and Alcyone in his own way. The feather-bed, as he brings it in, has a comic effect which it fails to have in the French poem, although there too it comes as a gift to Morpheus. Indeed, the whole soliloquy in bed (lines 240-269) was composed with humorous intent, as the *in my game* of line 238 makes plain. Worthy of special mention here is the proviso added to the description of the gifts promised to Morpheus: " this shall he have, if I knew where his cave might be " (lines 261-262). In effect, of course, the proviso cancels the promise and makes the whole thing more absurd than ever.

But the humorous touches are not restricted to the soliloquy. I cannot undertake to specify them all. It will be enough to point out that in this poem as elsewhere Chaucer's direct and indirect self-characterizations are meant to be funny. We must never forget that the poet's audience, or his public, as we now say, knew him personally. Knowing their man as they did, they would not be taken in when Chaucer said that never before then had he heard Morpheus spoken of, but his pretended lack of learning might well amuse them, and Chaucer expected his hearers to smile when he represented himself as ignorant of classical mythology. When he characterized himself as averse to fun-making (line 239), the smiles he got must have been broader still.

Chaucer's humor goes naturally with his lightness of touch, and with his beautifully colloquial style. Here he departs markedly from Machaut, whose French is polished but bookish and wanting in life and warmth. Now and then, it must be added, Chaucer shows himself a true son of his age and a true imitator of his French sources by falling into needless rhetorical elaboration. Such excessive elaboration appears, not only in individual passages, but also in the structure of the poem. It takes Chaucer 290 lines to put himself to sleep and start dreaming. One may contrast the Old English poem *Dream of the Rood*, where the poet's dream starts with the fourth line. Artistically speaking, the older poet gains much by making his introductory section short. But fourteenth-century taste favored the contrary procedure. Professor W. H. Clemen of Munich has given us an admirable discussion of the point. He says,[3]

> The story of Ceyx and Alcyone is for Chaucer the path by which he gradually gets closer to what he really wants to say. This story, as we shall see, is a parallel to the story told in the dream and leads up to it. Structurally considered, it means a further postponement of the actual theme of the poem, the choice of a bypath, an indirect form of expression, instead of an immediate beginning. This fondness for indirection, for a long artistic preparation, for an ornamental approach, is to be found in all Chaucer's early poems. He builds as it were a winding staircase of many steps, up which he slowly makes his way to his subject. This method of poetic composition . . . is alien to modern taste and regularly invites unfavorable criticism. Thus, R. K. Root says of the Ceyx-Halcyone episode: ". . . so slight is its connection with the main theme of the poem, that it constitutes a serious breach of artistic unity " (*Poetry of Chaucer*, p. 61). Nevertheless Chaucer's contemporaries, so far as we can judge, admired these long introductions and artificial frames or settings. The predilection for indirect means of expression, for adorning the train

---

[3] *Der junge Chaucer*, pp. 39-40. Quoted by the author's permission.

of thought with showy flourishes and an intricate scheme of presentation, was manifest in the style of the time. To it answers in the history of art that taste for complexity which stands out in the flamboyant style of late Gothic buildings. . . . [translation mine]

Luckily Chaucer had too much sense to yield himself unreservedly to the taste dominant in his time. And where he conformed to it, his genius made him put new life into the patterns within which he had to work.

We come now to the dream itself, the experience that Chaucer has been leading up to all along. Its main feature is a long dialog between himself and a knight clad in black, a dialog in which the man in black does nearly all the talking, Chaucer's part being limited to questions and comments meant to draw the man out, keep him talking until he has told his sad story in full. But the literary taste of the time being what it was, one must not expect the dreamer to meet the man in black at once. In the dream proper as well as in its preliminaries, the approach must be gradual and indirect. I will first give a summary of the dream up to the beginning of the dialog.

I dreamt (says Chaucer) that it was May, at daybreak. I lay in bed all naked, looking about me. I had been wakened by the singing of the birds. They were perched on the tiles of my roof and there they were busy making the most delightful music. My room was well ornamented, and all the windows were well glazed with clear glass, not one pane broken. It was a joy to behold it, for in the glazing was wrought all the story of Troy and Medea and Jason. And all the walls of my room were painted with fine phrases taken from all [parts of] the Romance of the Rose, both text and commentary. My windows were all shut, and through the glass the sun shone on my bed with bright beams. Also the heavens were so fair; blue, bright, clear was the air, and the weather was mild, neither hot nor cold. In all the sky there was not a cloud.

As I lay, it seemed to me I heard a hunter blowing his horn, and the noises that go with the gathering of a hunt. I was delighted, and took my horse and left my room, never stopping until I reached the field outside. There I joined the hunt, and hied me to the woods with the hunters. At last I spoke to a man, saying, " Tell me, comrade, who shall hunt here? " He answered back, " Sir, the Emperor Octovien, and he is hard by." When we came to the forest side, the hunt proper began. A stag was found but it got away and the hunter at last blew a signal to that effect.

I had left my tree, and as I walked along, a whelp came up to me. It was very friendly, behaving as if it knew me, but when I tried to catch it, it ran off. I followed it down a pathway which seemed to be little used, as it was thick with grass and flowers. The trees were tall, clean of branches almost to the top, and set from ten to twelve feet apart. Their leafy tops met overhead and made the wood a place of shade throughout. Before me and behind me the wood was full of deer, and overhead the trees swarmed with squirrels. To make a long story short, the forest had so many beasts that Argus himself could not have made an exact count of the wonders I dreamt in my dream.

But they roamed on, down the wood, with miraculous speed; so at last I was aware of a man in black, sitting under a huge oak-tree. " Lord," thought I, " who may that be? What ails him to sit here? " At once I went nearer, and saw that he was a handsome young knight. I came up right behind him, and there I stood as still as anything. He saw me not at all, because he let his head drop and in a sorrowful voice he composed ten or twelve lines of a riming poem, the saddest lament I have ever heard. It was a miracle that Nature could let anybody have such sorrow and not die. With a face piteously pale he said a lay, a kind of song, words without music. And here it is, for I can repeat it perfectly:

> 475   I have of sorwe so gret won
> That joye get I never non,
> Now that I see my lady bryght,
> Which I have loved with al my myght,
> Is fro me ded and ys agoon.
>
> Allas, deth, what ayleth the,
> That thou noldest have taken me,
> Whan thou toke my lady swete,
> That was so fair, so fresh, so fre,
> So good, that men may wel se
> Of al goodnesse she had no mete.

When he had made thus his lament, he grew so pale and looked so woebegone that I thought he was about to faint away, and I went forward and stood right at his feet and greeted him, but he said nothing. His sorrow was so great that he did not hear me, for he had well nigh lost his mind for grief. But at last he was aware of me, how I stood in front of him and took off my hood and had greeted him as politely and considerately as I knew how.

Chaucer's dream begins with an idealized scene. The dreamer finds himself abed in a beautiful room the decorations of which represent the world of books, the literary masterpieces that mean most to him. Outside, he hears the singing of birds, and sees nature at its best. Wherever he turns, everything is just as it should be, and life holds nothing but pleasure and beauty. This kind of opening is conventional enough, of course. The May morning with its choir of birds, indeed, can be traced back to classical antiquity, and the troubadours had taken it up long before Chaucer's time and made it popular. But Chaucer here gives to this old, shop-worn matter something of its original freshness and charm. His birds, sitting on the tiles of his roof and singing for all they are worth, have become more than a stereotyped literary device. They sing far better than real birds but they have a touch of reality about them none the less. One must believe that Chaucer in writing this opening for his dream got his inspiration, in part at least, from nature herself. Moreover, the opening which Chaucer used was needed, not only because it was prescribed by tradition, but also because it has a structural function in the dream as a whole, that of contrast with the main action. Nothing could be sharper than the opposition between the paradise with which the dream begins and the hell with which it ends.

Both this paradise and this hell are solitudes, be it noted. The poet lies alone in the one; he finds the black-clad man sitting alone in the other. Between the two comes the hunt, a lively social event which contrasts alike with what precedes and with what follows. The hunt of course has another function too: that of getting the poet out of bed and into the forest, where in due time he will meet the puppy and be led to the man clad in black. On top of that, the story of the hunt adds to the complexity of the dream and thereby makes its appeal to the current taste for complication already discussed. But there is also a conventional element here. As all the world knows, the medieval lord, when he was not waging war, spent his time hunting and hawking. The description of a hunt, therefore, had as fit a place in courtly poetry as the hunt itself had in courtly life. A hunting scene would make many members of the poet's audience prick up their ears who otherwise had no interest in poetry and attended his readings simply because they had to or because it was the fashionable thing to do. Certainly courtly poets were accustomed to include hunting scenes in their poems. A familiar case is *Sir Gawain and the Green Knight*. It seems likely, then, that Chaucer when he put the hunting scene into his dream was conforming to traditional practice. It is noteworthy that the whole episode takes only 43 lines, and of these only 15 deal with the hunt itself (lines 372-386). By letting the stag escape Chaucer was able to cut his hunting scene astonishingly short. It seems reasonable to conclude that he had no special interest in hunting as a literary theme, though authorities on this medieval sport tell us that he knew what he was talking about.

The next episode is that of the whelp which came up to Chaucer and made friends with him. This whelp answers to the lion in Machaut's *Dit dou Lyon*, who behaves in much the same way. Such behavior in a lion is strange; we are in a world of marvels. By turning the lion into a puppy, Chaucer replaced the marvelous with the familiar. He also gave to the creature the charm and the appeal which very young things have. The little beast became interesting in its own right. But it has a definite function in the economy of the dream: it brings Chaucer to the man clad in black. It does this by running off, down a pathway, when Chaucer tries to catch it. Chaucer follows, of course. We hear no more of the whelp, but why should we? Its duty is done. The pathway leads the poet to his man. The puppy belongs to a class of animals very familiar in medieval story: animals which flee before the hero and entice him to follow. Such an animal commonly serves as an emissary of a fairy mistress, and by its tactics it brings the hero to her, as it does in Marie de France's *Graelent*. Chaucer used the pattern familiar in such stories but made it serve his own purposes.

The forest that Chaucer came to by following the puppy belongs to a world not our own. To quote,

> 419 And every tree stood by himselve
> Fro other wel ten foot or twelve.
> So grete trees, so huge of strengthe,
> Of fourty or fifty fadme lengthe,
> Clene withoute bowgh or stikke,
> With croppes brode, and eke as thikke—
> They were nat an ynche asonder—
> 426 That hit was shadewe overal under.

The great height of the trees (from 240 to 300 feet) is less remarkable than the regularity of their spacing and the symmetry and uniformity of their growth. Chaucer's source here is the description of the dream-garden in the *Roman de la Rose*. We learn from passages like these what medieval perfectionists did to nature to make it beautiful. Chaucer and his fellows did not like it wild, and though they took delight in its tamer aspects, such as green fields and flowery meadows, a forest had to be reduced to order and system before it could give them esthetic satisfaction. Not until the eighteenth century did a taste establish itself for the natural scenery which we now hold in highest regard.

The dream-forest was full of wonderful wild beasts, but Chaucer went on until he came upon a man: a knight clad in black. Chaucer came up to him from behind, and overheard him composing a lament for his dead lady. We have already looked at this lament, and have seen that it falls into two stanzas, the first of five lines, the second of six. By overhearing it, Chaucer (and so his audience) has learned why the knight is clad in black and is so sad at heart. He comes forward and speaks to the knight in order to help him if he can. At first the knight was too deep in sorrow to answer him or even to be aware of him but finally he came to, as it were, and at this point the dialog begins. We have reached the main part of the dream at last. The dialog between Chaucer and the knight may be summarized thus:

Knight: I pray thee, be not wroth; truly I neither heard nor saw thee. *Chaucer*: Ah, good sir, no matter; I am right sorry if I have intruded. Forgive me, if I have made a mistake. *Knight*: No forgiveness is needed, for nothing has been said or done amiss. *Chaucer*: Sir, the hunt is over. I think the stag is gone; the hunters cannot find him anywhere. *Knight*: I care not for that. My thought is not at all about that. *Chaucer*: By our Lord, I believe you. Your face tells me as much. But, sir, will you hear one thing? It seems to me I see you in great sorrow. If you would tell me all your woe, I should like to heal you if I can. Tell me of your sorrows. Perhaps that may ease your heart. *Knight*: Many thanks, good friend, but no man can console me. Nothing can cure me, no remedies, no medicines. Whoso seeth me may say he hath met with sorrow, for I am sorrow and sorrow is I. False Fortune hath played a game of chess with me. She stole up on me and took my queen, and when I saw my queen gone, alas, I could no longer play. Alas, that I was born. *Chaucer*: Ah, good sir, say not so. Remember Socrates, who cared not three straws what Fortune did. If you kill yourself, you will be damned. Many have slain themselves but they were fools. But there is no man alive here who would make this woe for a queen. *Knight*: Thou knowest full little what thou sayest; I have lost more than thou thinkest. *Chaucer*: How may that be? Good sir, tell me all about it. *Knight*: Willingly; come sit down. I will tell thee if thou wilt listen with all thy wit. *Chaucer*: Yes, sir. *Knight*: Swear thy troth to it. *Chaucer*: Gladly. *Knight*: Do it then. *Chaucer*: I shall right gladly hear you fully, so God save me, with all the wit I have, as well as I know how.

Knight: In God's name! Sir, from my first youth, ever since I knew what love was, I have served him faithfully, body, heart, and all. This was many a year before my heart was set on anyone. I chose love for my first vocation. One day I happened to come to a place where I saw the fairest company of ladies ever seen together. One of them outshone the rest as the sun outshines the moon and stars. To make a long story short, it was my sweet one, and I fell in love at first sight. My heart told me it would be better to serve her without requital than to be happy with another. Her hair, her eyes, her bearing, her face, her voice, her figure were all that heart could wish, and she was as good as she was beautiful. Her name was good fair White [English for Blanche], and it suited her. As I said, my love was fully set on her, for indeed that sweet woman was my all, my joy, my life, my fate, my well-being, and all my bliss, my world's welfare and my goddess, and I was hers fully and altogether. *Chaucer*: By our Lord, I believe you indeed. Truly your love was well bestowed. I know not how you could have done better. *Knight*: Better? Nothing like as well. *Chaucer*: I believe it, sir, by God! *Knight*: You may well believe it. *Chaucer*: Sir, so I do; I am sure it seemed to you that she was the best, and the fairest to behold, whoever had looked at her with your eyes. *Knight*: With my eyes? Nay, everyone that saw her said and swore that it was so. And even if they had not, I would still have loved her best. I must needs love her. But no, it was not a matter of need. I wanted to love her. When I first saw her I was right young, and had much to learn, but I used the wits I had to love her as best I could, to do her honor and to serve her. When I saw her of a morning it would make me happy all day. And to this day she sits so in my heart that, by my troth, I would not leave my lady out of my thoughts for all the world.

Chaucer: Now, by my troth, sir, it seems to me you may be able to get shrift without repentance. *Knight*: Repentance! nay, fie! Should I now repent of loving? Nay, then I should be a traitor indeed. Nay, while I am alive here I will never forget her. *Chaucer*: Now, good sir, you have certainly told me how you first saw her and where. There is no need to repeat it any more. But would you tell me about your first addresses to her, and how she first came to know that you loved her. And tell me also what you have lost, the thing I heard you speak of before. *Knight*: Yea! thou knowest not what thou sayest; I have lost more than thou thinkest. *Chaucer*: What loss is that? Won't she love you? Is it so? Or have you done something amiss, so that she has left you? Is it this? For God's love, tell me all. *Knight*: Before God, I shall. For a long time she knew not that I loved her. I dared not tell her what was in my heart, for fear it would offend her. But I made songs in her praise. Here is the first one:

> 1175 Lord, hyt maketh myn herte lyght,
> Whan I thenke on that swete wyght
> That is so semely on to see;
> And wisshe to God hit myghte so bee
> That she wolde holde me for hir knyght,
> 1180 My lady, that is so fair and bryght.

One day I bethought me what woe and sorrow I was suffering for her, and she knew nothing of it. What was I to do? I bethought me that Nature never gave to anybody so much beauty and goodness without giving mercy too. In hope of that I told my tale. I had to tell it or die. I know not how I began. Many a word I skipped in my story, for pure fear. Bowing to her, I hung my head. I did not dare look at her, not once, for my wits failed me. I said "mercy" and no more. It was no fun. At last, when my courage came back a little, I besought her to be my sweet lady, and I swore ever to be steadfast and true and love her always and never have another lady. And when my tale was done, it seemed to me that all I said meant nothing at all to her. I cannot now reproduce her words, but this was the gist of them: she said no. Alas, the sorrow I suffered that day. I dared say nothing more, but stole away. And sorrow and I were bedfellows for many a day, because my love for her was no sudden fit of passion but a feeling that never left me. Another year it befell that I thought I would try to make her know and understand my woe. And she well understood the feelings of my heart, and it seemed a pity that I should die for love of her, since there was no harm in me. So when my lady saw all this she gave me fully the noble gift of her mercy, keeping safe her honor always. So help me God, that moment I was raised up, as from death to life, and thenceforth we lived in perfect happiness. *Chaucer*: Sir, where is she now? *Knight*: Now? Alas that I was born. That was the loss that before this I told thee that I had lost. Bethink how I said before this, "Thou knowest full little what thou sayest; I have lost more than thou thinkest." God knows,

alas, that was she. *Chaucer*: Alas, sir, how? what may that be?
Knight: She is dead. *Chaucer*: Nay. *Knight*: Yes, by my troth.
Chaucer: Is that your loss? By God, it is a pity.

In one of Machaut's poems, the *Jugement dou Roy de
Behaingne*, a lady who is mourning the death of her lover
meets a knight whose lady has left him. This meeting,
and the dialog that follows, served Chaucer as his chief
source for the meeting and dialog between himself and the
man in black of his dream. The man in black replaces the
lady of Machaut's poem, and Chaucer himself plays the
role which Machaut gave the knight. In composing this
part of his poem Chaucer also drew upon other poems
of Machaut's, notably the *Remede de Fortune*. But the
source material which Chaucer used took new shape in
his mouth. The French poet had his characters debate
their respective sorrows, the question being which one was
worse off. Each failing to convince the other, they finally
ask the King of Bohemia to judge between them, and he
passes judgment in favor of the knight. Such debates on
courtly-love topics are familiar in medieval literature, but
to us they seem singularly arid, and Machaut's poem,
though cleverly done, has not a spark of genuine feeling in
it from beginning to end. Chaucer took this unpromising
material and made it over. His man in black is no debater,
though traces of the old debating technic survive. He is
a mourner, and his words are an outpouring of his feelings.
As we know, he stands for John of Gaunt, and his grief
is no fiction, invented by the poet for debating purposes,
but a sad reality. Chaucer's sympathy and his wish to
comfort the mourner are likewise no literary concoction
but come from the heart. The tone and spirit of Chaucer's
dialog with the man in black differ correspondingly from
what we find in Machaut's debate.

Before the dialog began, Chaucer had overheard the
knight's lament for his dead lady. In other words, he knew

from the start what the matter was. But in the dialog itself he shows no awareness of the truth, and not until the very end, when the knight says " she is dead," does he come to understand the situation. This inconsistency has long bothered the critics. Kittredge in his second Johns Hopkins lecture tried to explain it. He said,[4]

> He owes his knowledge of the lady's death to overhearing the knight, who was too much absorbed to notice either his steps or his greeting. With instinctive delicacy, therefore, he suppresses his knowledge, and invites the knight's confidence in noncommittal terms, on the ground of pity for his obvious sufferings. And when the knight speaks eagerly, though not plainly, . . . and the Dreamer notes that words are indeed a relief, as he had hoped, it is not for him to check their flow. Let him rather hide his knowledge still, and tempt the knight to talk on and on.

This is ingenious but not wholly convincing, for inconsistencies may be seen elsewhere in Chaucer's compositions, inconsistencies equally glaring and not so easy to rationalize. To me it seems possible enough that here Chaucer deliberately sacrificed the virtue of consistency to gain the greater virtue of dramatic irony. Such irony could be had only if the audience knew in advance the reason for the knight's sorrow whereas the knight's questioner (that is, Chaucer) remained unaware of the truth to the end. But Chaucer was telling the story of the dream in the first person, and therefore the information that the knight's lady was dead had to come to the audience through Chaucer. The poet's way of dealing with this difficulty was to ignore it. By the device of overhearing he gave the audience the advance information they needed. This done, he proceeded to forget what he had just overheard, and the questions he asked the knight came from a mind completely ignorant of the facts.

The ironical effects made possible by this device add to

[4] *Chaucer and his Poetry,* pp. 52 f.

the dialog points of tension, moments of excited interest, foreign to the story that the knight tells, a story which follows the familiar course of a conventional, idealized love affair. But Chaucer has to pay for what he gets: his own part in the dialog becomes a fool's part, for who but a fool could forget so quickly and so thoroughly? Yet Chaucer manages to make artistic use of the invincible stupidity which he attributes to himself. He is an amusing fool. He butts in where he has no business, insists on having his curiosity satisfied, and in general behaves as only a fool can behave with impunity. The knight recognizes that his questioner is well-meaning, however foolish, and treats him with the consideration which a gentleman has for hopelessly witless people. But Chaucer nearly always says the wrong thing, or says the right thing the wrong way, and the knight reacts sharply enough, though his irritation soon passes in each case. This action and reaction make a humorous pattern repeated again and again in the course of the dialog. Thereby Chaucer introduces a comic element into the very heart of his elegy, and this without spoiling the elegiac effect, a piece of technical virtuosity beyond praise. The oath-taking passage (lines 745-758) is perhaps the most obviously humorous part of the dialog, but wherever Chaucer speaks one is justified in looking for humor and one usually finds it. Be it added that in nearly all his writings Chaucer has something to say about the feebleness of his wits. It is a stock joke, certain to raise a laugh or at least a smile.

Throughout the dialog the man in black presents his love affair in strictly courtly terms. Marriage is nowhere mentioned, and the following passage makes it clear that the affair was not physically consummated:

> 1269 My lady yaf me al hooly
> The noble yifte of hir mercy,
> Savynge hir worship, by al weyes,—
> Dredles, I mene noon other weyes.

In other words, John of Gaunt's happy marriage with Blanche could not be represented as such but had to be turned into an extra-marital love affair for the sake of conformity to the conventions of courtly love. And as it would never do to have the Duchess give herself to a lover, the affair had to be presented as a love in which the desires of the flesh could not be satisfied and must be sublimated.

The dialog ends abruptly, with Chaucer s exclamation, " it is a pity! " The dream shifts back to the hunt; the hunters leave the forest; for that time the stag-hunting is over.

> 1314   With that me thoughte that this king
> Gan homwardes for to ryde
> Unto a place, was there besyde,
> Which was from us but a lyte:
> A long castel with walles white,
> Be seynt Johan! on a ryche hil
> 1320   As me mette; but thus hyt fil.

The king is presumably the knight in black; that is, John of Gaunt. He now rides home to a " place " (presumably Richmond) in the neighborhood. It is called a long castle, evidently a pun on *Lancaster*, and it is set on a rich hill, another pun on *Richmond*. The white walls and the oath by St John are meant to remind us of the Christian names of Duchess and Duke respectively. The high rank of the knight in black had been brought out, indirectly, in the dialog: he used *thou* in addressing Chaucer, whereas Chaucer used *ye* in addressing him. Now he is called a king, a description not strictly accurate but indicative of his royal birth and his importance in the English scheme of things.

The dream is nearly over; three lines more remain.

> 1321   Ryght thus me mette, as I yow telle,
> That in the castell ther was a belle,
> As hyt hadde smyten houres twelve

And with that Chaucer woke up, to find himself lying in his bed, with the book that he had been reading still in his hand. We now see that the story of Ceyx and Alcyone led naturally to the dream, as it, like the dream, had for its subject the sorrow of one whose mate was dead. The story in the book inspired the dream about the man in black by an association of ideas familiar in the psychology of dreams. Indeed, we may even conjecture that the idea of composing an elegy on the Duchess came to Chaucer through an actual reading of this very story, quite apart from dream psychology. Certain touches in the dream itself lend support to the theory that Chaucer in this poem tried to make his fictitious dream realistic; that is, like a real dream. As Kittredge wisely puts the matter (pp. 69 f.),

I do not contend that Chaucer carried out his dream-psychology in a thoroughgoing and consistent manner. That would have destroyed the continuity required in a narrative. But assuredly, in various details, he brought the experiences of the Dreamer, with admirable art, near to the actual phenomena of the dream-life.

Here, of course, Chaucer's treatment of his material differed greatly from that of previous composers of love visions. But it must be added that there is nothing dream-like about the dialog proper. On the contrary, its realistic touches are those of actual conversation. Here again Chaucer put life into a lifeless conventional literary form, the debate on questions of courtly love. From the beginning of his literary career he set his own stamp on everything he took.

CHAPTER III

THE HOUSE OF FAME

WE HAVE SEEN that Chaucer in composing the *Book of the Duchess* patterned his poem on the love-vision then fashionable but actually wrote an elegy. In making the *House of Fame* he took a like pattern of courtly-love poetry and used it for a poem of entertainment. Here his procedure was far more drastic than it had been in the earlier poem, where he told the story of John of Gaunt's love for Blanche and made this story the culminating feature of his dream. In the *House of Fame* the machinery of courtly love, once it has been used to explain the course of events, becomes negligible, and though the poet tells the love-story of Dido and Æneas, he subordinates it to another theme.

But the most revolutionary thing about the *House of Fame* is the shift of stress from instruction to entertainment. The poetry of courtly love in Chaucer's day was didactic in purpose. The story proper amounted to little, and Machaut and his fellows were chiefly concerned to teach the rules to be followed by courtly lovers in their love affairs. The teaching was done by precept and by example. The story of a love affair was told, not for its own sake but as an exemplum. It served as an illustration of how lovers ought to behave, or of how they ought not to behave, as the case might be. Other poems, as we have seen, served as vehicles for debates on nice points of courtly-love theory and practice. Gods and goddesses of pagan antiquity might also be brought in, and personified

42

abstractions like Mirth, Beauty, and Courtesy played parts appropriate to their names. To the modern reader these conventional poems of courtly love are almost intolerably tedious. Nowadays only scholars read them, and even they read them only for professional reasons, not for pleasure.

Passing from Machaut and his fellows to Chaucer is like passing from the schoolroom to the playground. Not that the didactic element is lacking in Chaucer's poems. The knight in black of the *Book of the Duchess* is a model lover, and he was intended to be just that. But Chaucer makes the story of the love affair interesting for its own sake, and though the poem is an elegy he enlivens even the dialog with touches of humor, a feature alien to his French sources. In the *House of Fame* Chaucer's liveliness and especially his humor have freer play than they could possibly have in an elegy, and the narrative becomes entertaining indeed, a little masterpiece of fun and fantasy. But before going on with the discussion, we had better go through the poem itself, to see how it is made and what it is made of.

The *House of Fame* is 2158 lines long. It is written in iambic tetra-meter couplets, and falls into three " books." The first of these begins with a " proem " on dreams; the proem ends with the announcement that on December 10 the poet had a wonderful dream which he will now tell. But before he tells it he makes invocation to the god of sleep, who with his thousand sons sleeps in a cave on a stream fed by the river Lethe. Next come three prayers: first, to the god of sleep for success in telling the dream aright; secondly, to the Christian God, that he bless those who hear the story of the dream and " take it well "; thirdly, to Christ, that he curse those who from evil motives misjudge it. After the prayers the poet calls upon his audience to listen to the dream. He begins the story by saying that he went to bed as usual on the night of December 10 and fell asleep wonderfully soon. He dreamt he was in a temple of glass, elaborately decorated with a great variety of precious things. He did not know where he was, but he knew he was in a temple of Venus, for he saw her naked figure portrayed floating in a sea, with her husband Vulcan, her son

Cupid, her doves, her comb, and her rose garland. As he roamed about in the temple, he found a wall with a tablet of brass on which was written the beginning of the *Æneid* of Vergil. Chaucer gives the lines in English. There follows a synopsis of the *Æneid*, divided into fifteen parts or scenes. One of these, the twelfth, is no less than 177 lines long. It deals with Æneas's desertion of Dido and Dido's suicide, to which Chaucer adds comments of his own and parallel cases drawn from classical story. The tenth part, in which the story of Dido begins, is also disproportionately long; it comes to 32 lines. The other parts are all short, some of them very short; thus, the eleventh part is only three lines long. After examining these parts or scenes, " graven " on the temple wall, Chaucer left the temple in order to see if there was any man stirring who could tell him what country he was in. But he discovered that he was in a desert, a sandy waste. Looking upwards, he saw an eagle high in the sky. It was much bigger than any eagle he had ever seen, and glittered like gold.

The second book begins with a proem that falls into three parts: first, the poet calls upon his hearers to listen, promising that they will hear a dream more marvelous than the most famous dreams of ancient story; secondly, he invokes Venus and the Muses to help him; thirdly, he appeals to Thought (that is, the memory) to show all the virtue that is in her. He then resumes the story of the dream. The eagle swooped down upon him, snatched him up in its claws, and carried him off into the vast spaces of the sky. At first Chaucer was frightened out of his wits, but the eagle spoke to him (for it had the gift of speech) and assured him that he had nothing to fear. Jupiter, the god of thunder, had taken pity on Chaucer, who had served Venus and Cupid so long without reward, and had depended on books for all his information. Jupiter therefore sent the eagle to take Chaucer to a palace called the House of Fame, where he could have a good time and hear more love stories than there are grains of sand. Chaucer did not understand how the stories reached the House of Fame, but the eagle explained matters so learnedly and so simply that everything became clear to Chaucer and he agreed that it must be as the eagle said. The eagle now taught Chaucer geography a while, until it soared so high that the earth became a mere point. Then it began to teach Chaucer astronomy, but Chaucer soon rebelled at that; he had learned enough and refused to listen to any more learned lectures. After a while they approached Fame's house, set between heaven and earth; before they reached it they could hear the buzz of talk with which it was filled. The eagle put Chaucer down in a road near by, and told him to walk in and make himself at home. But Chaucer first wanted to know if the noise he heard was made by people on earth or in the palace of Fame. The eagle explained that the people were on earth but their speech could be seen as well as heard in the palace, where each speech took the shape of the person that spoke it. With that Chaucer took leave of the eagle and went forward to the palace. The eagle waited outside.

The third book begins with an invocation to Apollo. Then Chaucer concludes the story of his dream. He found the house set on a high hill of ice. He climbed the hill and saw before him a castle so beautiful that no description could do it justice. Its outside walls were adorned with many pinnacles, each holding niches in which stood all kinds of minstrels and tellers of tales. There Chaucer heard famous harpers, pipers, and trumpeters of old playing their instruments. There he saw jugglers, magicians, witches, and other wonderworkers such as Medea, Circe, and Simon Magus. But when he saw he was free to go where he liked he went on till he found the castle gate, and went in at once. There he met a crowd of heralds, gorgeously dressed, and each wearing a coat-of-arms. There were so many of these coats that it would take a book 20 feet thick to describe them all. In the hall itself, which was plated with gold throughout, and studded with jewels, he saw Fame sitting on a throne made of a single ruby. She had a way of varying in size: one moment she would be tiny; the next, she stretched from earth to heaven. She had as many eyes as birds have feathers, and as many ears and tongues as beasts have hairs. She had wings on her feet and wore many jewels. The nine Muses, gathered about her throne, filled the air with songs in her praise. On her shoulders she upheld those of great fame: Alexander and Hercules.

Two rows of pillars made a passage-way from the doors of the hall to the throne. On each pillar stood a writer of antiquity, or a group of writers, engaged in upholding the fame of their particular subject. Thus, Josephus and seven helpers, standing on a pillar of lead and iron, bore up the fame of the Jews. The hall was as full of writers as trees are of rooks' nests. While Chaucer was looking at all this, groups of petitioners came into the hall and knelt before Fame, begging her to grant their petitions. Some of the petitions she granted, some she refused, and to some of the groups she gave the opposite of what they asked for. Her decision in each case was arbitrary, so far as Chaucer could tell, without regard for justice or anything other than caprice. Chaucer describes nine such groups of petitioners.

After seeing what happened to them, he fell into conversation with a man who asked him, " Art thou come hither to have fame? " Chaucer said no. " But what dost thou here then," said the man. Chaucer answered, " to learn new tidings, I know not what, tidings of love or such glad things. For certainly he that made me come hither said to me that I should both hear and see wonderful things in this palace. But these be no such tidings as I have in mind." The man then offers to lead Chaucer to another house where he will hear the new tidings he has not heard in the palace where he now is. Chaucer went out with him and saw, near by, a whirling house made of wickerwork. It was indeed a house of tidings, as he could tell from the roar of speech that came from it. All its many doors were wide open day and night, but Chaucer had to have the help of the eagle to get inside, so swiftly did the house revolve. When he was in, he found the house so crowded that he had hardly a foot of space to stand in, though there ought to have been plenty of room, as the house was 60 miles long. Everybody there was engaged in telling some piece of news to his neighbor, who then would pass it on to another, making changes in it as he did so. When the news had got ripe, so to speak, by passing from mouth to mouth long enough, it flew out of the house of tidings and made its way to Fame, who decided what would become of it. Chaucer ` roamed about in the house, listening, until he heard a great noise in a corner where love tidings were being spread. He and many others made their way thither in a kind of stampede. At last he saw a man who seemed to be of great authority,—and here the poem breaks off, unfinished.

Now that we have before us an outline of the poem we can with profit compare it further with the *Book of the Duchess.* First let us look at the way the dreams are introduced. In the earlier poem the introductory matter leads us, step by step, from Chaucer's insomnia to the book he read because of it and on to the story in that book which informed him of Morpheus, the god of sleep, and inspired him to pray to Morpheus for sleep. The prayer is granted and with sleep comes a dream which the poet likewise owes to Morpheus, if we may go by the story of Ceyx and Alcyone, in which the god of sleep serves also as a bearer of dreams. The chain of causality never breaks, though it may get pretty thin. In other words, the course of the introductory action brings about the dream, and to some extent determines the chief feature of the dream: a lament for a dead spouse.

How different it all is in the *House of Fame*! Here the poet goes to bed one night as usual, falls asleep almost at once, and has a wonderful dream. Before this we get introductory matter — a good deal of it — but it has no organic connection with the dream. The invocation is a conventional feature going back to classical antiquity. The proem is equally conventional, belonging as it does to the tradition of dream poetry which Chaucer was follow-ing. Both serve to give to our poem a sophisticated literary flavor from the start. They are prefixed to the story of the dream by way of rhetorical ornamentation, not because they are really needed to explain why Chaucer had a dream or why the dream took shape as it did. For the same reason Chaucer prefixed a proem to his second book and an invocation to his third. Both are decorative rather than organic features of the poem.[1]

If now we compare the opening of the *House of Fame* with that of the *Roman de la Rose*, we see that the French poem gave Chaucer a structural model which he followed but elaborated. The French poet tells us that he went to bed as usual and fell fast asleep. Like Chaucer, he prefixed to this statement some general observations about dreams. But the discussion of dreams in the *Roman de la Rose* is only 20 lines long, whereas Chaucer devoted no less than

[1] The so-called proem of the second book actually includes, besides the proem proper, no less than three invocations: to Venus, to the Muses, and to Thought (i. e. the mind, or memory). The first of these Chaucer took from Boccaccio's *Teseide* i. 3; the other two, from Dante's *Inferno* ii. 7-9. The invocation of the third book is based on Dante's *Paradiso* i. 13-27, though Chaucer has made significant changes.

58 lines to the subject. Again, the French poem has no invocation, but after the general discussion of dreams goes on to the particular dream which the poet dreamt. Most important of all, Chaucer's opening differs greatly in tone and point of view from the opening of the *Roman de la Rose*. The French poet takes a strong stand; he opposes the view that dreams are lies and fables, and asserts vigorously that they have significance. Chaucer begins and ends his discussion with a pious prayer: may God turn every dream to our good. Into this envelope of conventional piety he crowds all the theories he knows about dreams, but he makes none of these theories his own. On the contrary, he is the complete agnostic; he simply does not know. To quote a typical passage:

12   I not; but whoso of these miracles
     The causes knoweth bet then I,
     Devyne he; for I certeinly
     Ne kan hem noght, ne never thinke
     To besily my wyt to swinke
     To knowe of hir signifiaunce
18   The gendres, . . .

In part, this is a conventional gesture of humility or modesty, something to be expected of writers. Like statements of ignorance or unworthiness still appear in books. But Chaucer goes further. He does not even have an opinion on the subject, and he assures his hearers that he has no intention whatever of overworking his wits in order to learn something about it. He is content to leave all this headwork to the " grete clerkys " that undertake such things; he wishes them well in their task, but he will have none of it himself. All this was meant to be funny. Chaucer's audience knew perfectly well that he was a man of learning and anything but a lazy-bones. In consequence, they could not and did not take seriously what he said about his mental indolence.

The invocation which follows is likewise humorously meant, in part at least. Chaucer put it in, no doubt, for the sake of rhetorical elaboration, but when it took shape in his hands he could not resist giving it a certain lightness not usual in the rhetorical craftsmanship of those days. I am not referring to the fact that he prays to Morpheus as well as to God and Christ. The sequence strikes us as incongruous, but pagan and Christian deities appear together so often in medieval invocations that their association must be reckoned conventional. At most this association might imply that the prayers to God and Christ, like the one to Morpheus, had only a stylistic function. It is hard for us to tell, but I think they had a religious function too. On top of that, a humorous element is conspicuous (the main thing, indeed) in the prayer to Christ, and appears in the other two prayers as well. Thus, the prayer to Morpheus is made subject to a proviso: it holds, provided that he really has control of dreams. In a modern mouth, a humorous prayer to God would normally indicate that the man who said it did not take God seriously. Certainly this holds good of the Anglo-Saxon world. Not so in the Middle Ages. Chaucer's prayer to Christ is definitely funny, but Chaucer did not mean to be irreverent, and his audience found the prayer amusing but not shocking.

Leaving the introductory matter and going on to the dream itself, let us continue our comparison of the *Book of the Duchess* and the *House of Fame*. In the earlier poem Chaucer seems to have taken some account of dream psychology; certain touches of his are best so explained. Nothing of the kind appears in the *House of Fame*, where the dream is used, conventionally enough, as a vehicle for wonders impossible in actual life. Such wonders are also to be found in the *Book of the Duchess*, but there they are subordinated to a main action drawn from life itself, however idealized and stylized, whereas in the *House of Fame* the main action is marvelous throughout.

In his earlier dream Chaucer first finds himself in a room with glass windows on which was depicted the story of Troy, while on the walls was recorded the Romance of the Rose. This room reminds one of the temple of glass in the later dream, where the story of Troy again serves for decoration, even Lavinia appearing in both room and temple. But the contrast is great between the desert in which the dream temple is set and the May garden which surrounds the dream room. So complete is this contrast, indeed, that one is tempted to connect the two by polarity. Did Chaucer give the temple a setting intentionally opposed to the setting he had given the room of his earlier poem? We shall never know, but the opposition is a fact, and I think it worthy of mention.

Further systematic comparison of our two poems would lead us into speculations ingenious rather than plausible. In the following, therefore, the *House of Fame* will be our chief concern. Here the poet's dream turned into a search for new stories, but it began with a very old story, the tale of Æneas, an offshoot of the Troy legend known to Chaucer as to us through the Vergilian epic. In the dream a series of episodes from the life of Æneas serves, appropriately enough, to decorate the walls of his mother's temple.[2] Chaucer tells the story of the *Æneid* not directly but by using a highly conventional and artificial device: he describes these wall decorations in the dream temple of Venus. Most of his descriptions are very sketchy indeed, but he makes much of the love story of Dido and Æneas, for which he could draw on Ovid's *Heroides* as well as Vergil's *Æneid*. Here Chaucer's interest obviously lies not

[2] Chaucer found both temple and decorations in his source (*Æneid* i. 446 ff.), but there the temple was Juno's, not Venus's, and the decorations depicted events in the Troy story proper.

in the love affair itself but in its conclusion: Æneas's abandonment of Dido and Dido's suicide. Moreover, he shows no interest in the complexities and shadings of the story as Vergil tells it. In particular, he presents Æneas as a villain pure and simple, though at the very end of his account (lines 427-432) he protects himself in a perfunctory way against critics who might object to his simplification of the story. His handling of Dido and Æneas contrasts strangely with his treatment of a like love story in *Troilus and Criseyde*, where the lovers are presented with a richness and fulness unmatched in medieval literature. It is tempting to explain the difference on the theory that Chaucer composed the *House of Fame* before he had reached the height of his powers as a literary artist.

Whatever the explanation, we have before us, in the Dido story of the first book, little more than an exemplum. The stripping of the narrative down to its bare bones is enough to indicate the exemplary character of the story. But Chaucer gives us, besides, plenty of moralizing comments and adds a number of parallel cases, each an example of a lover's faithlessness to his lady. The didacticism of this part of our poem stands out so clearly that there is no need to labor the point.

What has this story to do with the rest of the poem? More precisely, what trait or feature makes the story of Dido suitable for inclusion in the *House of Fame*? We cannot fully answer this question now. Indeed, we may not be able to answer it convincingly at all. But it will not be anticipating too much to say that our poem is well named. It deals with Fame, and *fame* is a word which in Middle English may mean rumor, report, gossip, reputation good or bad, and the like. Now Dido in the lament which Chaucer puts in her mouth mentions Fame and makes much of fame. To quote:

345 O, welawey that I was born!
     For thorgh yow is my name lorn,
     And alle myn actes red and songe
     Over al thys lond, on every tonge.
     O wikke Fame! for ther nys
     Nothing so swift, lo, as she is!
     O, soth ys, every thing ys wist,
     Through hit be kevered with the myst.
     Eke, though I myghte duren ever
     That I have don, rekever I never
     That I ne shal be seyd, allas,
     Yshamed be thourgh Eneas,
     And that I shal thus juged be:
     " Loo, ryght as she hath don, now she
     Wol doo eft-sones, hardely."
360 Thus seyth the peple prively.

It seems from this that Dido slew herself not because she
lost her lover but for fear of ill fame and its consequences.
If so, Chaucer may here be giving us a foretaste of the
workings of Fame (and fame) which he describes so well
in the third book of our poem. In any case, the tale of
Dido along with everything else in the dream temple
belongs to the preliminaries, not to the main action, which
begins with the eagle.

When Chaucer in his dream has looked at the decorations of the temple he goes outside to find out what country
he is in. There he sees that the temple is set in a desert,
a sandy waste.

489 Ne no maner creature
     That ys yformed be Nature
     Ne sawgh I, me to rede or wisse.
     " O Christ! " thoughte I, " that art in blysse,
     Fro fantome and illusion
     Me save! " and with devocion
     Myn eyen to the hevene I caste.
     Thoo was I war, lo! at the laste,
     That faste be the sonne, as hye
     As kenne myghte I with myn ye,

Me thoughte I sawgh an egle sore,
But that it semed moche more
Then I had any egle seyn.
But this as sooth as deth, certeyn,
Hyt was of gold, and shon so bryghte
That never sawe men such a syghte,
But yf the heven had ywonne
Alle newe of gold another sonne;
So shone the egles fethers bryghte,
508 And somwhat dounward gan hyt lyghte.

When Chaucer finds out that he is alone in a wilderness
of sand, without a soul to counsel him or guide him, he
is terrified and appalled. He even fears that he has lost
his mind, and prays to Christ to save him from phantom
and illusion. He looks to heaven with devotion, hoping
for an answer to his prayer, and the answer comes in the
shape of a golden eagle. The earnestness of tone in this
passage is remarkable. But what does it mean? Are we
to take the passage symbolically? If so, what is the
symbolism?

Early in the second book we begin to see the light.
The eagle in explaining to Chaucer why he was being
carried off told him that Jupiter felt sorry for him and
wanted to do him a good turn. The god had noticed that
Chaucer, although he had served Cupid and Venus faithfully and long, and had written many poems about love,
never got the slightest reward for his pains. And there
was something else that the god had noticed:

643 And also, beau sir, other thynges;
That is, that thou hast no tydynges
Of loves folk yf they be glade,
Ne of noght elles that God made;
And noght oonly fro fer contree
That ther no tydynge cometh to thee,
But of thy verray neyghebores,
That duellen almost at thy dores,
Thou herist neyther that ne this;

> For when thy labour doon al ys,
> And hast mad alle thy rekenynges,
> In stede of reste and newe thynges
> Thou goost hom to thy hous anoon;
> And, also domb as any stoon,
> Thou sittest at another book,
> Tyl fully daswed ys thy look,
> And lyvest thus as an heremyte,
> 660   Although thyn abstinence ys lyte.

In other words, Chaucer had drawn his material wholly from books, and had lost contact with life. Jupiter therefore had the eagle take Chaucer to the House of Fame. There he could enjoy himself and thus receive some reward for his services to Cupid. There, too, he could hear stories from the lips of men, instead of getting them at second hand from books. See also lines 2007-2026.

The temple set in the sandy waste may be taken, then, to stand for the literary life Chaucer was leading before the eagle carried him off: composing courtly-love poems and reading books. Jupiter decided that the poet was getting stale and needed a change. Chaucer does not tell us in so many words how he himself felt about it, but his prayer for deliverance from phantom and illusion indicates that he took the situation much more seriously than Jupiter did. The god did not consider that he was saving Chaucer from anything. He was giving him not salvation but recreation, combined with a new and inexhaustible source of supply for stories of love and other things. Under the eagle's friendly ministrations Chaucer quickly won back his usual good spirits and humorous outlook. The return to himself is marked by the following passage:

> 555   Til at the laste he to me spak
> In mannes vois, and seyde, " Awak!
> And be not so agast, for shame! "
> And called me tho by my name,
> And, for I shulde the bet abreyde,

Me mette, " Awak " to me he seyde
Ryght in the same vois and stevene
That useth oon I koude nevene;
And with that vois, soth for to seyn,
My mynde cam to me ageyn,
For hyt was goodly seyd to me;
566   So nas hyt never wont to be!

The eagle, when it spoke to the poet, took the voice of
Chaucer's wife, in order to make him feel at home. The
trick worked all the better because the eagle spoke in a
kindly tone of voice which Chaucer's wife did not use.
This little joke of Chaucer's at his wife's expense, one of
the most ancient jokes known to man (though our poet
gives it a fresh turn), sets the tone for the rest of the
second book. Thenceforth comedy holds the stage. And
since the eagle provides most of the comedy, it is time
for us to have a good look at this remarkable creature.

Chaucer got the golden eagle from Dante (*Purgatorio*
ix. 19 ff.), but in Chaucer's hands this noble bird, this
symbol of divine grace is changed almost beyond recognition. In our poem the eagle obviously serves to take the
poet away from temple and desert to a place where he will
find an abundance of new stories. But the eagle is not
merely a means of transportation; it also gives Chaucer
information and helps him in other ways. Moreover, the
eagle is a character in the story in its own right. And
what a character! Chaucer's genius for comedy here
reached a height of achievement which he never surpassed
and rarely equaled. It is impossible to get the full flavor
of the eagle's amazing personality without reading the
second book of our poem from beginning to end, and I
can imagine no more delightful literary experience than
such a reading. But here I shall have to content myself
with a sample: the conclusion of the eagle's very learned
lecture on sound-waves and the comments which follow:

823   " Now have I told, yf thou have mynde,
       How speche or soun, of pure kynde,
       Enclyned ys upward to meve;
       This, mayst thou fele, wel I preve.
       And that same place, ywys,
       That every thing enclyned to ys,
       Hath his kyndelyche stede:
       That sheweth hyt, withouten drede,
       That kyndely the mansioun
       Of every speche, of every soun,
       Be hyt eyther foul or fair,
       Hath hys kynde place in ayr.
       And syn that every thyng that is
       Out of hys kynde place, ywys,
       Moveth thidder for to goo,
       Yif hyt aweye be therfroo,
       As I have before preved the,
       Hyt seweth, every soun, parde,
       Moveth kyndely to pace
       Al up into his kyndely place.
       And this place of which I telle,
       Ther as Fame lyst to duelle,
       Ys set amyddys of these three,
       Heven, erthe, and eke the see,
       As most conservatyf the soun.
       Than ys this the conclusyoun,
       That every speche of every man,
       As y the telle first began,
851   Moveth up on high to pace
       Kyndely to Fames place.

       Telle me this now feythfully,
       Have y not preved thus symply,
       Withoute any subtilite
       Of speche, or gret prolixite
       Of termes of philosophie,
       Of figures of poetrie,
       Or colours of rethorike?
       Pardee, hit oughte the to lyke!
       For hard langage and hard matere
       Ys encombrous for to here
       Attones; wost thou not wel this? "

And y answered and seyde, " Yis."
865 " A ha! " quod he, " lo, so I can
Lewedly to a lewed man
Speke, and shewe hym swiche skiles
That he may shake hem be the biles,
So palpable they shulden be."

First the eagle gave a brilliant lecture on sound-waves, explaining the whole thing in language so simple that anybody with any sense at all could understand it. Then the lecturer proceeds to ask Chaucer if he didn't think he had heard a good lecture. " By God, you ought to like it! For hard words and a hard subject both at once are tiresome to listen to; you know that perfectly well, don't you? " Chaucer said " yes." And now the eagle is exultant. " Aha! Indeed, I know how to speak in such a plain way to a plain man and make things so clear to him that he can shake bills [the bird's substitute for shaking hands] with my explanations, so palpable should they be." Such a bird as this eagle is not to be met with every day. Nowhere, indeed, outside the pages of Chaucer, shall we find anything like it.

But though the eagle makes most of the comedy in the second book, its passenger, so to speak, does his part too, and the heavenly journey, a literary motif very familiar to the Middle Ages, here takes a character all its own. Chaucer once again has taken a device hitherto used for high and holy things and made it serve a comic purpose. The cleverness and originality of the performance go with a lack of respect for the old literary sources, or perhaps it would be better to say that Chaucer disregarded, if indeed he did not parody, the values traditionally associated with the old literary forms and devices. In time he would contrive devices of his own, but that time was not yet.

The goal of his journey, the House of Fame, was familiar to him, and to the Middle Ages generally, in the *Meta-*

morphoses of Ovid (xii. 39-63) . But Chaucer makes two
houses out of Ovid's one. The Roman poet had put Fame
in an *arx* ' stronghold.' This answers to Chaucer's *castel*
(lines 1161, 1176, etc.) , set on a hill doubtless inspired by
Ovid's *summa* (line 43) . But Chaucer provides another
building, a house of tidings. His description of what goes
on in this house is based on Ovid, but the house itself
resembles Ovid's in two respects only: its innumerable
entries and ever-open doors. It is made of wickerwork
(not of brass or bronze) , is shaped like a cage, stands in a
valley hard by the castle, and has the gigantic length of
60 miles. Most remarkable of all, it whirls about con-
tinually, and at such a rate of speed that Chaucer can
get in only with the help of the eagle. Chaucer presumably
learned about whirling houses by reading romances. He
may have learned of wickerwork houses by actual obser-
vation in Wales.

Chaucer's castle, the House of Fame proper, with its
decorations, denizens, displays and petitions, owes to Ovid
only a few details. Fame herself is presented as the goddess
of renown and notoriety, and as the sister of the goddess
Fortune. She draws her ammunition, so to speak, from the
adjoining house of tidings, the center for rumors, gossip,
scandal, news, stories and the like. This house, too,
belongs to her, though she lives in the castle. Chaucer's
description of her is based on Vergil (*Æneid* iv. 173-183) ;
the Roman poet in turn for sundry details drew on
Homer's description of Eris (*Iliad* iv. 440 ff.) . In Vergil it
is Fama's function to spread rumors; she therefore moves
from place to place. But Chaucer followed Ovid in housing
her and made her *arx* or castle a gorgeous palace, where
she sat on a throne and dispensed renown or notoriety,
or denied these favors, as the whim moved her. Chaucer
seems to have used traditional accounts of the goddess
Fortune in creating his character of Fame, and he in-

directly acknowledges this debt in the passage where he makes Fame sister to Fortune (lines 1546 f.) .

Vergil makes Fame monstrous in appearance and wicked in character, and here he represents classical antiquity in general. Chaucer took over Vergil's description with fewer changes than one might expect. Thus, the variation in size which Vergil attributes to Fama is well enough out of doors but might be expected to prove embarrassing for a goddess seated on a throne in the great hall of a palace, yet Chaucer kept this feature of the Vergilian description nevertheless, presumably because it was so striking a peculiarity. In other ways, besides, he ignored the courtly setting which he had given her. Chaucer usually omitted or left undeveloped the allegorical figures that he found in his sources. Here his procedure was different: he changed Fame from a personification into a person. For illustration I quote part of one of her speeches:

> 1776   " Fy on yow," quod she, " everychon!
> Ye masty swyn, ye ydel wrechches,
> Ful of roten, slowe techches!
> What? false theves! wher ye wolde
> Be famous good, and nothing nolde
> Deserve why, ne never ye roughte?
> Men rather yow to hangen oughte!
> For ye be lyke the sweynte cat
> That wolde have fissh; but wostow what?
> He wolde nothing wete his clowes.
> Yvel thrift come to your jowes,
> And eke to myn, if I hit graunte,
> 1788   Or do yow favour, yow to avaunte! "

This is Fame's answer to a group of petitioners. She calls them swine, wretches, thieves, and tells them they ought to be hanged. Such language from a goddess, sitting on a throne, indicates how far Chaucer is willing to go in turning allegorical characters into human beings. Fame was traditionally wicked; Chaucer makes her vulgar as well. Her speech is true to life, but the life it is true to is not what one would expect in courtly circles.

Let me conclude by trying to answer, however briefly, this question: what did Chaucer do with the literary material he used in composing this poem? His matter was mainly representative or symbolic in kind. Instead of presenting this matter in the usual cut-and-dried fashion, with everything neatly arranged and labeled, and the symbolism carefully explained, Chaucer tried to present it as a series of real events, things that had really happened to him. He either left it to the reader to draw a given moral or, if he drew it himself, he did so incidentally and by the way, putting his comments into the narrative quite unsystematically as the spirit moved him. He made his descriptions as lively as he possibly could, and strove always first for entertainment, with edification as a by-product. In so doing, he brought new life into bones long dry and dead.

CHAPTER IV

THE PARLIAMENT OF FOWLS

OUR STUDY of Chaucer's poetic art began with the
Book of the Duchess and continued with the House
of Fame. In these poems Chaucer used a conventional
pattern of presentation but departed markedly from tradition both in matter and in style. The poem to which we
now come, the Parliament of Fowls, goes with the other
two. It will be convenient to start our account of it with
a summary of its salient features.

The Parliament of Fowls is a poem of 699 iambic pentameter verses.
These fall into seven-line stanzas with the rime-scheme ababbcc,
except for the roundel inserted before the last stanza. The poem
opens with some comments on love, but Chaucer hastens to add that
he knows about this subject not from experience but from books.
He goes on to say that he does a great deal of reading, for fun and
for lore. Not long ago he happened to see an old book which interested
him so much that he spent a whole day reading it. The book was
Cicero's Dream of Scipio, an account of a dream the younger Scipio
had in which his grandfather [by adoption] Africanus came to him
and told him of life after death. Chaucer for lack of light had to
stop reading at nightfall. He went to bed, his mind busy with the
problems he had read about in Cicero's book. At last, however, he
fell asleep and dreamt that Africanus came to him just as he had
come to the younger Scipio. Here Chaucer puts in some speculations
about dreams. Africanus told Chaucer he wanted to reward him for
reading the old book. Here Chaucer inserts a prayer to Venus to help
him tell his dream as it should be told, and then resumes the narrative once more. Africanus took him to a gate, the entrance of a walled
park. On each side was written a message to lovers. The two
messages contradicted each other, and between them they brought
Chaucer to a standstill, but Africanus shoved him in, saying that

61

neither message was for Chaucer, since he did not serve Love, but if he did not know how to love he could at least look on, and what he saw would give him material for his writing. He then took Chaucer by the hand and they went in. From this point we hear nothing more of Africanus.

Chaucer now describes the park, taking up first the trees, of which he names 13 kinds; secondly, the garden with its flowers and spring-fed pools alive with fishes; thirdly, the birds and beasts; fourthly, the instrumental music and the murmur of the breeze; fifthly, the mild climate and wholesome spices and grasses which kept everyone there from growing sick or old and made everyone a thousand times happier than words can express, in this paradise of perpetual day. After describing the park Chaucer goes on to describe its denizens, beginning with Cupid and his daughter Will (i. e. carnal appetite), and proceeding to a group made up of Pleasance, Array, Lust, and Courtesy (i. e. Pleasantness, Adornment, Pleasure, and Kindness), with Craft (i. e. the art of doing). Delight and Gentleness stood together under an oak. He saw Beauty unadorned, Youth full of fun, Foolhardiness, Flattery, and Desire, Messagery and Meed (i. e. the sending of messages and giving of bribes). Next he saw a temple, with women dancing about it and doves sitting on its roof. Before it sat Peace and Patience, surrounded by Behest (i. e. Promise) and Art and their folk. Within the temple he heard sighs so hot that they kindled new fires on the altars, and he saw that Jealousy brought about all the sorrows that lovers bear. As he went he saw the god Priapus standing in the chief place within the temple. In a corner he found Venus and her porter Riches. She lay on a bed of gold, half naked; beside her sat Bacchus and Ceres. Two young people were kneeling before her, calling on her for help. The walls of the temple were hung with broken bows of former votaries of Diana, and many love stories were painted on the walls.

Leaving the temple, Chaucer took a walk in the park and came to a clearing where he saw the goddess Nature sitting on a hill of flowers. About her was gathered a multitude of birds, for it was St Valentine's day (Feb. 14), when every bird comes there to choose its mate. Nature marshalled the birds in their appointed order, the birds of prey having the highest place, then the little birds that eat worms and the like; lowest in the dale sat the water-fowl, and the birds that eat seed sat on the green. Chaucer saw and described briefly a number of different kinds of birds belonging to these four groups. Nature held on her hand a female eagle, the princess, so to speak, of the whole assembly. And now Nature opened the parliament of birds with a speech from the throne. After a few introductory words she said that the bird of highest rank, the male eagle, should be the first to choose a mate, and that the others should follow him in order of rank. But in every case the choice made would hold only if the one chosen accepted the proposal.

The eagle chose the female eagle that Nature held on her hand. He made his proposal in the conventional language of courtly love. The female was too embarrassed to answer, and another eagle, of lower rank than the first, took advantage of the situation to make his plea, couched in like terms but with less elegance. A third eagle also plead his cause, so that the female eagle had three proposals to deal with. Chaucer reported only one speech of each eagle, but the three rivals kept at it all day long, until other birds began to get restive, and interrupted the proceedings. There followed a hot debate between the friends and the foes of courtly love, until Nature called the parliament to order and told the birds to select speakers, one for each of the four kinds present. Each speaker would then speak for the group he represented. This was agreed to, and the birds of prey elected a falcon to speak for them. The falcon thought that the arguments of the three suitors did not prove anything, and that the test should be battle. The three eagles were ready to fight, but the falcon would not have it so. The fighting he had in mind had already been done. In his opinion, the lady should take the foremost of her three suitors, the one whose knighthood, estate, and birth were most eminent. The water-fowl chose the goose to speak for them. She said nothing about the point at issue (that is, which suitor should the female eagle take), but attacked the whole business of courtly love, saying, " If she is not willing to love him, let him love another." This moved the sparrowhawk to speak up, though he was not an official spokesman. He ridiculed the goose, calling her a fool and telling her she would be better off to hold her peace. The fowls of higher rank all laughed at this, but the turtle-dove, who spoke for the seed-fowl, took the goose's words more seriously. She was moved to indignation and defended courtly love, saying, " God forbid a lover should change." She thought a lover should remain faithful to his lady however coldly the lady treated him, and even death should make no difference. The duck, another unofficial spokesman, made fun of the turtle-dove's views, and thereby drew down on herself the denunciations of the falcon. The cuckoo, who spoke for the worm-eating fowls, now added his bit to the discussion. " I don't care how long you argue," he said, " if only I can have my mate in peace." The merlin denounced the cuckoo roundly for this, calling him a glutton and a murderer, and wishing him a solitary life the rest of his days.

Nature at this point put a stop to the debate. She called on the female eagle to make her choice, advising her to take the first suitor, but leaving her free to do as she liked. The eagle asked for a year's respite, saying, " I don't want to serve Venus and Cupid as yet." Nature granted her boon, told the three lovers that a year was not so long a time for them to hold out, and gave the other birds each his mate. The birds were delighted and each pair began to bill and coo. But before the parliament broke up, a chorus of birds sang the following roundel:

680   Now welcome, somer, with thy sonne softe,
That hast this wintres wedres overshake,
And driven away the longe nyghtes blake!

Saynt Valentyn, that art ful hy on-lofte,
Thus syngen smale foules for thy sake:
Now welcome, somer, with thy sonne softe,
That hast this wintres wedres overshake!

Wel han they cause for to gladen ofte,
Sith ech of hem recovered hath hys make,
Ful blissful mowe they synge when they wake:
Now welcome, somer, with thy sonne softe,
That hast this wintres wedres overshake,
692   And driven away the longe nyghtes blake!

With the noise that the birds made in flying away Chaucer woke up, and started reading other books. He is still at it, he tells us, in the hope that thereby he may " dream something for to fare the better."

Throughout the narrative which I have just sketched Chaucer serves as reporter of what he sees and hears, not as a participant in the action. He never says a word to anybody, not even to Africanus, his guide, though Africanus of course talks to him, and after he gets into the garden of love his guide vanishes from the scene. In the *Book of the Duchess*, on the contrary, the poet talks briefly with one of the hunters, has dealings if not speech with the little dog, and carries on a long conversation with the man in black. In the *House of Fame* the poet is a mere spectator, once he gets to his destination. But he talks to both his guides: the golden eagle and the man near him in the great hall where Fame is holding audience. His conversation with this man shows that he thought of himself as present and visible like anybody else, whereas in the *Parliament of Fowls* nobody seemed aware of his existence. Here his part was strictly passive: he obeyed his guide and kept his eyes open for " mater of to wryte " (line 168). In this matter, then, the *Book of the Duchess* and the *Parliament of Fowls* stand at opposite poles; the *House of Fame* stands between them, but considerably closer to the latter.

In the *Book of the Duchess* no personified abstractions appear as characters, though some are mentioned, and the man in black characterizes Fortune at length. In the *House of Fame* one abstraction, Fame, appears as a character; others mentioned are Nature, Thought, Love, Fortune, Philosophy, and Adventure (note also the trumpets Clear Laud and Slander). In the *Parliament of Fowls* many personified abstractions actually appear on the stage, although only Nature has a speaking part. Chaucer got from the *Teseide* of Boccaccio (vii. stanzas 54-59, 64) the throng of abstractions in the garden of love. His description of Nature rests on the much longer one of Alanus de Insulis in his *Planctus Naturae*, to which Chaucer himself refers us for details (lines 316-318). The love-vision poetry of Chaucer's time swarms with such personified abstractions, many of whom make long speeches, but Chaucer spares us these and uses nearly all his personifications for decorative purposes only. In particular be it noted that the poet's guides or mentors are never personifications.

With the personified abstractions go the gods and god-

desses, likewise a heritage from classical antiquity. After
the conversion of the western world to Christianity the
poets continued to use these divinities, who indeed had
become little more than literary machinery long before the
end of the pagan period. Chaucer adorns many of his
poems with pagan deities and other figures taken from
classical mythology, following a fashion which was to
persist almost to our own day. Most of these figures come
in as mere literary allusions, but now and then they have
a more important part to play. Thus, Venus could hardly
have been left out of the garden of love in the *Parliament
of Fowls*. Chaucer uses such classical material freely in
all his dream poems.

The *Parliament of Fowls* opens with an aphorism, the
familiar one attributed to Hippocrates but here used in a
very un-Hippocratic way:

> The lyf so short, the craft so long to lerne,
> Th'assay so hard, so sharp the conquerynge,
> The dredful joye, alwey that slit so yerne:
> Al this mene I by Love, that my felynge
> Astonyeth with his wonderful werkynge
> So sore iwis, that whan I on hym thynke
> Nat wot I wel wher that I flete or synke.

This opening conforms to the rhetorical rule that a poem
should begin with a maxim, pithy saying or the like.[1]
The *House of Fame* begins similarly, with a pious prayer
of general application. In his next stanza Chaucer makes
a very neat transition from love to books and his own
reading:

> For al be that I knowe nat Love in dede
> Ne wot how that he quiteth folk here hyre,
> Yit happeth me ful ofte in bokes reede
> Of his myracles and his crewel yre.
> There rede I wel he wol be lord and syre;
> I dar nat seyn, his strokes been so sore,
> But " God save swich a lord! "—I can na moore.

[1] See J. M. Manly, in *Proceedings of the British Academy* 12.102.

The third stanza continues the subject of Chaucer's reading habits and goes on to a particular book which in the succeeding stanzas he tells us about in some detail. The reading of this book led to his dream.

The elaborate, indirect approach to the dream which we find here reminds us at once of the *Book of the Duchess*, where likewise the dream grew out of the reading of a book. In this case, however, Chaucer read the book by night, not by day as in the *Parliament*, and he came to read the book because he was troubled with sleeplessness, brought about by the pangs of unrequited love. It will be seen that the preliminaries are more complicated in the earlier poem, and it takes Chaucer 290 lines to get to the dream itself, whereas in the *Parliament of Fowls* the dream begins with line 95. In the two poems Chaucer makes use of the same device to introduce the dream, but in his repetition of the device he varies it considerably. Such repetition with variation is characteristic of Chaucer's poetic art. Another example of it is the quarrel motif, used repeatedly in the *Canterbury Tales*, but always with a good deal of variation. Note also lines 2007-2026 of the *House of Fame*, a repetition of lines 614-698.

The Proem of the *House of Fame* is given over to a discussion of dreams. Among other things, the causes of dreams come up for consideration. We get something of this in the *Parliament of Fowls* as well.

> 99   The wery huntere, slepynge in his bed,
>   To wode ayeyn his minde goth anon;
>   The juge dremeth how his plees been sped;
>   The cartere dremeth how his cartes gon;
>   The riche, of gold; the knyght fyght with his fon;
>   The syke met he drynketh of the tonne;
>   The lovere met he hath his lady wonne.
>
>   Can I not seyn if that the cause were
>   For I hadde red of Affrican byforn,
> 108   That made me to mete that he stod there;

Chaucer inserts this passage into the story of the dream. It interrupts the narrative, but not seriously so, since Africanus has not yet begun to speak, though he has already appeared to the dreamer. The stanza beginning with line 99 was taken from Claudian.[2] The thought is familiar, of course. Shakespeare has Mercutio say much the same thing in his Queen Mab speech in *Romeo and Juliet*.

After the first speech of Africanus we get another interruption: Chaucer inserts a stanza calling upon Venus to help him " to rime and also to compose " (line 119). This interruption answers to the Invocation of the *House of Fame* much as the preceding interruption answers to the Proem. The two digressions, set the one before, the other after the speech of Africanus, balance each other and have a rhetorical function: they serve as Proem and Invocation respectively, though incorporated in the narrative proper. Their true function is marked by their digressive character. Chaucer here shows himself a master of rhetoric indeed. In the opening of his new poem he manages to repeat (with variations) not only the opening device used for the *Book of the Duchess* but also the ones used for the *House of Fame*!

The two inscriptions over the gate of the park, one on each side, and giving contradictory advice to lovers, were obviously done in imitation of Dante's inscription over the gate of hell (*Inferno* iii. 1 ff.). Love is hell for many, and the inscription in black warned would-be lovers what might happen to them if they entered the garden of love. But there was also the inscription in gold, which held out alluring prospects. Chaucer could not tell which piece of advice to follow, whether to go in or stay out, and indecision stopped him in his tracks. But Africanus shoved him in, saying, " this writing is not meant for thee, . . . for thou

[2] In Sextum Consulatum Honorii Augusti Praefatio, lines 3-10.

of love hast lost thy taste. . . . But nevertheless, although thou be dull, yet what thou knowest not how to do, yet canst thou see. . . . And if thou hadst skill to compose, I shall show thee matter to write of." This is meant to be funny, of course, like nearly everything said about Chaucer in all his works, irrespective of whether he says it himself or puts it in the mouth of somebody else. The humor is emphasized by the shoving and, for those who know Dante, includes the inscriptions over the gate. We have no way of knowing how many people in Chaucer's audience would chuckle over the turn the poet gave to the Dante passage, but in all likelihood there were few such connoisseurs at the English court. Yet Chaucer himself surely relished his little joke even if nobody saw the point when he read the poem to his courtly audience.

The promise of Africanus to show Chaucer matter to write of makes the purpose of the dream clear. The eagle in the *House of Fame* also made much of this purpose, although it mentioned another purpose as well: recreation. Here then the two poems have much in common, and in both, as we have seen, the poet looks and listens but takes no part in what is going on about him. A like purpose appears in the *Book of the Duchess*, but here the poet has to ask questions and win the confidence of the man in black in order to get the full story that he is seeking. In other words, the method of getting information used in the earlier poem differs radically from the method used in the two later poems.

The garden of love is an earthly paradise the features of which we need not linger on. But the lists or catalogs included in Chaucer's description of the garden call for a few words of comment. The catalog as a literary device is probably as old as literature itself. We get it in Homer, for instance. The oldest poems that we have in English are the three sixth-century catalogs (technically known as thulas) incorporated in the seventh-century poem *Widsith*. Chaucer names most of the personified abstractions in catalog style, but he uses this form of presentation more strictly in his list of trees and, later on, in his list of birds. In both these lists the name of the particular tree or bird is systematically accompanied by a descriptive epithet or short characterization. The list of lovers (lines 288-292) is given in a form more rigorous still: the names speak for themselves. The lists add to the complexity and therefore to the richness of the artistic effect. In using them, Chaucer was following rhetorical precept, but the rhetoricians in turn were only rationalizing a poetic practice that goes back to prehistoric times and needs no justification. Lists are still used by poets, and their poetic value has not changed much down the centuries. If the names mean nothing to you the list becomes a mere sequence of words which you are likely to skip. But if the names are familiar to you they arouse associations in your mind and the list becomes a series of allusions freighted with values beyond calculation.

With line 295 (200 lines after the dream begins) Chaucer reaches his main theme, the parliament of birds held on St Valentine's day by order of the goddess Nature, who presides over the proceedings. It is wholly appropriate that this parliament should be held in a wooded part of the garden of love, for it is the purpose of the meeting to see to it that each bird shall have a mate. The parliament is devoted to the subject of love, and all the speeches bear on the problems of love-making and mating. But the debate does not begin at once. Before Nature calls the meeting to order at line 383, we have descriptions of Nature herself, of the place of meeting, and of the way in which the birds are seated or assigned places to stand (the members of the parliament are represented as standing or sitting, not as perching). Then follows the catalog of birds already discussed. After that, Chaucer repeats, with the usual variation, what he said earlier about the purpose of the meeting, and adds a very important piece of information: that Nature held on her hand a female eagle,

373   of shap the gentilleste
      That evere she among hire werkes fond,
      The moste benygne and the goodlieste.
      In hire was every vertu at his reste,
      So ferforth that Nature hireself hadde blysse
378   To loke on hire, and ofte hire bek to kysse.

This paragon of a bird is evidently the heroine of our story, the center about which the doings of the parliament revolve. Her place on Nature's hand symbolizes her importance in the action. But she has nothing to say until the meeting is nearly over. When she does speak, her words end the debate. Nature for that reason does not give her the floor until the debate has run its course.

The female eagle belongs to the birds of prey, the aristocrats of the parliament. They " were set highest " (line 324). Below them came the worm-eating fowls. The water-fowl " sat lowest in the dale " (line 327). Since our story is a fable, it seems reasonable enough to conjecture that this three-fold division answers to the division of medieval society into the nobility and gentry at the top, the tradesmen of the towns in the middle, and the peasantry at the bottom. The fourth group, the seed-eating fowls who " sat on the green " (line 328), are not classified in terms of high and low, and it has therefore been conjectured that they represent the clergy. There is nothing in the text of the poem inconsistent with this scheme of representation, but it remains a guess.

Still more problematic is the relationship, if any, between Chaucer's parliament of birds and the English parliament of his day. Nature opens the session with a speech from the throne reminiscent of the ceremonial speech at the beginning of a session of Parliament, but she could hardly have done anything else and this parallel is not worth much. Her instructions to the four groups of birds to choose spokesmen remind us of the Speaker of the House of Commons, but the correspondence is far from exact, as each group of birds chooses a spokesman, making a total of four. Moreover, the lower classes had no representation whatever in a medieval parliament: the Commons in Chaucer's day consisted of gentry from the counties and well-to-do burgesses from the towns. The water-fowl can be given a parliamentary connection only by making them poach on the preserves of the worm-eating fowls, a counsel of desperation which cannot be reconciled with the text of the poem. At most, then, one may say that Chaucer, through his knowledge of English parliamentary practice, got the idea of having spokesmen but changed the number from one to four to suit his particular purpose.

Although the birds hold their parliament in order to choose their mates, nearly the whole meeting is devoted to something rather different: the pleas of three male eagles for the favor of the female eagle that Nature holds on her hand. The three lovers are seeking not a mate but a mistress, as the royal eagle tells us in so many words (line 416). Chaucer gives us only the first round of pleading, the first speech of each of the three eagles. But he tells us that the speaking lasted from the morning till nearly sunset. The samples which Chaucer gives us all follow the regular courtly-love pattern. Thus, the royal eagle says, " I am all hers, and will ever serve her." He wants to be her servant, to obey her orders, to do whatever she says. This relationship of mistress and servant is the fundamental thing in courtly love. The royal eagle presents beautifully the code which governs the courtly lover in his relation to his mistress. The other two eagles also speak well, but their pleas lack the perfection which the plea of their royal rival shows. In other words, the royal eagle has a superiority in speech consonant with his higher rank.

Chaucer enjoyed greatly the love debate, in spite of its length. At any rate, he praised the speeches very highly:

> 484 Of al my lyf, syn that day I was born,
> So gentil ple in love or other thyng
> Ne herde nevere no man me beforn, . . .

But not all the audience appreciated them. The goose, for instance, said, " All this is not worth a fly " (line 501). Likes and dislikes here go with social distinctions. The birds of prey and the seed-eating birds understood and believed in courtly love, but the worm-eating birds and the water-fowl could make nothing of it, and found it silly. Yet it was the inability or unwillingness of the pleaders to stop which finally brought rebellion in the ranks. As the sun got lower and lower in the sky

> 491 The noyse of foules for to ben delyvered
> So loude rong, " Have don, and lat us wende! "
> That wel wende I the wode hadde al toshyvered.
> " Com of! " they criede, " allas, ye wol us shende!
> Whan shal youre cursede pletynge have an ende?
> How sholde a juge eyther parti leve
> For ye or nay, withouten any preve? "
> The goos, the cokkow, and the doke also
> So cryede, " Kek, kek! kokkow! quek, quek! " hye
> 500 That thourgh myne eres the noyse wente tho.

The goose and the cuckoo, speaking (without authority) for water-fowl and worm-fowl respectively, went so far as to volunteer to say their verdict " fair and quick." The turtle-dove, one of the seed-eating birds, told the officious fowls they could wait a while yet, and added that it is better to keep quiet than to meddle with things you know nothing about. But Nature saw that something had to be done. She ruled that each of the four groups of birds should choose a spokesman to " say the verdict for all you birds " (line 525) . This set things straight for the moment, and the falcon, speaker for the birds of prey, pronounced in favor of the royal eagle, though not in so many words. But then trouble started up once more. The debate of the rival lovers had been stopped at last, but the other debate, the quarrel about the merits of courtly love as such, rose to the surface again. The goose, as we have seen, had already had something to say on this subject. She now came forward a second time. To quote,

> 554   The water-foules han here hedes leid
> Togedere, and of a short avysement,
> Whan everych hadde his large golee seyd,
> They seyden sothly, al by oon assent,
> How that " the goos, with here facounde gent,
> That so desyreth to pronounce oure nede,
> 560   Shal telle oure tale," and preyede " God hire spede! "

The poet's hearers had already listened to one speech of the goose (lines 501-504) and therefore knew what the water-birds meant by " her refined eloquence." But to make assurance doubly sure Chaucer immediately gave his audience another taste of her quality:

> 561   And for these water-foules tho began
> The goos to speke, and in hire kakelynge
> She seyde, " Pes! now tak kep every man,
> And herkeneth which a resoun I shal brynge!
> My wit is sharp, I love no taryinge;
> I seye I rede hym, though he were my brother,
> 567   But she wol love hym, lat hym love another! "

Such " eloquence " and such views were made for ridicule, and the sparrowhawk supplied it. But the heretical advice shocked the turtle-dove, and when the seed-fowl chose her for spokesman and asked her to speak her mind, she expressed with real eloquence the orthodox doctrine of courtly love:

584 Though that his lady everemore be straunge,
  Yit lat hym serve hire ever, til he be ded.

So far, the duck had contributed only " quek, quek "
(line 499) to the proceedings. But now she spoke up:

589 " Wel bourded," quod the doke, " by myn hat!
  That men shulde loven alway causeles,
  Who can a resoun fynde or wit in that?
  Daunseth he murye that is myrtheles?
  Who shulde recche of that is recheles?
  Ye quek! " yit seyde the doke, ful wel and fayre,
595 " There been mo sterres, God wot, than a payre."

The goose was a fool, and the sparrowhawk answered her
by pointing out that fact. But the duck made some telling
points, and the falcon himself, official spokesman for the
birds of prey, took the floor to put her in her place.

596 " Now fy, cherl! " quod the gentil tercelet,
  " Out of the donghil cam that word ful right!
  Thou canst nat seen which thyng is wel beset!
  Thou farst by love as oules don by lyght:
  The day hem blent, ful wel they se by nyght.
  Thy kynde is of so low a wrechednesse
  That what love is, thow canst nat seen ne gesse."

This speech of the falcon's is one of the most important
in the whole poem. According to the falcon, water-fowl
(the " kynde " to which the duck belongs) are a social
class so low that they are incapable of understanding or
even of guessing what love is. The love which the falcon
has in mind is courtly love, of course. A peasant does not
know how to love; he is of the dunghill and the finer
emotions mean nothing to him. A churl has little indeed
in common with a lady or gentleman. He belongs to another world, a world to which culture and refinement of
any kind are alien and incomprehensible. The falcon here
expresses a view generally held and indeed taken for
granted in the Middle Ages. Courtly love in particular

was for the upper classes only, as its very name indicates. We shall soon see that the middle classes, the worm-eating birds of our poem, had no part in it either, if their spokesman truly represents them.

We have already noted that the falcon, the spokesman for the birds of prey, spoke to the point when he said his verdict (lines 533-553). The three eagles had been debating all day, and it was the duty of the spokesmen to decide which eagle had made the best case for himself. The falcon did his duty, but the next spokesman, the goose, fool that she was, left the point at issue and took up something else: in flat contradiction to the code of courtly love, she advised a lover whose lady would not love him to turn to another lady. This led to a series of speeches which we have just reviewed. The series ends with a speech by the falcon, a speech which closes the debate on fidelity in love and, by bringing the falcon forward again, reminds us that he had spoken a little earlier on a different subject: had said his verdict on the three eagles. And if the falcon's reappearance does not remind *us* of his first appearance and what he said then, it seems to have reminded the cuckoo at any rate, for the cuckoo now pushed himself forward as spokesman for the worm-eating fowls and said his verdict, going back to the point at issue which the goose had ignored, and which the speakers that followed her had not taken up, so absorbed were they in debating the goose's advice to lovers. Be it noted that the worm-eating fowls did not choose the cuckoo for their spokesman; he chose himself. His verdict, then, may be looked upon as personal rather than representative of his kind. But Chaucer does not have any worm-eating fowl dispute the cuckoo's verdict or object to his serving as spokesman. In other words, the poet does not make it clear to what extent the cuckoo was really representative of the worm-eating fowls. He leaves this question open, and we shall have to leave it open too.

The cuckoo first addresses himself to the three debaters, saying, " If only I can have my mate in peace, I don't care how long you debate." Then he turns to the parliament, and says his verdict: " Let each of them be without a mate all their lives! This is my counsel, since they cannot compose their differences." This is obviously no proper verdict. It is most unreasonable of the cuckoo to expect the three lovers to agree. Each claims that he loves the lady best and most. It would be self-stultification indeed for any of them to admit that after all he did not love the lady as well or as much as another loved her. Moreover, the cuckoo's verdict punishes all three lovers instead of giving the lady to one of them, and the lady loses all her lovers. Worst of all, the cuckoo by his words makes it plain that he does not take the debate seriously. Courtly love means nothing to him. It is this that brings down upon him the wrath of the merlin.

> 610 " Ye, have the glotoun fild inow his paunche,
> Thanne are we wel! " seyde the merlioun;
> " Thou mortherere of the heysoge on the braunche
> That broughte the forth, thow [rewthelees] glotoun!
> Lyve *thou* soleyn, wormes corupcioun!
> For no fors is of lak of thy nature—
> 616 Go, lewed be thou whil the world may dure! "

By this time Nature had had enough. The spokesmen had got into heated arguments with each other and with other birds, so that the verdicts on the original debate had themselves grown into a series of little debates. Only one of the spokesmen, the falcon, had said a verdict which made sense, and even he had not said outright what he meant. The falcon had left it to the female eagle to choose a lover, though he had made it pretty plain which lover she ought to choose, and Nature followed the same course.

But she promised to grant the female eagle's first prayer, and this proved to be a prayer to put off any decision " until this year be gone " (line 647). Nature perforce agreed, and told the suitors,

> 660   Beth of good herte, and serveth alle thre.
>   A yer is nat so longe to endure.

In the foregoing I have said nothing about Chaucer's sources for the doings of the birds in parliament assembled. Gatherings of birds are well known in medieval literature, but the particular turn that Chaucer gave to this meeting does not appear elsewhere; the closest parallel is Oton de Grandson's *Songe de St Valentin*, which likewise combines bird parliament and *demande d'amours*, but, as we have seen, Chaucer reports very little of the love debate and makes much of the clash between the birds of higher and lower rank over courtly love itself. The partiality which Nature shows for one of the contestants, a departure from the pattern proper to the love contest, has been explained on the hypothesis that the poem is an occasional one in which the royal eagle stands for some royal personage. But neither the prayer of the female eagle for a year's delay nor the behavior of the fowls of lower rank fits in well with a poem intended to compliment a king or prince. In some ways Chaucer's performance reminds one of an earlier Middle English poem, *The Owl and the Nightingale*, but we cannot prove that he knew this work.

The *Parliament of Fowls* is usually dated in 1381-1382, on grounds which Professor B. H. Bronson in a recent paper (*ELH* XV 247 ff.) has shown to be untenable. Mr Bronson rightly took the north-northwest of the invocation to Venus as geographical rather than astronomical in reference, but he took Chaucer's compass points too seriously, I think. The geography here is surely humorous, and my guess is that Chaucer was specifying the location of some lady who had come to visit him in his room. If he was facing south as he began to write his dream down, a lady looking over his shoulder would be north-northwest. Whether the lady deserved identification with Venus or not I have no means of knowing, but I feel sure she would not have objected to the compliment.

Mr Bronson in the same paper pointed out certain features of our poem which he took to be signs of revision. In particular, he argued that the female eagle held on Nature's hand originally had only one suitor, the royal eagle. If so, we have an explanation for the goose's use of the singular rather than the plural in lines 566-567:

> I seye I rede him, though he were my brother,
> But she wol love him, lat him love another.

There can be no doubt, I think, that the goose was talking about the royal eagle here. But it does not follow that he had no rivals. The falcon had just said his verdict, and this verdict was in favor of the royal eagle, whose suit Nature too had expressly favored. The goose, I take it, thought that settled the matter, and simply ignored the unsuccessful suitors, going on to something else, as we have already seen. In my opinion the loose ends and inconsistencies in our poem do not support the hypothesis that Chaucer revised his work. He wrote that way in the first place, and what seem to be faults actually serve his stylistic purpose. A conversational style of writing cannot be neat and orderly without spoiling the effect aimed at. With life goes imperfection.

Chapter V

THE LEGEND OF GOOD WOMEN

S O FAR we have taken up Chaucer's longer poems in what appears to be their chronological order (though certainty in this matter is not to be had, apart from the *Book of the Duchess*). Our next poem, however, was composed later than *Troilus and Criseyde*. In the prolog of the *Legend of Good Women* the god of Love rebukes Chaucer for having told the story of Cressida, and he bids the poet make amends by celebrating in song women who proved faithful rather than faithless to their lovers. If nevertheless we look at the *Legend* first, we do so because it has the form of a love-vision and therefore appropriately follows the three love-visions we have just examined.

To be precise, only the prolog of our poem is cast in the love-vision form. In the Gg version, the prolog ends with the following couplet:

> 544 And with that word, of slep I gan awake,
> And ryght thus on my Legende gan I make.

In the F version, the end of the dream is nowhere marked in so many words, but the final couplet implies, I think, that the poet has waked up:

> 578 And with that word my bokes gan I take,
> And ryght thus on my Legende gan I make.

Moreover, the penance imposed on Chaucer for his " mis-saying " incidentally makes it clear that the legend proper does not belong to the dream:

F 481   Thou shalt, while that thou lyvest, yer by yere,
        The moste partye of thy tyme spende
        In makyng of a glorious legende
        Of goode wymmen, maydenes and wyves,
        That weren trewe in lovyng al hire lyves;
        And telle of false men that hem bytraien,
        That al hir lyf ne do nat but assayen
        How many women they may doon a shame;
        For in youre world that is now holde a game.
        And thogh the lyke nat a lovere bee,
  491 Speke wel of love; this penance yive I thee.

Chaucer was to spend most of his time, the rest of his life, making a glorious legend of good women: that is, celebrating the lives of women faithful to their lovers (and so to Love) even unto death. He actually composed only nine such lives, and left the ninth one unfinished. It has been conjectured that he began making them in 1386, at the behest of Queen Anne, and that he stopped working on them in 1394, after the queen's death. If so, he did, on the average, one life a year during the period of composition.[1] But this numerical correspondence, however neat, may represent mere coincidence. Be it noted that one of the lives (the fourth) tells of two women, Hypsipyle and Medea; they were taken together because they had the same lover, Jason, who proved faithless to both. Chaucer thus made nine lives but celebrated ten saints of Love in song.

In medieval times the word *legend* meant a saint's life. The transfer of this technical term from Christianity to the cult of courtly love naturally gave it a new meaning. The lives of Chaucer's ten good women were saintly for Cupid and his votaries, not for the authorities of the Christian Church, who had other views of hallowhood. The appearance of Cleopatra as the leading saint of Love makes clear from the start what was good about Chaucer's ten

---

[1] See J. L. Lowes, *Geoffrey Chaucer*, p. 163.

women. They achieved that supreme goodness known as saintliness by giving their all for Love, even life itself. It was Cleopatra's suicide after her lover's death that made her a saint of Cupid. By dying of her own free will she proved her complete devotion to Anthony and so to the god of Love. The pagan character of all this needs no emphasis; it speaks for itself. But it differs greatly from the paganism of classical antiquity. The cult of courtly love, rooted in the lusts of the flesh and fed by the love literature of the ancients, grew up in the shadow of the Church and took shape accordingly. In particular, the lover's worship of his mistress owed much if not all to the Christian environment in which it flourished. Only by spiritualizing its fires could medieval love become courtly.

The F version of the prolog may be summarized as follows:

The poet begins by pointing out that our knowledge of heaven and hell comes, not from experience but from hearsay or books. But God forbid that we should believe only what we have knowledge of by experience. Truth is not so restricted. We learn much from books: historical truth and the wisdom handed down from the past. Where no other evidence is to be had we ought to believe what books tell us. Chaucer himself is fond of reading and believes what he reads. He thinks so highly of books that no amusement can take him from them, except sometimes on a feast-day. But when May comes, with its birds and flowers, farewell his book and his devotion (lines 1-39).

Chaucer is also very fond of a particular flower, the daisy. In May he gets up early every morning to see the daisy open. He loves it and will always love it. In the evening he runs to see the daisy close when the sun sets. This flower loves the sun and hates darkness. The poet laments his lack of words to praise the daisy as it ought to be praised, but calls on lovers to help him, whether they are " with the leaf or with the flower," men who know how to express themselves (i. e. poets). He hopes they will not mind if he repeats what they have said, since he is doing it in honor of love and in the service of the flower. He now turns to the flower itself and prays it to inspire him to song (line 40-96).

At this point Chaucer goes back to the subject of books. He will explain in due time why he brought up this subject. You cannot say everything at once in rime (lines 97-102).

Returning now to the daisy, Chaucer tells us of what happened to him on the first day of May. He got up very early, driven by a thirst to see the daisy open. He knelt by it in the meadow until it had opened. It smelt so sweet and looked so lovely that no other plant could be compared with it. Winter was gone and spring had clothed the earth anew in green. The birds that had escaped the fowler were singing to their mates, making love in courtly style. All singing as one, they bade the summer welcome. Zephyrus and Flora breathed on the flowers and made them open. It seemed to Chaucer that he could spend all May in the meadow without sleep or food or drink. He lay down on his side and made ready to stay there all day, looking at the daisy (lines 103-187).

Here Chaucer puts in an apologetic passage. In spite of his praise of the daisy he is not taking sides with the party of the flower against the party of the leaf. He does not know who are on either side. This poem is to be about something else: stories current before the strife between flower and leaf was begun (lines 188-196).

The poet now resumes his story of what happened to him on May day. When the sun set and the daisy closed, he went home and had a bed made for himself out of doors, in an arbor. There he fell asleep in an hour or two (lines 197-209).

Chaucer's Dream

I dreamt that I lay in the meadow, to see the daisy. From afar the god of Love came, walking in the meadow, and leading by the hand a queen clad like a daisy. The god was clothed in silk and wore a sun for crown. His face shone so bright that I could hardly look at him. He looked at me so sternly that my heart turned cold. The queen he held by the hand was so womanly, benign and gentle that no creature half so beautiful could be found anywhere (lines 210-246).

Here Chaucer interrupts the story of the dream to say a ballad which he has composed in praise of the queen. He adds that the ballad does not overpraise her, for she surpasses all. Besides, she kept him from dying for fear of Love's words and face, as his hearers will find out at the proper time (lines 247-281).

The story of the dream is now resumed. Behind the god of Love, says the poet, I saw some 19 ladies coming, royally clad, and after them came three or four times as many women as I thought could possibly have lived on earth since God made Adam. And these women were each one true in love. When they saw the daisy they all knelt down and sang with one voice, " Weal and honor to troth of womanhood, and to this flower that bears all our worth in symbol! Its white crown bears the witnessing." All the company then sat down, the god of Love in first place, next to him the queen, and then the others in order of rank. For a time there was silence. At last the god of Love looked at me and said, " Who kneeleth there? " I answered, " Sire, it is I," and came nearer to him and saluted him. He said, " What dost thou here, so nigh my own flower, so boldly? A worm would be worthier to come near my flower than thou art." " And why, sire," said I, " if it please you." " Because," said he, " thou art in no way deserving of it. It is my relic, worthy and delightful, and thou art my foe. Thou canst not deny it, for thou hast translated the Romance of the Rose, which is a heresy against my law, and of Cressida thou hast said as it pleased thee, making men trust women less. By St Venus, who is my mother, if thou live thou shalt repent this cruelly." (lines 282-340) .

Then the queen spake and said, " God, for courtesy's sake you must give him a chance to reply to these accusations. If you were not a god you might have been misinformed. Also, this man is foolish, and so he might have done it without meaning any harm. Or somebody might have made him do it. Or he may now be very sorry he did it. It was not so bad to translate the work of others as it would have been if he had made it up himself. A righteous lord ought to keep such things in mind and not play the tyrant. A king ought to deal justly with his subjects. And if he can make no excuse but asks for mercy, you ought to be merciful. The man has served you well in other poems. I ask you not to hurt this man, if he shall swear that he will mend his ways and write about women who are faithful to their lovers." The god of Love answered, " Madam, you are so good and true that I cannot deny your request. Do with him as you like." And turning to me he said, " Now go thank my lady here." I rose and knelt before her and said, " Madam, may God reward you for coming to my help. But truly I did not think I was doing wrong. It was my intention to further troth in love and to make men beware of falseness and vice." She answered, " Let be thy arguing. Thou art forgiven; hold to that. Now I will say that penance thou shalt do for thy sin. Thou shalt spend the greater part of thy time, from now on, in making a glorious legend of good women who were true in loving, all their lives; and tell of false men that betray them. And though it does not please thee to be a lover, speak well of love. Now go thy way; this penance is not a heavy one." The god of Love smiled, and then said, " Knowest thou who this lady is? " I answered, " Nay, sire, but I see well she is good." Love said, " Hast thou not in a book the story of Queen Alcestis, who was turned into a daisy? " I answered and said, " Yes, now I know her. Well hath she repaid me for my love of her flower. It is no wonder that Jove translated her to the skies." Then Love said, " It was a great negligence of thine not to put her in the ballad thou made: ' Hide, Absalom, thy tresses.' Now I charge thee to put her in thy legend. And now farewell, I charge thee no more. I must go home to paradise with all this company. But serve always the fresh daisy, and begin thy legend with Cleopatra. I know that thou canst not rime everything that such lovers did in their day; it would be too long to read and to hear. It will be enough to repeat the gist of the stories found in old authors." (lines 341-577).

With this speech of the god of Love, Chaucer's dream ends. The poet adds that he took up his books and got to work on his legend.

In one Chaucerian manuscript (commonly called Gg) another version of the prolog of the *Legend* has come down to us. For many years philologists have disagreed at length about the two versions, the question at issue being that of priority: which version is the earlier? For my part I follow ten Brink and others in giving priority to version F (the B of Skeat's edition), the version which I have just outlined. Without arguing the matter, I will indicate briefly the most important changes Chaucer made in doing his revised version (Gg, the A of Skeat). He changed the time of the dream from the beginning to the end of May, and brought it in much earlier in the poem (with line 104 instead of line 210). He shortened considerably the passages about the daisy and the birds. He spoke of the queen by name when he described her at her first appearance, instead of holding her name back until nearly the end of her long speech. He incorporated the ballad into the dream, putting it in the mouths of the ladies of Love's train, who sang it instead of the short song they sang in the earlier version. He took Love's words about the ballad

to heart, changing the last line of each stanza by replacing
" my lady cometh " with " Alceste is here." He lengthened
Love's denunciation of Chaucer from 21 to 71 lines. He
also made the queen's defense of the poet somewhat longer.
He shortened Love's last speech from 40-odd lines to less
than 20 lines. He made many other smaller changes,
some of which are improvements, though others are not.[2]

It may be well to give a few illustrations of Chaucer's
changes. The last couplet of the prolog, quoted above in
both versions, shows improvement in revision, as it is
obviously desirable that the dream be brought clearly and
plainly to an end. In other cases the revision tightens the
structure and straightens things out at the expense of
attractive features of the earlier version. A good example
is the second passage about old books, which reads in F
as follows:

> 97 But wherfore that I spak, to yive credence
>   To olde stories and doon hem reverence,
>   And that men mosten more thyng beleve
>   Then men may seen at eye, or elles preve,—
>   That shal I seyn, whanne that I see my tyme;
> 102 I may not al at-ones speke in ryme.

The poet anticipates that his hearers by now may be
wondering why he brought up the subject of old books and
old stories at all, as he soon dropped it and began talking

[2] In making the Gg version Chaucer canceled 126 lines of the F version:
50-52, 57-60, 64-65, 68-70, 83-96, 101-107, 109-117, 144, 152-179, 181, 183-
187, 201, 229-231, 247, 271-275, 297-299, 321, 334, 348-349, 357, 368, 380,
496-497, 539-540, 543, 552-565, 568-577. He composed 93 new lines for the
Gg version: 54, 72, 85-88, 91, 105, 138-141, 161-162, 164, 199-200, 247, 258-
263, 268-312, 324-327, 344-345, 348, 360-364, 368-369, 400-401, 414-415,
527-532. He revised the following lines in such a way as to lengthen or
shorten the passage: F 71-72 and 81-82 answer to Gg 69-70; F 139 and 143,
to Gg 127; F 180, to Gg 50 and 90; F 202 and 211, to Gg 106; F 212-213,
to Gg 142-145; F 332, to Gg 264-265; F 339-340, to Gg 316; F 358, to Gg
333-334; and F 541-542, to Gg 533. The revision may involve canceling part
of the line; thus, F 56 became Gg 58 by cancellation of " And I love it,
and " together with replacement of " ever ylike " by its semantic equivalent
" as wel in wynter as in somer."

about a flower, the daisy, a subject remote from dusty tomes. But instead of saying why he began his poem as he did, Chaucer says, " I shall tell you when the proper time comes. I can't tell you everything at once." This is a Chaucerian touch, if there ever was one. In the revision, Chaucer dropped lines 101-102 and changed the other four lines to the following:

81 But wherfore that I spak, to yeve credence
To bokes olde and don hem reverence,
Is for men shulde autoritees beleve,
There as there lyth non other assay by preve.

This is feeble stuff, so far. But the poet goes on to say,

85 For myn entent is, or I fro yow fare,
The naked text in English to declare
Of many a story, or elles of many a geste,
As autours seyn; leveth hem if yow leste!

Here everything is made perfectly clear, but the light-heartedness is gone, in spite of the effort at levity in the last line.

A different case is the first passage about old books, which ends thus in F:

27 Wel ought us thanne honouren and beleve
These bokes, there we han noon other preve.
And as for me, though that I konne but lyte,
30 On bokes for to rede I me delyte,
And to hem yive I feyth and ful credence,
And in myn herte have hem in reverence
So hertely, that ther is game noon
That fro my bokes maketh me to goon,
35 But yt be seldom on the holyday,
Save, certeynly, whan that the month of May
Is comen, and that I here the foules synge,
And that the floures gynnen for to sprynge,
39 Farwel my bok, and my devocioun!

Chaucer changed this passage a good deal, when he made his revision of the prolog:

27 Wel ought us thanne on olde bokes leve,
There as there is non other assay by preve.
And as for me, though that my wit be lyte,
30 On bokes for to rede I me delyte,
And in myn herte have hem in reverence,
And to hem yeve swich lust and swich credence
That there is wel unethe game noon
That fro my bokes make me to goon,
35 But it be other upon the halyday
Or ellis in the joly tyme of May:
Whan that I here the smale foules synge
And that the floures gynne for to sprynge
39 Farwel my stodye, as lastynge that sesoun!

The change in line 39 was surely made in a moment of poetical aberration (though Robinson's pointing makes it worse and is unjust to the poor poet). Most of the other changes were made to get rid of the run-on lines. In the earlier version there were three of these: 27, 32, and 36. In the later version, all the lines are end-stopped. In other passages of the revised version Chaucer did the same thing, and he seems to have looked upon a run-on line as metrically inferior, though not to be ruled out altogether.

It will be worth our while to look at the changes in this passage more narrowly. By comparing the two versions we can look over the poet's shoulder, so to speak, while he is at work and learn something about one aspect, at least, of his poetic art: his technic of revision. It would be possible to write a whole book about this technic of his in the *Legend of Good Women*. Here we have only a few pages for the study of a single passage, and it would be perilous to base any generalizations on our gatherings, but I think our time will be well spent none the less.

We might as well begin at the beginning, with line 27. As it stands, this line does not make a complete unit of thought; the thought is completed by the first two words of line 28. Chaucer's problem was to make the thought complete within the limits of the line. He got the space needful for this by canceling the verb *honouren,* which was something of a metrical filler anyhow, and contenting himself with one infinitive. The *and* after *honouren* had the function of linking the two infinitives. Now that one of the infinitives was canceled, the link served no further purpose and had to be canceled too. These cancelations left Chaucer with two feet to fill in line 27. He might have shifted " these bokes " of the next line into the blank space, but the line he would have made by so doing could have been given a satisfactory scansion with difficulty if at all. He therefore gave himself a little more leeway by canceling the prefix *be-* of his second infinitive, thus changing the verb-form into a simple *leve.* Into the space of five syllables thereby made available in line 27, Chaucer put the phrase " on olde bokes," filling the line neatly enough from a metrical point of view and completing the thought beautifully within the limits of the line. The phrase actually used, " on olde bokes," was obviously inspired by the " these bokes " of the earlier version, taking shape as it did to fit the metrical and syntactical conditions of Chaucer's problem.

In the foregoing I have made no effort to reconstruct the course of events in a sequence true to psychological reality. I do not know what this sequence was, and I see no way of finding out. Chaucer may perfectly well have started by deciding to shift " these bokes " to line 27, and only then may he have looked at that line to see what he could dispense with there. But I am inclined to think that he began by brooding over his problem, and that he ended with a solution which came to him in a flash, all at once. Certainly he need not have gone through any such conscious procedure as that which I have outlined. But whether he analyzed and then synthesized consciously or unconsciously, his mind worked on the problem before it solved it, and the elements which his mind had to consider before the problem could be solved are the elements which I have pointed out. Whether these elements were considered one at a time or together we shall never know, but we do know that they were all considered.

Chaucer's problem in line 28 differed greatly from the problem he solved in line 27. When he shifted " these bokes " or their equivalent to line 27, he thereby made a blank space in line 28, a space which had to be filled to satisfy the metrical requirements of the line. His problem, then, was one of expansion or augmentation. What was left of line 28 had to be given a new wording which would fill up the line. The poet had to say the same thing in more words. A little prolixity was needed. He expanded *noon other preve* ' no other experience ' to *non other assay by preve* ' no other test by experience.' This statement is more precise as well as longer than the earlier one, but the great reason for changing the wording was to make the statement longer, not to make it more precise. In other words, the problem here was metrical, not semantic. The same applies to the expansion of the first part of the line: from *there we han* ' where we have ' to *there as there is* ' there where there is.' In this case the metrical requirements made it needful to cancel the pronoun and change the verb, but there is no real difference in the thought.

The change in line 29 amounts to little. There is no change at all in the thought, but the wording of the revised version is such that the personal pronoun *I* does not come in. Chaucer also gets rid of the *I* in line 31. The earlier version has three *I*'s in as many lines (29, 30, and 31), of which only one is kept in the later version, the one in line 30. This change is to be reckoned a stylistic improvement, an avoidance of repetition.

Line 30 is left unchanged. Lines 31 and 32 are made

to change places, and the first two words of line 33 are
canceled. These words, " so hertely," belong grammatically
to line 32 and keep that line from being end-stopped.
Their cancelation, then, turns line 32 (or line 31, as it
becomes in the revised version) into an end-stopped line.
But the idea behind the canceled words needs expression,
and Chaucer found means to get this idea in without
giving up the systematic end-stopping which he liked to
have. To express this idea he used the word *swich* ' such '
(that is, ' so much ') . He found he could not insert *swich*
into line 32, because that would destroy the metrical
pattern of the line. He therefore put line 32 right after
line 30, and brought the old line 31 down to the position
of line 32. The pattern of this line (the new 32) included
a word-pair connected by the conjunction *and*, and
Chaucer kept the pairing, though he changed one member
of the pair. The second member of the pair was modified
by the adjective *ful*, and it was easy to substitute *swich*
for this *ful*; there is even a connection in meaning, though
of course not a complete equivalence. The first member
of the pair had no modifier, but before it came an *I* which
could be dispensed with, and Chaucer put another *swich*
where the *I* had stood. He had to have two for the sake
of symmetry, one modifier for each member of the word-
pair. But " swich feyth and swich credence " did not fully
satisfy him, in spite of its symmetrical structure. The two
words of the word-pair mean very much the same thing,
and Chaucer saw no point in the semantic repetition. The
second member of the pair, *credence*, was the rime word
and could not be changed, but *feyth* was easier to handle.
Chaucer replaced it with *lust* ' interest,' a very satisfactory
solution indeed.

With " so hertely " canceled, the rest of line 33 needed
expansion, the problem here being like that in line 28.
Chaucer turned the trick readily enough, by inserting the

adverbs *wel* and *unethe* 'hardly' before *game*. This changed the meaning a little, but so little that the change hardly mattered. Line 34 was left as it was, except for one subtle change: the indicative *maketh* was replaced by the subjunctive *make*. This change goes with the expansion of line 33; in both cases the statement, unqualified in the earlier version, has become slightly less positive.

In both versions the rest of the passage specifies the exceptions to the rule set down in lines 33-34. These exceptions are two in number: the holiday and the month of May. In the earlier version the two exceptions are not on the same footing: Chaucer said he left his books seldom on holidays but he made no such qualification about his behavior in May. In the later version, however, Chaucer treated the two exceptions in the same way: he marked their equality by using the correlative pair *other . . . or ellis* 'either . . . or else.' The first member of the correlation, *other*, replaces the "seldom" of line 35; the second member, *or ellis*, replaces the "save, certeynly" of line 36. The correlation carried with it a parallelism in the structure of the two lines, a parallelism not to be found in the earlier version, where line 35 ends with a prepositional phrase whereas line 36 ends with a clause which runs on into the next line. Chaucer took the consequences of the correlation which he had set up and made the two lines parallel in structure throughout: "upon the halyday" (line 35) corresponds in formal pattern to "in the joly tyme of May," though the correspondence is not absolutely rigid, since the second prepositional phrase has a somewhat more complicated structure than the first. Both lines, too, are end-stopped, whereas in the earlier version only line 35 is end-stopped. The change from *month* to *tyme* in line 36 has the effect of removing the alliteration, and this may have been Chaucer's reason for making the change; in line 1 of the poem the change he makes has the same effect.

The insertion of *joly* makes a happy solution of the metrical problem here.

The last three lines of the passage are integrated with line 36 in the earlier version, but this integration could not be kept if lines 35 and 36 were to be correlated and made parallel. Chaucer therefore took the other tack and made the last three lines an independent grammatical unit, serving to make more specific what happened to him in the jolly time of May but without any syntactical linkage to line 36. The significant changes here are the cancelation of *is comen* and the replacement of *and* by *whan*. These two changes, both in line 37, remove the two links which in the earlier version bind lines 36 and 37 together. Line 37, shortened by the cancelation, was made metrically complete by inserting the adjective *smale* before *foules*. Line 38 was left unchanged. The changes made in line 39 were not needed, so far as I can see. I have already expressed my opinion of them. I wish Chaucer had let the line stand as it was. But there is no accounting for tastes.

Chaucer's revision of lines 27-39 did not involve any major operations. The lines stayed where they were (except for 31 and 32, which exchanged places), the thought remained the same, and the number of lines in the passage was not altered. But elsewhere Chaucer made changes much more radical. Thus, line 118 of the earlier version reappears, somewhat changed in wording, as line 225 of the later version, a very great shift indeed in place. In other cases Chaucer made two lines out of one or the reverse. I will give an example of each.

Line 358 of the earlier version reads thus:

> Envie ys lavendere of the court alway.

In his revision Chaucer expanded this to two lines:

> 333 Envye—I preye to God yeve hire myschaunce—
> Is lavender in the grete court alway.

He accomplished the expansion very simply: by inserting a parenthetical ejaculation after the first word, *envye*, and by putting the adjective *grete* in front of *court*. But this is not the whole story. He also canceled line 357 of the earlier version, and revised lines 354-356. In other words, his expansion of lines 358 was not done in isolation, but was accompanied by other changes in the context.

Another interesting piece of revision is the following. The earlier version reads:

> 138　This was hire song, " The foweler we deffye,
> 　　　And al his craft." And somme songen clere
> 　　　Layes of love, that joye it was to here,
> 　　　In worship and in preysinge of hir make;
> 　　　And for the newe blisful somers sake,
> 　　　Upon the braunches ful of blosmes softe,
> 144　In hire delyt they turned hem ful ofte,

Here we have seven lines. In the revision Chaucer reduced the passage to five lines:

> 126　This was here song, " The foulere we defye."
> 　　　And some songen on the braunches clere
> 　　　[Layes] of love, that joye it was to here,
> 　　　In worshipe and in preysyng of hire make,
> 130　And for the newe blysful somers sake,

How did he go about it? He canceled line 144 altogether, and made lines 139 and 143 into a single line, canceling in the process the first half of line 139 and the second half of line 143. He put the new line thus made into second place in the passage, the place that line 139 has in the earlier version. Unluckily the scribe who copied the revised text messed it up a bit. To be precise, he made two mistakes in copying. His worst mistake was to skip the word *layes*, the first word in the third line of the passage. But he made another mistake too: instead of putting the particle *and* where it belonged, at the head of the second line of the passage, he wrote it after the word *love* of the third line. In this position it makes no sense, of course. Both the scribe's mistakes, it will be seen, do things to the third line (line 128 of the revised version of the prolog). In the MS this line reads:

Of love and that joye it was to here,

and as it stands the line is obviously defective, both metrically and grammatically. Skeat saw this, of course, and mended the line by inserting the word *May* after *and*. This would be well enough if the line occurred in isolation. But in fact we have the earlier version to go by, and in making emendations we had better stick to Chaucer's wording. Skeat might well have found the proper reading of line 128 if he had not got into trouble with line 127. This line, as it stands in the MS,

Some songen on the braunches clere,

scans beautifully, though the pentameter here is trochaic rather than iambic, as not infrequently in Chaucer's verse. But Skeat did not see this, and emended the line, making it read thus:

Somme songen layes on the braunches clere.

This emendation actually changes the line from a pentameter to a hexameter, and must therefore be rejected. But Skeat's emendation, unfortunate in itself, had a still more unfortunate consequence. When Skeat went on to line 128 he had already used the word *layes* in line 127, and it was therefore not available to him when he tried to set straight the truly defective line in the text: line 128. This being his unhappy situation, he had to resort to conjecture pure and simple, instead of following the guidance of Chaucer himself (i.e. the earlier version of the text).

I have dealt with this passage at some length because

it illustrates what can happen to a text in the hands of a careless scribe and an editor who rushes to conclusions. Skeat was a very great scholar, perhaps the greatest of all Chaucerian scholars. The debt which we owe to him is incalculable. But he was not exempt from human frailty. Like Homer, he could nod. Here he fell into elementary mistakes, both of scansion and of method, with results deplorable indeed. The moral for students is simple: never take on faith the emendations which an editor makes. Study the passage for yourself, and see what *you* can make of it without going beyond the author's own words.

The earlier version, as I have already pointed out, made a great deal more of the birds and their love-making than Chaucer chose to keep in the revised version. One of the omitted passages is of particular interest to the student of Chaucer's sources. It reads:

> 160   Al founde they Daunger for a tyme a lord,
> Yet Pitee, thurgh his stronge gentil myght,
> Forgaf, and made Mercy passen Ryght,
> Thurgh Innocence and ruled Curtesye.

Here we have a number of personified abstractions, characters who played important parts in the love-visions so popular in Chaucer's day. We found such personifications in all Chaucer's earlier love-visions, though only Fame and Nature were given speaking parts. Here the personified abstractions appear once more, and as usual they get short shrift. But in the revision they vanish from the scene. Evidently Chaucer's interest in such figures, never great, became less and less as time went on. He used them because he found them in his sources, but here at least he made bold to discard them together.

Philological scholarship has dug up and exhibited in detail the sources which Chaucer used in composing the prolog of the *Legend of Good Women*. The material about the daisy came from a number of French poems, chiefly the *Lay de Franchise* of Chaucer's contemporary Eustace Deschamps. The love-vision proper, in which the god of Love accuses the poet and Alcestis defends him, owes much, in structure and in detail alike, to Froissart's *Paradys d'Amours*, and something to certain poems by Machaut and others. Chaucer refers to some of these sources in a well-known passage:

> Gg 61   For wel I wot that folk han here-beforn
> Of makyng ropen, and lad awey the corn;
> And I come after, glenynge here and there,
> And am ful glad if I may fynde an ere
> Of any goodly word that they han left.
> And if it happe me rehersen eft
> That they han in here freshe songes said,
> I hope that they wole nat ben evele apayd,
> Sith it is seyd in fortheryng and honour
> 70   Of hem that eyther serven lef or flour.

This apology for using the work of others is made with a modest gesture conventional enough but presumably sincere. In the last line quoted the poet mentions " them that either serve leaf or flower." He is here referring to the two parties into which the English court seems to have been divided at that time, the one devoted to service of the leaf, the other to service of the flower. The vogue for such rival parties arose in France and spread to England. We know none too much about them, but there is an English poem of the fifteenth century, *The Flower and the Leaf*, which throws some light on the subject.

The main feature of the prolog is, of course, the trial of the poet, in which the god of Love serves as both judge and accuser, with Queen Alcestis as defender of Chaucer and counselor of the god. In the revision the trial scene is greatly expanded at the expense of the rest of the prolog. Lines 496-497 of the earlier version mention Queen Anne of England, wife of Richard II, though not by name:

> And whan this book is made, yive it the quene,
> On my behalf, at Eltham or at Sheene.

These are the last two lines of the dialog between Chaucer and Alcestis, in which she tells him what to do by way of penance. Her final instructions, just quoted, are to be taken as her most important utterance. If so, it follows that Alcestis spoke for Queen Anne, and that the English queen commissioned Chaucer (commanded him, indeed) to compose the *Legend of Good Women*. In the revised version of the prolog these two lines were left out, and it is commonly supposed that Chaucer left them out because the Queen had died. If so, the revision took place in the year 1394 or later.

The god of Love adds his instructions to the queen's, telling Chaucer (1) to write of Alcestis " in thy legend . . ., when thou hast made other small ones before "; (2) to begin with Cleopatra; and (3) to be brief. The third injunction is of particular interest. The god says:

> 570 I wot wel that thou maist nat al yt ryme,
> That swiche lovers diden in hire tyme;
> It were to long to reden and to here.
> Suffiseth me thou make in this manere,
> That thou reherce of al hir lyf the grete,
> After thise olde auctours lyste to trete.
> For whoso shal so many a story telle,
> 577 Sey shortly, or he shal to longe dwelle.

Here Chaucer is protecting himself. He has his orders from the queen, but he wants to do as little work as possible on this particular task. He therefore puts in the god of Love's mouth specific instructions that the poet is to repeat only the gist of what he finds in the old authors. In the revision of the prolog Chaucer kept instructions (1) and (2) but left out instruction (3). It would seem to follow that he needed no further protection. If so, he presumably had been relieved, by Queen Anne's death or otherwise, of the obligation to keep working on the *Legend*. Be it added that Chaucer did not " make of this wife " (i. e. Alcestis) in the *Legend*, although he kept Love's instruction that he do so. Perhaps he thought that what he had said of her in the prolog was enough.

But why did Chaucer bother to revise the prolog at all? What purpose was the revision intended to serve? I wish I could answer this question, but I cannot. I can only say that, whatever Chaucer's purpose, we are lucky indeed to have the two versions. Without the revised version of the prolog of the *Legend of Good Women* we should know far less than we do about Chaucer's way of making.

Of the *Legend* itself, as distinguished from its prolog, little need be said. Chaucer wrote these very short lives because he had to, not because he wanted to. Both versions of the prolog make delightful reading, each in its own way (I like the earlier one better, myself, though the craftsmanship of the later one is more finished), but the nine lives of the ten saints of Cupid were done in a perfunctory spirit and we could do without them. They are worth reading; Chaucer never wrote anything truly worthless. But they are not worth reading over and over and living with. It is just as well that Chaucer did not finish the *Legend of Good Women*.[3]

[3] By kind permission of the Clarendon Press, this chapter includes parts of a paper of mine forthcoming shortly in the Proceedings of the First International Conference of Professors of English.

CHAPTER VI

TROILUS AND CRISEYDE

WE BEGAN with a look at Chaucer and his times. We then took up some of Chaucer's minor poems: the four longer ones, all cast in the form of a love-vision. We saw that Chaucer left two of these unfinished. The *Canterbury Tales* likewise was never finished; when Chaucer died he had written only a small part of the gigantic work the dimensions of which he set down for his readers in the general prolog (lines 791-795). But Chaucer's other major work, *Troilus and Criseyde*, is complete. The poet here, and here alone, gives us a full-length masterpiece with a beginning, a middle, and an end. Here a whole building stands before us, a monumental work of art, noble in design, ample in scale, and perfected in all its parts. No long poem so high in artistic worth had been composed in the English tongue for 600 years. If the *Troilus* does not have the grandeur and the splendor of *Beowulf* or *Paradise Lost*, it has merits of its own so great that we can name it in the same breath with these peaks of English narrative poetry.

Troilus and Criseyde is a story of courtly love, a story which the poet tells in 8239 lines, grouped into five books.[1] The meter is the iambic pentameter which Chaucer favored in his later verse, and the lines of verse fall into stanzas with the rime-scheme ababbcc. This is the stanza that Chaucer used in the *Parliament of Fowls*. The scene

[1] Book I has 1092 lines; Book II, 1757; Book III, 1820; Book IV, 1701; and Book V, 1869. It will be noted that the first book is by far the shortest, and that the last book is the longest.

of the story is set in ancient Troy, and the events take place during the siege of Troy by the Greeks. Troilus himself is mentioned in the *Iliad*; he was one of the many sons of King Priam. But no story about him is known to us from classical or even post-classical times, though in a sixth-century Latin account of the fall of Troy attributed to a certain Dares Phrygius we are told that Troilus was second only to Hector among the Trojan champions. Dares included in his account a list of Trojans and Greeks, with brief word-pictures of those listed. Troilus, Briseide, and Diomede appear in this list. The *Historia* of Dares served the twelfth-century French poet Benoit de Sainte Maure as a source for his *Roman de Troie*, and here for the first time, so far as we know, Troilus figures in a love story. Benoit may have thought that such a hero as Dares represents Troilus to be deserved to have a love affair. At any rate, he took the three characters Troilus, Briseide, and Diomede of Dares's list and invented a story in which Briseide, after she left Troy, became faithless to her lover Troilus and took Diomede for her new lover. Benoit also gave Briseide the Trojan soothsayer Calchas for father.

Benoit's story makes part of his huge *Roman de Troie*, and it remains a mere episode in the *Historia Trojana* of Guido delle Colonne, a retelling in Latin of the French *Roman*. But Chaucer's Italian contemporary Boccaccio made a separate story out of it, and amplified it by telling in detail how Troilus and his mistress became lovers (Benoit had done no more than tell the story of Briseide's faithlessness). Here the go-between Pandaro played an important part. This character was one of Boccaccio's major contributions to the story. He got the name from the Troy legend. Pandaro's double function as friend and go-between may have been inspired by the Galehot of the

Lancelot story.[2] Boccaccio also changed the name of the lady from Briseide to Criseida, for reasons obscure to us. The new name answers to Homer's *Chryseis* much as the old one answers to his *Briseis*.

Boccaccio's reworking of the story (to which he gave the title *Filostrato*) was Chaucer's chief source for *Troilus and Criseyde*. He also made some use of two other works of Boccaccio's: *Filocolo* and *Teseide*. He used, besides, Benoit's version of the story, and now and then he brought in this and that from a variety of other authors, classical and medieval. He handled all this material with his customary freedom, and added much of his own. Chaucer's tale is 2559 lines longer than the *Filostrato*, and the difference marks not stuffing but a breadth and depth of presentation foreign to Boccaccio's poem, which is a well told but superficial story of courtly love, a story the characters of which move brightly about on the stage and play their obvious parts with easy and engaging competence. Chaucer took these characters and made them over. Troilus became the perfect courtly lover, a hero of love indeed. His rival Diomede became a bold seducer, urging his suit in courtly-love terms but showing no signs of being truly in love. Pandarus and Criseyde were turned into persons so complex that our poem could be hailed as the first psychological novel.[3] The changes in characterization have their effects on the course of the narrative; in particular, Pandarus plays a much more active part in Chaucer's version of the story than Pandaro plays in the *Filostrato*, and the parts of Troilus and Criseyde thereby become more passive. But the plot of the English poem remains simple, as the following outline of it will show.

[2] See T. A. Kirby, *Chaucer's Troilus*, pp. 110-114.

[3] So Kittredge, in his fourth Johns Hopkins lecture; see *Chaucer and his Poetry*, pp. 109, 112.

Young Troilus, heroic son of King Priam of Troy, was fancy-free and a scorner of love until one day at a religious service he saw and fell in love with Criseyde, a young and beautiful widow whose father, the Trojan soothsayer Calkas, had gone over to the Greeks, leaving his daughter behind in Troy. Troilus went home and went to bed, so love-sick that he longed for death, which would at any rate put him out of his misery. An older friend of his, Pandarus, Criseyde's uncle, came to see him one day and found him in this sad state. Troilus was very loath to tell what ailed him, but Pandarus finally wormed his secret out of him and volunteered to serve as go-between and help the lover win the lady. Troilus thankfully accepted his services, and thenceforth Pandarus devoted himself to the love-affair, running to and fro between lover and lady, bearing letters, arranging meetings, and finally bringing the affair to a head and a successful issue. The lovers then spent many nights together in perfect happiness, but fate or fortune soon parted them. Calkas persuaded the Greeks to offer their prisoner Antenor in exchange for Criseyde, and the Trojans accepted the offer. Criseyde had to leave Troy and go to the Greek camp. She told Troilus that she would contrive to come back in ten days' time, but she never returned and took the Greek champion Diomede for lover. Troilus long refused to believe her unfaithful. When he at last came to know the truth, he fell into despair and resolved to seek his death on the battle-field. There in the end, after many heroic feats of arms, he was slain by Achilles. His soul went up to the seventh sphere of heaven. Thence he looked down on this earth and saw the futility and vanity of earthly things. The story ends with an orthodox Christian moral: stop following blind impulse which cannot last, and cast all your heart on heaven.

Troilus and Creseyde is now usually dated in 1385 because of the astronomical conjunction mentioned in the text (iii. 624-5):

> The bente moone with hire hornes pale,
> Saturne, and Jove, in Cancro joyned were,

an event which actually took place in May, 1385.[4] The poem could not have been written before 1382 if the *A* of the following passage stands for Queen Anne:

[4] See R. K. Root and H. N. Russell, *PMLA* XXXIX 48 ff.

i. 169   Among thise othere folk was Criseyda,
          In widewes habit blak; but natheles,
          Right as oure firste lettre is now an A,
          In beaute first so stood she, makeles.

The *now* would be very much to the point indeed if this
passage was written in 1382, when Anne became Queen
of England by her marriage to Richard II. How long it
took Chaucer to finish his poem we have no means of
learning, but it seems not unreasonable that he was still
working on it in 1385.

The poem opens with a stanza in which the poet an-
nounces his subject and calls on Tisiphone to help him
compose the verses:

          The double sorwe of Troilus to tellen,
          That was the kyng Priamus sone of Troye,
          In lovynge, how his aventures fellen
          Fro wo to wele, and after out of joie,
          My purpos is, er that I parte fro ye.
          Thesiphone, thow help me for t'endite
          Thise woful vers, that wepen as I write.

The first four lines of the poem give us a remarkably complete summary of the story: time, place, theme (namely,
love), and course of events. We learn also the name and
station of the hero. We gather, too, that the poem is to
be a tragedy, in the medieval sense of that word, as defined
by the monk in the *Canterbury Tales* (B 3163 ff.).
Chaucer himself calls his poem a tragedy:

v. 1786   Go, litel bok, go, litel myn tragedye,
           Ther God thi makere yet, er that he dye,
           So sende myght to make in som comedye!

' Go, little book, go, my little tragedy, and may God send
to thy maker, before he die, the strength to match thee
with some comedy.' The poet actually lived to match
the *Troilus* with a comedy, the *Canterbury Tales*, though

he died before the matching was complete. One is tempted to take it that Chaucer, when he wrote the lines just quoted, already had the Canterbury pilgrimage in mind.

But the tragedy of Troilus is to be one of a particular kind: the poet's purpose is to tell his hero's double sorrow in love. Not a few *casus virorum illustrium* are falls in which love plays a part, but these commonly involve worldly misfortune besides. Love proved Anthony's undoing but it was the armed forces of Octavianus at Actium that brought him down. How different the case of Troilus! When he fell in battle at the hands of Achilles he got what he was seeking: his *coup de grace.* He had already fallen, in effect, and went about in a living death from which his slayer released him. The tragedy of Troilus is one of the heart alone. To the very end our hero played with success the worldly part which he was playing at the beginning: an upholder of Troy second only to his brother Hector. No change in outward circumstance but an inward change from bliss to wanhope made the tale of Troilus a tragedy.

The unusual course of this tragedy, the feature that makes the sorrow double, is brought out in the fourth line of the poem:

> Fro wo to wele, and after out of joie.

There are not two sorrows, be it noted, but two periods of sorrow: at the beginning and at the end. The first of these comes from falling in love, and turns into a period of bliss when the lady takes pity on her lover and grants him her favors. The second period of sorrow comes when the lovers have to part, and reaches the depths of despair when the lover becomes convinced of his lady's faithlessness. The three periods, the two of sorrow, the one of bliss, together make up our hero's course of love, a love which is one and the same throughout but which throws the lover into a state now of sorrow, now of bliss, depending on what the lady does. In the usual tragedy the hero begins on the heights and descends into the depths. Here however he makes two descents, with a very great height between, and much of the story is the tale of his *ascent* to that height. The tragedy of Troilus thus has a complexity all its own, a sequence of woe and joy and woe again in which contrast heightens the height and deepens the depths until the catastrophe makes it a tragedy indeed.

But the first as well as the second descent is from a height, and this height Chaucer ignored when he reduced his story to the formula " double sorwe." Chaucer's formula applies to Troilus while he was a lover. But the hero first appears on the stage fancy-free, and in the high spirits that go with his consciousness of freedom. We get a good picture of him on this height, and then we see him fall into the depths by falling in love with Criseyde. From a structural point of view the high point at the beginning of the hero's ups and downs ought to be matched by a high point at the end. Chaucer meets this structural need by making Troilus fancy-free once more. The hero dies for love, as a courtly lover should. But in so doing he wins freedom from the bonds of love, and his soul rises " ful blisfully " up to the seventh sphere of heaven. From this height he looks down on " this litel spot of erthe " and sees the vanity of worldly things. The hero's translation to heaven makes it possible for Chaucer to eat his cake and have it too. The poem is a tragedy but it ends on the heights. The hero after death gains the happiness which his virtues did not bring him in this life. His martyrdom to love is richly rewarded, though the thing for which he died vanishes in the process. His purgation from earthly impulse, indeed, makes part of his reward.

Be it added that the ascent of Troilus to heaven seems to have been an afterthought on Chaucer's part. Stanzas

259-261 (lines 1807-1827) of the fifth book are wanting
in two of the manuscripts, and if one reads the text with
care one sees that these stanzas interrupt the stream of
thought, which flows naturally and smoothly when one
proceeds directly from the hero's death (line 1806) to
stanza 262 (lines 1828-1834):

> Swich fyn hath, lo, this Troilus for love!
> Swiche fyn hath al his grete worthynesse!
> Swiche fyn hath his estat real above,
> Swich fyn his lust! swich fyn hath his noblesse!
> Swych fyn hath false worldes brotelnesse!
> And thus bigan his lovyng of Criseyde,
> As I have told, and in this wise he deyde.

The *fyn* here six times mentioned is obviously not the
hero's translation to heaven nor yet the disposition which
Mercury made of him there, but his death at the hands
of Achilles. One can only speculate on Chaucer's reasons
for inserting the three stanzas. Structurally, as we have
seen, they make a neat balance, matching as they do the
fancy-free Troilus at the beginning of Book I. But the
poet may have put them in simply because he liked the
corresponding passage in Boccaccio's *Teseide* (xi. stanzas
1-3) and thought he could work it in here to better effect
than in the knight's tale of the Canterbury collection.[5]

A line so drawn as to mark the high and low points
of the action of our poem, in terms of the hero's emotions,
would take the form of the letter *W*, the three high points
marking Troilus's high spirits (1) before he fell in love,
(2) when he and Criseyde became lovers in the fullest
sense, and (3) when he reached heaven, after his death,
while the two low points would mark his low spirits (1)

---

[5] The *Teseide* is the source of the knight's tale, but Chaucer did not
include Arcite's translation in his version of the story. Perhaps it was only
when he came to the death of Arcite (in composing the knight's tale) that
it occurred to him to give this heavenly journey to Troilus instead.

when he confessed his love-sickness to Pandarus, and (2) when he found that his parting gift to Criseyde had come into Diomede's possession. But it would be better to draw the line as a curve, in such a way as to mark periods of high and low spirits instead of high and low points. Whatever the method of marking, the movement of the poem conforms throughout to the feelings of its hero. We have here the tragedy of Troilus; what happens to the other characters is important only as these happenings affect the hero. Chaucer starts out to tell " of Troilus . . . in loving," and this remains his subject to the end.[6]

Chaucer calls on a Fury to help him compose his poem; in the fourth book he invokes all three Furies. He gives two explanations for his appeal to Tisiphone, a positive and a negative. It is as fitting for a woeful wight (i. e. the poet) to have a dreary companion as it is for such a wight to have a sad face in telling a sorrowful tale (lines 12-14). Moreover, he dare not ask Love for help, even though he would die without it, because the god has always found him unpleasing (lines 15-17). In lines 8 and 9 he gives another clue:

> To the clepe I, thow goddesse of torment,
> Thow cruwel Furie, sorwynge evere yn peyne.

This description of Tisiphone reflects the medieval view that the Furies not only made others suffer but also themselves had perpetual suffering to bear, a view which rested on post-classical if not on classical authority. A goddess sorrowing as well as tormenting may have seemed to the poet a helper more suitable than the god of Love, who inflicted torments on others but had no sorrows himself.

Chaucer calls on Tisiphone to

---

[6] The restriction to the hero's love-affair is reiterated and emphasized in Book V, lines 1765-1769.

i. 10   Help me, that am the sorwful instrument
         That helpeth loveres, as I kan, to pleyne.

Later he describes himself as one " that serves the god of
Love's servants " (line 15). He cannot himself be a
servant of Love, for the god will have none of him, but
he will do what he can:

i. 47   For so hope I my soule best avaunce:
         To prey for hem that Loves servauntz be,
         And write hire wo, and lyve in charite,

         And for to have of hem compassioun,
         As though I were hire owne brother dere.

Chaucer never tires of telling us how hopeless his own
case is when it comes to love. In the *Book of the Duchess*
we learn that his lady is still cold, after he has given her
eight years of devotion. In the *House of Fame* we get a
much fuller statement of the poet's sad situation. The
eagle tells Chaucer that Jupiter

614   hath of the routhe,
         That thou so longe trewely
         Hast served so ententyfly
         Hys blynde nevew Cupido,
         And faire Venus also,
         Withoute guerdon ever yit,
         And neverthelesse hast set thy wit
         (Although that in thy hed ful lyte is)
         To make bookys, songes, dytees,
         In ryme, or elles in cadence,
         As thou best canst, in reverence
         Of love, and of hys servantes eke,
         That have hys servyse soght, and seke;
         And peynest the to preyse hys art,
628   Although thou haddest never part.

Here, as in the *Book of the Duchess*, Chaucer's want of
success in love is clear: he is still " withoute guerdon "
and never had part in the things he wrote of. Even worse

is his state as Africanus presents it in the *Parliament of Fowls*. He tells Chaucer not to concern himself with the two inscriptions over the gate leading to the garden of love:

> 158   For this writing nys nothyng ment bi the,
> Ne by non, but he Loves servaunt be:
> For thow of love hast lost thy tast, I gesse,
> As sek man hath of swete and bytternesse.
>
> But natheles, although that thow be dul,
> Yit that thow canst not do, yit mayst thow se.

By this time the poet has turned into a mere spectator. He can report what he sees and hears; nothing else is left open to him. Much the same may be said of him as we find him in the *Troilus*, but here the tone is different: service through reporting, not mere reporting, has become the thing; high seriousness has replaced the light, humorous touch of sharp-tongued Africanus.

This high seriousness also comes out in a feature peculiar to the *Troilus* passage: the emphasis on prayer. An invocation is a prayer, of course, but the precative form is highly conventional and in his earlier invocations Chaucer took it lightly enough. For illustration I quote Chaucer's prayer to God in the Invocation of the *House of Fame,* Book I:

> 81   And he that mover ys of al
> That is and was and ever shal,
> So yive hem joye that hyt here
> Of alle that they dreme to-yere,
> And for to stonden alle in grace
> Of her loves, or in what place
> That hem were levest for to stonde,
> And shelde hem fro poverte and shonde,
> And from unhap and ech disese,
> And sende hem al that may hem plese,
> That take hit wel and skorne hyt noght,
> Ne hyt mysdemen in her thoght
> 93   Thorgh malicious entencion.

The lightness of touch here is evident, and needs no comment, but the jocular treatment of love in lines 85-87
should not be overlooked. Nothing comparable can be
found in the opening of the *Troilus,* where all the petitions
are earnest indeed. After the one to Tisiphone, which we
have already taken up (though not in full), Chaucer
manages to bring in an indirect prayer to Love, although
he has just explained the invocation to the Fury by saying
that he dare not pray to Love. This indirect petition reads,

> 19 But natheles, if this may don gladnesse
>   To any lovere, and his cause availle,
>   Have he my thonk, and myn be this travaille.

Here the first *this* means the poem and *he* means the god
of Love. Then comes the long passage addressed to " lovers
that bathe in gladness " (lines 22-46). It falls into a
number of petitions. The poet asks such lovers (1) to
remember the " passed heaviness " that they have felt
and the adversity of others; (2) to bear in mind how
they have experienced Love's assurance in plaguing them;
(3) to pray for those that are in Troilus' case; (4) to pray
for the poet; (5) to pray for those that are in despair over
a love that will never be regained; (6) to pray for those
that are slandered; (7) to pray for those sunk in a despair
out of reach of Love's grace; and (8) to pray for those that
are at ease in love. This series of petitions was obviously
done in imitation of the so-called bidding prayer which
commonly preceded the sermon in a religious service, and
in composing the passage the poet kept something of the
tone and spirit of his model.

Chaucer ends the introductory section of the poem as
follows:

> 52 Now herkneth with a good entencioun,
>   For now wil I gon streght to my matere,
>   In which ye may the double sorwes here
>   Of Troilus in lovynge of Criseyde,
> 56 And how that she forsook hym er she deyde.

These lines take us back to the first five lines of the poem, lines which they repeat in a somewhat varied form, with the addition of a promise (line 53) to get on with the story proper. The direct address to the audience (line 52) answers to line 5 in the earlier passage, where the poet likewise speaks directly to his hearers. This is a conventional feature, and it need not follow that the poem was actually read to an audience, but such a reading would be possible enough, of course. The device of variation enables the poet to give us two new items of information about the story: we learn who it was that Troilus fell in love with and why it was that he fell into a second period of sorrow. The statement that she forsook him also carries with it the implication that he had earlier won her for mistress, but this is nothing new, as his success has already been announced in the *wele* of line 4.

The device of repetition reminds one of the *House of Fame*, where the poet begins and ends his introductory remarks about dreams (lines 1-58) with a pious wish which by virtue of its repetition serves as a kind of envelope for the introductory matter. The first eight stanzas of the *Troilus* show a like technic, but here the repetition brings the poet back to his story with a directness and immediacy not found in the other poem. In both poems the repetition gives to the introductory passage a rounded effect, though in the *House of Fame* this effect is greatly weakened by the postscript (lines 59-65) which the author added to his Proem. In the *Troilus* the poet managed to avoid such a weakening by putting at an early point in the concluding lines his promise to get on with the story, instead of tacking the promise on after the repetition, as he did in the *House of Fame*.

The practice of giving to the reader in advance a good idea of what will happen in the course of the story was traditional; it goes back to classical antiquity, where it belonged first of all to the epic, and took the form of a more or less elaborate announcement of the subject, combined with an invocation of the Muse. Chaucer conformed to this conventional way of opening a long narrative poem. We have already seen what he did with it, and how he adapted it to a story of love. Such an opening necessarily served to diminish the element of suspense, but if the audience already knew the story there would be no great amount of suspense in any case. Moreover, suspense counted for little in medieval story-telling; instead, we find an extensive use of foreshadowing.

The first eight stanzas of the poem serve to open the narrative as a whole. They also make the Proem of the first book, though in the manuscripts they are not marked as such. Tisiphone is an appropriate helper for this book, which deals mostly with the sorrows of the hero after he has fallen in love and before his lady has shown him any favors. For the second book the poet invokes Clio, the Muse of history; for the third, he invokes Venus, but also calls on Calliope, the Muse of epic poetry. At the end of this book he addresses Venus, Cupid, and the nine Muses, and from his words we gather that all these helped him make the book, though in its Proem he mentions only Venus and Calliope. But now his helpers " wol wende " (line 1812), and in the Proem of the fourth book he invokes Mars and the Furies. The fifth book has no proem and no invocation, though the first stanza of this book answers, after a fashion, to the proems of the earlier books.

The various proems have the function of indicating the course of events, each in its own way. The Proem of Book I marks out the course of the action in the poem as a whole; that of Book IV, in the last two books; those of Books II and III, in their respective books. The proems serve, besides, to give the rhetorical elaboration which literary custom prescribed for the opening of a book. The invocations incorporated in the proems make part of this elaboration and help to indicate the nature of the action that is to follow.

The five openings differ considerably in length and otherwise. The opening of Book I is the longest (eight stanzas or 56 lines), as befits its importance. The other openings have the following lengths: Books II and III, seven stanzas or 49 lines each; Book IV, four stanzas or 28 lines; Book V, one stanza or 7 lines. The first opening may be analyzed as follows. Eight lines (1-5 and 54-56) give information about the story. Line 52 calls the audience to attention. It is very appropriately followed by a line in which the poet gives assurance that he will now start telling his story without (further) delay. The invocation to Tisiphone takes only six lines (6-11), and the last two of these are almost wholly devoted to a description of the poet as " the sorrowful instrument that helps lovers (as well as he knows how) to lament." The seven lines that follow serve two purposes at once: they explain (1) why the poet is invoking Tisiphone rather than the god of Love, and (2) why he is no more than a sorrowful instrument. In lines 47-51 the poet recurs to this instrumental theme and develops it further. Lines 19-21 make an indirect prayer to Love, as we noted above. All this comes to 31 lines. The remaining 25 lines, nearly half the opening, are given over to the passage addressed to "lovers that bathe in gladness," a passage also discussed above. The whole makes an intricate and skilfully wrought rhetorical pattern in which at every turn Chaucer uses his favorite device of repetition with variation.

The opening of Book II is seven stanzas long. It falls into three parts. First comes a stanza indicating the course of the action:

> Owt of thise blake wawes for to saylle,
> O wynd, o wynd, the weder gynneth clere;

> For in this see the boot hath swych travaylle,
> Of my connyng, that unneth I it steere.
> This see clepe I the tempestous matere
> Of disespeir that Troilus was inne;
> But now of hope the kalendes bygynne.

This stanza, inspired in part by the opening of Dante's *Purgatorio*, begins with a metaphor (lines 1-4) which the poet then proceeds to explain (lines 5-6), using a fool-proof technic not without humorous overtones.[7] The last line of the stanza may also be taken for an explanation of "the weder gynneth clere." In the poet's use of "the boot hath swych travaylle, of my connyng" one catches, besides, the apologetic note, or at any rate the gesture of modesty which Chaucer is so fond of making.

The invocation to Clio, Muse of history, makes the second part of the opening of the book. It comes to only four lines (8-11), and of these only the first three belong to the invocation proper, the fourth line serving to explain that Clio's is the only help that the poet needs in this particular book. The rest of the opening is given over to an apology to lovers. The poet begs them to excuse him for the want of passion in his narrative, which is a mere translation of a Latin original.[8] He wishes neither thanks nor blame for his work; all credit and discredit should go to the author he is translating. Besides, they have no more right to expect him (i. e. Chaucer) to speak with feeling about love than to expect a blind man to be a good judge of hues. They must also bear in mind that the language of love, and the ways of love-making generally, have changed much in a thousand years. If for this reason Troilus's wooing seems odd to any lover present, the poet reminds him that there are many roads to Rome, and that

---

[7] Compare ii. 904-905, where the humor is more obvious.

[8] This in fact did not exist; Chaucer here as elsewhere in the poem used vernacular sources almost exclusively. He represented his source as Latin in order to give to his poem greater prestige and authority.

customs differ in different countries. Indeed, of all the lovers in the audience, hardly three have the same methods of making love. Moreover, ladies are not alike and have to be wooed differently. Chaucer ends the apology by saying that inasmuch as he has begun he is determined to follow his author if he finds he knows how to; that is, he is determined to go on with the poem, guided by his source.

The opening of Book III agrees with that of Book II in length but differs greatly from it in thought and structure. The differences answer to the change in the hero's fortunes. In the second book Troilus begins to hope; in the third, he wins his lady's love and favors. Chaucer accordingly starts Book III with an invocation to Venus. In so doing he identifies the planet with the goddess, and his first words apply to the planet:

> O blisful light, of which the bemes clere
> Adorneth al the thridde heven faire!
> O sonnes lief!

But he goes on to speak of the goddess without the slightest transition, thus marking the identification as complete:

> O Joves doughter deere,
> Plesance of love! O goodly debonaire,
> In gentil hertes ay redy to repaire!
> O veray cause of heele and of gladnesse!
> Iheryed be thy might and thi goodnesse!

The series of apostrophes prepares us for the injunction or prayer with which the stanza closes (line 7). In this closing line the poet specifies for praise two characteristics of Venus: her might and her goodness. He develops both characteristics in the stanzas that follow, devoted to a love now heavenly, now earthly, a love in which flesh and spirit may mingle and even fuse. The second stanza is divided almost equally between might (lines 8-11) and goodness (lines 12-14), though the separation is not rigid, as *vapour eterne* shows goodness, *may endure* power. The two are presented together in the first part of the third stanza,

> Ye Joves first to thilke effectes glade
> Thorough which that thynges lyven alle and be
> Comeveden,

where Jove serves as creator and Venus takes character from the God of the Christians, but in the rest of the stanza Jove is merely the pagan deity, subjected to the power of his pagan daughter.

The fourth stanza, and the first two lines of the fifth, celebrate Venus as one who exercises her power for the good of all. She makes Mars peaceful, and raises lovers to moral heights which otherwise they could not reach. She brings about unity and friendship too. There follows a passage in which we learn the secret of Venus's might:

> 31 Ye knowe al thilke covered qualitee
> Of thynges, which that folk on wondren so,
> Whan they kan nought construe how it may jo
> She loveth hym, or whi he loveth here,
> 35 As whi this fissh and naught that comth to were.

Knowledge is power, for her at least. Chaucer ends his account of her greatness thus:

> 36 Ye folk a lawe han set in universe,
> And this knowe I (by hem that lovers be):
> That whoso stryveth with yow hath the werse!

Here the emphasis is on power but *lawe* carries with it an implication of right and justice, and so of goodness. Venus has set for people a law universally applicable, and whoever opposes her is certain to be overcome. The poet's parenthetical remark that his knowledge comes from lovers, not from his own experience, brings in, once more,

the familiar motif of Chaucer's dulness in matters of the
heart.

After praising Venus's power and goodness, the poet
proceeds to pray to her for help in his present task:

> 39   Now, lady bryght, for thi benignite,
>   At reverence of hem that serven the,
>   Whos clerc I am, so techeth me devyse
>   Som joye of that is felt in thi servyse.
>
>   Ye in my naked herte sentement
> 44   Inhielde, and do me shewe of thy swetnesse.

Here he calls himself the clerk of those that serve Venus,
and one is reminded of his earlier description of himself
as one that serves the servants of the god of love (i. 15).
He speaks of his heart as naked because it is void of the
passion (*sentement*) which in Book II he undertook to do
without (line 13), but which he now prays for. The old
trait yet again!

But Chaucer is not content to invoke Venus. He calls
on Calliope besides, the Muse of epic poetry:

> 45   Caliope, thi vois be now present,
>   For now is nede. Sestow nought my destresse,
>   How I mot telle anonright the gladnesse
>   Of Troilus, to Venus heryinge?

Here, almost at the end of the opening (contrast the opening of Book II), we learn what the course of events in
the book will be. That the hero will win his lady is
clearly implied in lines 41-44, but now we are told specifically that the poet must tell at once "the gladness of
Troilus." For such a task he needs all the help he can
get, and at the end of the book he thanks the Muses as a
group for what they have done in his behalf. It would
appear, then, that the Calliope of our opening stands for
all the Muses, of whom she is the chief. The poet ends the

opening with a pious prayer, setting aside the pagan machinery of his tale for the moment:

> To which gladnesse who nede hath God hym bringe!

He has already brought in the God of the Christians in line 12, to emphasize and enrich the goodness which he makes a characteristic of Venus. But now he gives to the opening as a whole a conclusion as Christian as he can contrive. In praying that God bring the gladness of consummated love to whoever needs it (that is, to all true lovers) he implies that this gladness comes from God.

With the Proem of Book III the author makes a fresh start, without linkage to the end of Book II. He proceeds quite otherwise when he begins Book IV. The last three lines of the third book read,

> My thridde bok now ende ich in this wyse,
> And Troilus in lust and in quiete
> Is with Criseyde, his owen herte swete.

The Proem of the fourth opens thus:

> But al to litel, weylaway the whyle,
> Lasteth swich joye,

obviously a continuation of what has just been said. But the word *swich* not only makes a grammatical link between the two; it also marks a change of theme from the particular case of Troilus to earthly happiness in general, the transitory nature of which the poet points out and laments. He goes on to blame Fortune for this, devoting the rest of the stanza to her wicked ways. With the second stanza the poet comes back to Troilus, telling his readers how Fortune treated his hero:

> From Troilus she gan hire brighte face
> Awey to writhe, and tok of hym non heede,
> But caste hym clene out of his lady grace
> And on hire whiel she sette up Diomede.

In the rest of the stanza Chaucer describes his own

unhappiness over his hero's case, and we hear nothing more of Fortune in this Proem.

The third stanza deals with Criseyde, much as the second dealt with Troilus. The first four lines tell of her faithlessness:

> For how Criseyde Troilus forsook,
> Or at the leeste how that she was unkynde,
> Moot hennesforth ben matere of my book,
> As writen folk thorugh which it is in mynde.

Here Chaucer is careful to say that he must repeat the story " as people wrote through whom it is known," and he adds, in the last three lines of the stanza, further words of protection for himself: how sorry he is that these writers found grounds to make such a report of Criseyde; and if they lied about her, the reproach should fall on them. Chaucer's " book " (line 17) might well be taken to mean the poem as a whole, which he elsewhere (v. 1786) terms a book. In the fourth stanza, however, where he calls on Mars and the Furies

> This ilke ferthe book me helpeth fyne,
> So that the losse of lyf and love yfeere
> Of Troilus be fully shewed heere,

he speaks specifically of his fourth book, and *ilke* ' same ' points back to line 17. We know, therefore, that when he wrote the Proem of Book IV he expected to finish the poem in four books. In fact, of course, Criseyde is still in Troy when the fourth book ends, and she is still wholly faithful to Troilus. The specific events mentioned in the Proem of Book IV all occur in Book V. But the events that do occur in the fourth book make possible the disasters of the fifth, and Chaucer's general statement about Fortune in lines 8-9,

> From Troilus she gan hire brighte face
> Awey to writhe, and tok of hym non heede,

applies beautifully to the course of the action in Book IV.

One finds it odd that Chaucer failed to revise his Proem to make it agree with the body of Book IV, particularly since the manuscript evidence indicates that he made at least one revision of the poem. But he seems to have decided to let the Proem stand and make it serve for Books IV and V taken together. For this reason Book V lacks a proem. But the wording of line 26 restricts the Proem to Book IV, and this line at least ought to have been recast if the Proem was truly meant to be used for both books. The fact that this line was left unchanged makes it impossible for us to be sure of Chaucer's final intention, though it seems reasonable to suppose that he failed to revise line 26 by oversight only.

Book V opens with a stanza which serves as substitute for the wanting proem:

> Aprochen gan the fatal destyne
> That Joves hath in disposicioun,
> And to yow, angry Parcas, sustren thre,
> Committeth, to don execucioun;
> For which Criseyde moste out of the town,
> And Troilus shal dwellen forth in pyne
> Til Lachesis his thred no lenger twyne.

Here we have rhetorical elaboration and information about the course of events but no invocation, though the author addresses the Fates directly and this reminds one, at least, of the apostrophes found in the other openings. The information given repeats, with variation, what we had already learned in the Proem of Book IV. And there are other correspondences. Jove answers in a way to the Fortune, the Fates to the Furies of the Proem. But the personal touch so marked in the opening of the fourth book is wholly wanting in that of the fifth. Indeed, this opening stanza makes a perfunctory impression.

Our survey of openings remains incomplete without a look at the stanzas with which the narrative proper begins.

Here each book goes its own way. In Book I, the Proem is followed by a stanza (lines 57-63) sketching the story of the siege of Troy. Then comes a stanza introducing Calkas, the father of Criseyde. I quote its first three lines:

> Now fel it so that in the town ther was
> Dwellynge a lord of gret auctorite,
> A gret devyn, that clepid was Calkas.

The directness and simplicity of this beginning is obvious. In Book II, on the contrary, the narrative proper begins with an elaborate rhetorical dating:

> 50   In May, that moder is of monthes glade,
>   That fresshe floures, blew and white and rede,
>   Ben quike agayn, that wynter dede made,
>   And ful of bawme is fletyng every mede;
>   Whan Phebus doth his bryghte bemes sprede,
>   Right in the white Bole, it so bitidde,
>   As I shal synge, on Mayes day the thrydde,
>
>   That Pandarus, for al his wise speche,
> 58   Felt ek his part of loves shotes keene, . . .

In Book III the story is resumed, without preliminaries, at the point where it was dropped at the end of the preceding book:

> 50   Lay al this mene while Troilus
>   Recordyng his lesson in this manere:
>   " Mafay," thoughte he, " thus wol I say, and thus;
>   Thus wol I pleyne unto my lady dere; . . ."

In Book IV the narrative begins simply, but incorporates a rhetorical dating:

> 29   Liggyng in oost, as I have seyd er this,
>   The Grekes stronge aboute Troie town,
>   Byfel that, whan that Phebus shynyng is
>   Upon the brest of Hercules lyoun,
>   That Ector, with ful many a bold baroun,
>   Caste on a day with Grekes for to fighte,
> 35   As he was wont, to greve hem what he myghte.

It is in Book V, however, that rhetoric reaches its height. The opening of this book is followed by a stanza which dates the beginning of the action (namely, Criseyde's departure from Troy) in terms of the lapse of time (three years) since Troilus fell in love:

> 8   The gold y-tressed Phebus heighe on-lofte
> Thries hadde alle with his bemes shene
> The snowes molte, and Zepherus as ofte
> Ibrought ayeyn the tendre leves grene
> Syn that the sone of Ecuba the queene
> Bigan to love hire first for whom his sorwe
> 14 Was al that she departe sholde a-morwe.

From these beginnings it would appear that the poet was fond of starting the narrative proper with a rhetorical dating, but that he began simply enough if he left the date indefinite or dispensed with it altogether. In Book I he wisely did not try to date the Trojan War, and in Book III he was content to make the hero's preparations for the interview with Criseyde simultaneous with the whispering mentioned in the last stanza of the preceding book. Chaucer began the *Canterbury Tales* with an elaborate rhetorical dating in high style, and elsewhere in the Canterbury collection we find specific dates given with a like elaboration, though the rhetorical ornamentation is less pronounced: 10 a. m., April 18 (B 1-14) and 9 a. m., May 3 (B 4377-4387). The first of these datings introduces the host's speech on the flight of time; the second marks the beginning of the second part of the nun's priest's tale. By way of exception, Chaucer in the *House of Fame* twice gives the date of December 10, each time without using any rhetorical apparatus. He usually begins a narrative with an indefinite date (as *whilom* ' once upon a time ') or with no date at all, and such beginnings are regularly simple, conforming as they do to the familiar style of the folk-tale.

Chapter VII

TROILUS AND CRISEYDE (continued)

IN THE PRECEDING chapter we studied Chaucer's way of beginning the various books of *Troilus and Criseyde*. We now come to his way of ending them. The first book ends with a description of the state of things after Pandarus leaves Troilus and before the action of the second book begins. In stanza 153 (lines 1065-1071) we are told of Pandarus, in stanzas 154-156 of Troilus. The stanza about Pandarus is linked to the words of parting by lines 1062-1064, lines which belong at once to the body of the book and its ending. We learn that Pandarus is in no hurry; he is taking plenty of time to work out his plans before approaching his niece. The actual interval between the action of the first book and that of the second seems to be about a month; Troilus saw Criseyde and fell in love with her early in April (see lines 155 ff.), and Pandarus experienced his "teene in love" (ii. 61-62) on the third of May. Meanwhile Troilus, cheered by the hope that his friend may be able to help him, lies abed no longer:

> 1072   But Troilus lay tho no lenger down,
>   But up anon upon his stede bay,
>   And in the feld he pleyde the leoun:
>   Wo was that Grek that with hym mette aday!
>   And in the town his manere tho forth ay
>   Soo goodly was, and gat hym so in grace,
>   That ecch hym loved that loked on his face.

> 1079   For he bicom the frendlieste wighte,
>   The gentilest, and ek the mooste fre,

> The thriftiest and oon the beste knyght
> That in his tyme was or myghte be.
> Dede were his japes and his cruelte,
> His heighe port and his manere estraunge,
> And ecch of tho gan for a vertu chaunge.

This passage on the uplifting effects of courtly love answers to the longer one at the end of Book III; see below.

But the hero is not well yet. Book I ends with a stanza that makes things more precise:

> 1086 Now lat us stynte of Troilus a stounde,
> That fareth lik a man that hurt is soore,
> And is somdeel of akyngge of his wownde
> Ylissed wel, but heeled no deel moore,
> And, as an esy pacyent, the loore
> Abit of hym that gooth aboute his cure;
> And thus he dryveth forth his aventure.

The first line warns us of a shift of scene, and the last three lines bring out the passivity of the hero, who is constant in bearing what comes to him but leaves active measures to his physician. And it is of interest to note that the physician is not the lady (as in the *Book of the Duchess*) but the friend and go-between. The stanza wants formal linkage with the beginning of Book II, where *thise blake wawes* (line 1) and *this see* (line 3) symbolize the hero's despair after he fell in love, not his state as " an easy patient " after his physician's first visit. But though the two stanzas are not bound together syntactically, one may with reason connect the alleviation of the hero's pains with the clearing of the weather; the figures differ but the meaning is much the same.

The second book comes to an end at a critical point in the action, and the final stanza contrives to gain a maximum of suspense:

> 1751 But now to yow, ye loveres that ben here,
> Was Troilus nought in a kankedort,

That lay, and myghte whisprynge of hem here,
And thoughte, " O Lord, right now renneth my sort
Fully to deye or han anon comfort! "
And was the firste tyme he shoulde hire preye
Of love; O myghty God, what shal he seye?

Full suspense was impossible for the audience, it is true,
as they all knew that the hero's suit would prosper. But
Troilus himself feared the worst, though he hoped for the
best, and the poet by his art makes his hearers and readers
see things through the hero's eyes and react accordingly.
The direct address to the lovers in the audience not only
makes the last stanza more dramatic but also marks it off
from what precedes and makes up, to some degree at
least, for the want of a true break in the action. The
stanza has no connection with the Proem of Book III
but it is closely connected with iii. 50-58, lines which
present Troilus in the same situation and in the same
state of mind, though one notes a certain shift in tone and
weight. The integration between ii. 1751-1757 and iii. 50-
58 is so nearly complete, indeed, that one is tempted to
interpret the former stanza as a pseudo-ending only. But
perhaps it would be better to say that the ending of the
second book has a pattern all its own. It serves chiefly
to express the hero's feelings at the moment, and his state
of fearful hope, or hopeful fear, comes out with a vividness
beyond praise.

The pattern of the third book provides an ending in
which the poet addresses Venus and the Muses. Before
this formal conclusion Chaucer sets a series of five stanzas
describing the hero as happiness in love made him (lines
1772-1806). In these stanzas Troilus appears as perfect
in all respects, and his perfections are attributed to the
influence of Love upon him. To quote,

1804   Thus wolde Love, yheried be his grace,
           That pride, envye, and ire, and avarice
           He gan to flee, and everich other vice.

The uplifting effects of love had already been treated in the ending of the first book, but here they are more fully and more strikingly described. It seems in every way fitting that the poet should follow this inspired passage with his words in praise of those who gave him inspiration:

> 1807 Thow lady bryght, the doughter to Dyone,
> Thy blynde and wynged sone ek, daun Cupide,
> Yee sustren nyne ek, that by Elicone
> In hil Pernaso listen for t'abide,
> That ye thus fer han deyned me to gyde,
> I kan namore, but syn that ye wol wende,
> Ye heried ben for ay withouten ende!

> 1814 Thorugh yow have I seyd fully in my song
> Th'effect and joie of Troilus servise,
> Al be that ther was som disese among,
> As to myn auctour listeth to devise.
> My thridde bok now ende ich in this wyse,
> And Troilus in lust and in quiete
> Is with Criseyde, his owen herte swete.

For further discussion of this ending, see above (pp. 113, 118 f.).

In the fourth book Chaucer goes back to the pattern of conclusion which he used earlier; his last two stanzas simply tell us how his hero felt after the experiences which he underwent in the book:

> 1688 And after that they longe ypleyned hadde,
> And ofte ykist, and streite in armes folde,
> The day gan rise, and Troilus hym cladde,
> And rewfullich his lady gan byholde,
> As he that felte dethes cares colde,
> And to hire grace he gan hym recomaunde.
> Wher him was wo, this holde I no demaunde.

> 1695 For mannes hed ymagynen ne kan,
> N'entendement considere, ne tonge telle
> The cruele peynes of this sorwful man,
> That passen every torment down in helle.
> For whan he saugh that she ne myghte dwelle,

> Which that his soule out of his herte rente,
> Withouten more, out of the chambre he wente.

The lovers had just had their last night together, and Troilus left in utter misery, a misery that carries over to the fifth book, where lines 13-14 refer back directly to the end of the fourth and bind the two books together.

The ending of the fifth book is also the ending of the poem as a whole. It therefore makes complications not to be expected in the endings of the other books. First of all, where does the ending begin? The story proper is marked off from the matter which follows it by the final couplet of stanza 262 (lines 1828-1834),

> And thus bigan his lovyng of Criseyde,
> As I have told, and in this wise he deyde.

With line 1835, in other words, begins the second part of the ending of the poem. But the ending has a first part too; namely, the conclusion of the story proper. I put the dividing line between the body of the poem and its ending at the point where the poet stops telling about Troilus in detail and begins to summarize. The concluding stanzas of the story proper, then, I take to be stanzas 250, 251, 252, 258, and 262 (lines 1744-1764, 1800-1806, and 1828-1834):

> 1744 Gret was the sorwe and pleynte of Troilus;
> But forth hire cours Fortune ay gan to holde.
> Criseyde loveth the sone of Tideus,
> And Troilus moot wepe in cares colde.
> Swich is this world, whoso it kan byholde:
> In ech estat is litel hertes reste.
> God leve us for to take it for the beste!

> 1751 In many a cruel bataille, out of drede,
> Of Troilus, this ilke noble knyght,
> As men may in thise olde bokes rede,
> Was seen his knyghthod and his grete myght.
> And dredeles, his ire, day and nyght,

Ful cruwely the Grekis ay aboughte;
And alway moost this Diomede he soughte.

1758 And ofte tyme I fynde that they mette
With blody strokes and with wordes grete,
Assayinge how hire speres weren whette;
And, God it woot, with many a cruel hete
Gan Troilus upon his helm to bete!
But natheles Fortune it naught ne wolde
Of oothers hond that eyther deyen sholde.

1800 The wrath, as I bigan yow for to seye,
Of Troilus the Grekis boughten deere,
For thousandes his hondes maden deye,
As he that was withouten any peere,
Save Ector, in his tyme, as I kan heere,
But weilawey! save only, Goddes wille,
Despitously hym slough the fierse Achille.

1828 Swich fyn hath, lo, this Troilus for love!
Swiche fyn hath al his grete worthynesse!
Swiche fyn hath his estat real above,
Swich fyn his lust! Swich fyn hath his noblesse!
Swich fyn hath false worldes brotelnesse!
And thus bigan his lovyng of Criseyde,
As I have told, and in this wise he deyde.

Chaucer ends the story proper with a stanza (lines 1828-1834) the first five lines of which are done in high style, whereas the final couplet is done in a style so simple that it goes beautifully with the hortatory passage that follows. This stylistic division of stanza 262 into two parts answers to a change in the treatment of the theme. The first five lines are analytic as well as rhetorical, whereas the couplet puts the hero together again and presents his story as a whole, from beginning to end. But in spite of this change the stanza has unity enough: both parts sum up the action, lines 1828-1832 giving us a moralizing summary, lines 1833-1834 a factual summary, each presented strictly in terms of the hero.

This stanza originally followed stanza 258, as we saw

above (p. 107), and here I have left out, for the moment, the passage which Chaucer later inserted about the hero's translation to heaven. A feature of stanza 258 worthy of special note is the repetition, in lines 1800-1801, of the statement made in lines 1755-1756, a repetition which the author himself points out. He failed to develop the statement when he first made it, passing on to the hero's combats with Diomede. He therefore came back to his original generalization and proceeded to develop it properly (in lines 1802-1806). The words to the audience, " as I bigan yow for to seye," call attention to repetition and development alike.[1]

Between stanzas 252 and 258 the poet inserted five stanzas which digress from the story proper but make an important part of the ending of the poem. In stanza 253 Chaucer apologizes for not writing about his hero's martial feats, explaining that he has kept to the subject announced at the beginning, that " of his love," and referring his readers to Dares for a full account of Troilus's exploits in battle:

<blockquote>
1765   And if I hadde ytaken for to write
        The armes of this ilke worthi man,
        Than wolde ich of his batailles endite;
        But for that I to writen first bigan
        Of his love, I have seyd as I kan
        (His worthi dedes, whose list hem heere,
1771   Rede Dares, he kan telle hem alle ifeere),[2]
</blockquote>

In line 1769 Chaucer also apologizes for the inadequacies of his version of the love story: *I have seyd as I kan* ' I

---

[1] The meaning of lines 1804-1806 is obscured by the punctuation of the editors; the punctuation given above is my own. The poet tells us that Troilus was without an equal in his day except for Hector and with the one further exception that, by God's will, Achilles slew him.

[2] In fact, of course, Dares is so far from telling them all together that he tells none of them, though he makes the general statement that Troilus was second only to Hector as an upholder of Troy against the Greeks. Chaucer's reference to Dares is a mere device.

have said as well as I know how.' This is a conventional author's gesture of modesty, but, as we have seen, Chaucer likes to make it and brings it in on many occasions. It is obviously appropriate in the ending of the poem.

To this gesture he ties a whole stanza of further apology, addressed to women:

> 1772   Bysechyng every lady bright of hewe,
>   And every gentil womman, what she be,
>   That al be that Criseyde was untrewe,
>   That for that gilt she be nat wroth with me:
>   Ye may hire giltes in other bokes se.
>   And gladlier I wol write, yif yow leste,
> 1778   Penelopeës trouthe and good Alceste.

Here the poet apologizes for writing about a woman who was untrue to her lover. He excuses himself on the ground that he did not invent this feature of the story, and he tells the ladies that if they so wish he will write about women faithful in love, and do it more gladly. This stanza so clearly foreshadows the *Legend of Good Women* that one is tempted to take it for an addition to the poem, made when Chaucer decided (or started) to write the *Legend*. It may be, however, that our stanza came first, and gave Chaucer the idea of composing the *Legend*.

After stanza 254 comes a stanza in which apology yields first place to moralizing, though the poet continues to address the women of his audience:

> 1779   N'y sey nat this al oonly for thise men,
>   But moost for wommen that bitraised be
>   Thorugh false folk (God yeve hem sorwe, amen!)
>   That with hire grete wit and subtilte
>   Bytraise yow, and this commeveth me
>   To speke, and in effect yow alle I preye,
> 1785   Beth war of men, and herkneth what I seye!

Chaucer here tries to persuade the ladies that the moral of his poem is not " altogether for men only " but is also, indeed mostly, for women. Yet the moral he would have them draw is not the one we might have expected: be faithful to your lover. It would never do for him to teach them such a lesson; the implication that they needed (or might need) that kind of teaching would surely offend them, and would be discourteous besides. But though he could not with propriety warn them against actual or potential evil in themselves, he could perfectly well warn them against such evil in others. Now the tale obviously teaches virtuous men to beware of women. How can this moral be stretched so that it holds for virtuous people generally? The trick can be turned by expressing the moral in more general terms: beware of false folk. But Chaucer was not satisfied to do this. He preferred to phrase the moral in such a way that it holds for women only: beware of men. In making this the moral of *Troilus and Criseyde* the poet was making fun, of course. He could have found no moral for his tale more completely paradoxical, on the face of it, and therefore more amusing. And his fun-making went on, to the very end of the stanza. He tells the ladies of his audience to " beware of men and listen to what I say." There is one man they can believe, and Chaucer is that man.

Stanzas 254 and 255 obviously go together, and the moral, " beware of men," paradoxical and funny for *Troilus and Criseyde*, fits in all seriousness most of the tales that make up the *Legend of Good Women*. We may be sure that these two stanzas owe their being to a single inspiration, and that they are connected in some way with the *Legend*. They look more than ever like additions to our poem when we go on to stanza 256:

> 1786　Go, litel bok, go, litel myn tragedye,
> 　　　Ther God thi makere yet, er that he dye,
> 　　　So sende myght to make in som comedye!
> 　　　But litel book, no makyng thow n'envie,

> But subgit be to alle poesye,
> And kis the steppes where as thow seëst pace
> 1792   Virgile, Ovide, Omer, Lucan, and Stace.

This stanza with its serious, yet intimate tone would follow stanza 253 appropriately enough, but after stanza 255 it seems out of place. The break in the flow of the verse is so obvious that the editors commonly mark it with a dash, set at the end of line 1785.

In stanza 256 Chaucer has combined conventional features and given to the whole a personal stamp with more than his usual success. The author's address to his poem is such a feature; it goes back to classical antiquity. Chaucer no doubt knew various examples of its use in classical and medieval literature, and we can point to no particular one of them with assurance as his model. When he called his book little he presumably had in mind not its length but its importance. In other words, the thrice repeated *litel* is a modest gesture, and goes with the humility preached in the last three lines of the stanza. The warning against envy is a literary device much used in endings. The list of major authors in line 1792 also has a conventional character, though one finds it nowhere exactly duplicated. The same authors, with several others, appear in the *House of Fame*, lines 1456-1512. I have already discussed (p. 104 above) the first three lines of the stanza in another connection.

Stanza 256 is followed by a stanza in which Chaucer concludes his address to the poem:

> 1793   And for ther is so gret diversite
> In Englissh and in writing of oure tonge,
> So prey I God that non myswrite the
> Ne the mysmetre for defaute of tonge;
> And red wherso thow be, or elles songe,
> That thow be understonde, God I beseche!
> 1799   But yet to purpos of my rather speche.

Here the address has become little more than a device for linking the stanza to the preceding lines. Chaucer no longer tells his poem how to behave; instead, he prays to God in its behalf, and in effect, though not in form, he addresses the future copyists and readers of the poem, imploring them to be on their guard against the mistakes which an imperfect knowledge of the language may lead them to make. The poet's concern for a good text comes out also in the familiar lines addressed to his copyist Adam:

> Adam scriveyn, if ever it thee bifalle
> Boece or Troylus for to wryten newe,
> Under thy lokkes thou most have the scalle
> But after my makyng thow wryte trewe!
> So ofte adaye I mot thy werk renewe,
> It to correcte and eek to rubbe and scrape,
> And al is thorugh thy negligence and rape.

Here however the mistakes are due to negligence and haste, not to any *defaute of tonge*.

The last line of stanza 257 marks the end of the digressive passage and points back to the poet's " earlier speech " for the thread of the narrative now to be resumed. We are not told just where to find the loose end which is to be picked up, but, as we saw above, stanza 258 begins by repeating, in variant form, lines 1755-1756, a device which makes unmistakable the point of resumption. The editors commonly set a dash at the end of stanza 257, in spite of the obvious fact that line 1799 is there to prepare the reader for the resumption of the narrative in lines 1800 ff. The dash goes with the one after line 1785, and the two serve to enclose stanzas 256 and 257, thus marking them parenthetical. But, as we have seen, the truly parenthetical stanzas are 254 and 255, even though Chaucer by beginning stanza 254 with a participle has linked it grammatically to line 1769. In my opinion line 1769 once ended with a full stop and lines 1770-1771 were not parenthetical but simply made a separate sentence. This was immediately followed by the two stanzas in which Chaucer addressed his " little book." When the poet inserted the stanzas addressed to women he tied them very neatly to line 1769 with his " beseeching," but in so doing he made the final couplet of stanza 253 parenthetical, and thus gave to the stanza a closing awkwardness which it did not have when it was first written.

The insertion of stanzas 253-257 (lines 1765-1799) into the ending of the story proper amplified and elaborated this ending but left it essentially the same. The later insertion of stanzas 259-261 (lines 1807-1827), however, made a fundamental change in the nature of the ending. The story no longer ended with the hero's death and the summing up which formally closed the action. Between death and summary now came an account of the hero's translation to heaven:

> 1807 And whan that he was slayn in this manere
> His lighte goost ful blisfully is went
> Up to the holughnesse of the seventhe spere,
> In convers letyng everich element,
> And ther he saugh, with ful avysement,
> The erratik sterres, herkenyng armonye
> With sownes ful of hevenyssh melodie.

> 1814 And down from thennes faste he gan avyse
> This litel spot of erthe that with the se
> Embraced is, and fully gan despise
> This wrecched world, and held al vanite
> To respect of the pleyn felicite
> That is in hevene above; and at the laste
> Ther he was slayn his lokyng down he caste.

> 1821 And in hymself he lough right at the wo
> Of hem that wepten for his deth so faste,
> And dampned al oure werk that foloweth so
> The blynde lust the which that may nat laste,
> And sholden al oure herte on heven caste.

> And forth he wente, shortly for to telle,
> Ther as Mercurye sorted hym to dwelle.

Death was indeed a release for Troilus. His soul rose " full blissfully " to heaven, and there " with full contemplation " he saw the planets and heard the music of the spheres. From this point of vantage he considered intently the things of earth and realized their vanity in terms of the complete happiness of heaven. In particular, he laughed within himself at the woe of those he saw weeping so hard for his death.[3] On this particular he based two generalizations: (1) he condemned all we do " that follows in this way blind impulse that cannot last," and (2) he concluded that during our earthly life we " should cast all our heart on heaven." After making these generalizations Troilus went on to the heavenly abode which Mercury chose for him. One finds it noteworthy that the hero's love affair is not once referred to, directly or indirectly, in the whole passage. At most one may say that the affair makes part of " this foolish world " and like other mundane matters has become vanity to Troilus.

Chaucer presents his hero's insight, not as a lesson which earthly experience taught him but as wisdom which he won in virtue of his translation to heaven. From his station in the hollowness of the seventh sphere he could not fail to see the truth. But what had he done to earn a place in heaven? So virtuous, valiant, and famous a hero might well be rewarded thus in pagan antiquity, and Mercury's presence makes it clear that Chaucer here as elsewhere in the poem was using conventional machinery classical in origin. As we have already seen, he took the ascent to

[3] Chaucer does not tell us why his hero found the mourning funny; presumably it did not occur to him that any of his readers would need an explanation. Many modern readers miss the point, however, which is that Troilus by dying exchanged misery for happiness and earth for heaven and it therefore struck him as funny indeed that his friends should be grieving over an event which made him rejoice.

heaven from the *Teseide* of Boccaccio, where it crowns the heroic career of Arcite, but Boccaccio in turn was imitating the apotheosis of Pompey in the ninth book of Lucan's *Pharsalia*. Both Chaucer and Boccaccio may have used, besides, Cicero's *Somnium Scipionis* for this and that. Chaucer's exaltation of his hero, though an afterthought, makes a fitting end for the tale, since it gives to Troilus the supreme reward of virtue.

So far, we have been concerned with the first rather than the second part of the ending of the poem; that is, with the ending of the story proper (lines 1744-1834) rather than the matter which follows it (lines 1835-1869). We come now to the second or concluding part of the ending. It begins with an apostrophe which marks it off sharply from what precedes, but its first three stanzas none the less are stylistically linked to the last stanza (lines 1828-1834) of the first part. Lines 1828-1832 are done in a style continued in stanza 265:

> 1849 Lo here, of payens corsed olde rites,
> Lo here, what alle hire goddes may availle,
> Lo here, thise wrecched worldes appetites,
> Lo here, the fyn and guerdon for travaille
> Of Jove, Appollo, of Mars, of swich rascaille!
> Lo here, the forme of olde clerkis speche
> In poetrie, if ye hire bokes seche.

Moreover, lines 1849-1853 make a continuation of lines 1828-1832 in thought as well: they point the moral which the poet had already drawn in line 1832; namely, that the sad fate of Troilus exemplifies the transitory character of worldly things.[4] The two hortatory stanzas 263 and 264

---

[4] The insertion of stanzas 259-261 (lines 1807-1827) greatly weakened this argument, of course, as the hero, or at any rate his ghost, now had the happiest of all possible fates: he had been brought to the "full felicity that is in heaven above," and this presumably as a reward for virtuous living in his earthly abode. But Chaucer chose to let what he had written stand.

(lines 1835-1848) which come between, stanzas in which the poet urges young people to take warning by the example of Troilus and reject earthly for heavenly love, make a stylistic break in the passage, though in matter they depart but little from the context in which they are set. But we have already seen (p. 129) that the stylistic break actually comes, not at the end of stanza 262 but between its fifth and sixth lines: the final couplet of the stanza agrees in style with the engagingly simple hortatory stanzas. I take it, then, that the juxtaposition of two styles which Chaucer found needful in the final stanza of the story proper has its natural continuation in the three stanzas that follow, stanzas 263 and 264 conforming in style to the two lines immediately preceding them, and stanza 265 resuming the high style of lines 1828-1832.

It must be added that the hortatory stanzas have a highness of tone (though not of formal style, apart from the " O " with which the passage begins) and a depth of feeling not to be found in lines 1833-1834, the summary character of which precluded anything of the kind. These two stanzas are of Chaucer's very best, and their simple beauty shines the brighter for the rhetoric of their setting:

> 1835 O yonge, fresshe folkes, he or she,
>   In which that love up groweth with youre age,
>   Repeyreth hom fro worldly vanyte
>   And of youre herte up casteth the visage
>   To thilke God that after his ymage
>   Yow made, and thynketh al nys but a faire,
>   This world that passeth soone as floures faire.

> 1842 And loveth hym, the which that right for love
>   Upon a crois, oure soules for to beye,
>   First starf, and roos, and sit in hevene above;
>   For he nyl falsen no wight, dar I seye,
>   That wol his herte al holly on hym leye,
>   And syn he best to love is, and most meke,
>   What nedeth feynede loves for to seke?

Chaucer's plea to "young folks," and his denunciation of paganism which follows, make a striking contrast with the body of the poem, where he treats courtly love and pagan ways sympathetically enough. We have here, indeed, what amounts to a recantation, reminiscent of the so-called Retractation at the end of the *Canterbury Tales,* where "the book of Troilus" is named among the poet's "translacions and enditynges of worldly vanitees, the which I revoke in my retracciouns." Most modern readers find such endings esthetically disturbing. They feel that an author ought to keep to one point of view. But the Christian moral of the Troilus story is perfectly clear, and it is unreasonable to blame Chaucer for pointing it out. In so doing he followed a familiar and deeply rooted medieval literary convention, that of the religious ending. Such an ending might be perfunctory, but in a serious major work the moral application of the story would have to be taken seriously. Or so Chaucer thought, true man of the Middle Ages that he was. Moderns who think otherwise might well consider the possibility that Chaucer was right after all.

It has been suggested that Chaucer wrote his condemnation of courtly love and paganism to stave off ecclesiastical censure or worse. But we have no reason to think that a poem about courtly lovers whose love affair came to grief would have moved the authorities of the Church of England to action, in the midst of the great schism, and the classical paganism of the poem's setting would have disturbed these authorities even less. Moreover, we may be sure that Chaucer meant what he said. Himself worldly, he knew that unworldliness was the better part. Even the wife of Bath recognizes that

D 75   The dart is set up for virginitee.

Here however one notes with interest that Chaucer does

not commend the wife of Bath's solution to his young people in whom " love up groweth." The wife says,

> D 113   I wol bistowe the flour of al myn age
>   In the actes and in fruyt of mariage.

But Chaucer ignores this way out, in the *Troilus* at least. The lovers think of everything else when their parting impends, but it does not occur to them, or even to the scheming Pandarus, that marriage might keep them to-gether.[5] And in the conclusion of the poem the young people are urged to seek heavenly instead of earthly love; the sacrament of marriage is not even mentioned. Chaucer seems to have taken it for granted that love and marriage were incompatible. In this particular, if in no other, he clung to courtly-love teaching to the end of the chapter.

The poet likewise meant what he said in stanza 265 about the pagan gods. It was part of the tragedy of Troilus that he lived in a time and place far from the grace of God, the gift of Jesus Christ to mankind. Our virtuous hero had no access, in his life time, to the consolations and the joys of the faithful. He appealed to his gods for help in his misery, but he appealed in vain. Only after death did he win that insight which the Christian may win in earthly life. Chaucer rightly lays stress on the part which religion played in the action, even though that part proved negative rather than positive in its effects, since the religion was false and could do nothing for the hero.

This brings us to another function of the ending, perhaps the most important function of all. The poet, after he has told his story, looks back upon it and sees it in the large. His concluding stanzas give us some idea of what this comprehensive view revealed to him. We learn, among other things, that Chaucer came to see his tale in terms

---

[5] Line 555 of the fourth book might be taken as a reference to marriage, but the context points in another direction.

of his faith. When he began the poem it was his purpose (as he puts it) to tell the double sorrow of Troilus in loving, but when he came to the end he found he had made an exemplum, with a moral lesson which he could not dodge or overlook. His ending took shape accordingly. It differs in point of view from the body of the poem, but the difference makes the whole richer and nobler than it could have been otherwise. We must rejoice that Chaucer did not tell the story proper in the spirit of a preacher, making exemplary points as he went along, but we may congratulate ourselves that in the ending he brought his religious convictions to bear in words so informed with faith and so charged with beauty.

The last two lines of stanza 265 make a kind of apology for the pagan machinery:

> 1854 Lo here the forme of olde clerkis speche
> In poetrie, if ye hire bokes seche.

By attributing to classical models the " forme " he used, Chaucer is able to make these models responsible for the paganism of his poem. The attribution is right enough, for that matter, though the implication that the poet's immediate sources were classical gives a (designedly) false impression. One is reminded of the Latin source claimed in the proem of the second book.

Two more stanzas remain:

> 1856 O moral Gower, this book I directe
> To the and to the, philosophical Strode,
> To vouchen sauf, ther nede is, to correcte,
> Of your benignites and zeles goode.
> And to that sothefast Crist that starf on rode
> With al myn herte of mercy evere I preye,
> And to the Lord right thus I speke and seye:

> 1863 Thow oon and two and thre, eterne on lyve,
> That regnest ay in thre and two and oon,
> Uncircumscript, and al maist circumscrive,

Us from visible and invisible foon
Defende, and to thy mercy everichon
So make us, Jesus, for thi merci digne,
For love of mayde and moder thyn benigne.

Lines 1856-1859 serve as yet another modest gesture, conventional like the others: the poet directs his work to his friends Gower and Strode for any corrections they may find needful. The author's request carries with it a complimentary implication; the two friends would naturally feel flattered at being asked to correct Chaucer's poem. Here the compliment is the main thing; it seems altogether unlikely that Gower and Strode actually did any correcting, or were expected to do any.

Lines 1860-1869 bring the poem to a devotional close with a prayer drawn in part from Dante's *Paradiso* (xiv. 28-30). The *Canterbury Tales* likewise end with a prayer, and this way of closing was customary for literary works in Chaucer's day, as in the Middle Ages generally. It answers to the benediction at the close of a religious service, and reminds us that even works of entertainment might have a moral purpose besides. Here it is particularly appropriate, for it comes as the culmination of an elaborate and beautiful ending which grows more and more religious in tone and spirit as it proceeds. The closing prayer of *Troilus and Criseyde* takes us as near the throne of God as we are ever likely to get by the literary road.

The five endings differ markedly in length. That of Book I comes to 28 lines; Book II, 7 lines; Book III, 49 lines; Book IV, 14 lines; and Book V, 126 lines. The longest ending is naturally the one that ends the poem. The ending of Book III is also long, because it marks the height of the hero's bliss and sums up what he owes to Love and what the poet owes to Venus and the Muses. The ending of Book I is long enough to mark the flight of time and the change in the hero's fortunes. There is no true break in the action between Books II and III and between Books IV and V, and the endings of Books II and IV are correspondingly short. In general the endings meet with ease the needs that called them forth, and of the last we can say with J. S. P. Tatlock, " For a combination of grandeur and charm the ending is seldom matched in poetry." [6]

---

[6] *Modern Philology* XVIII 625.

CHAPTER VIII

THE GENERAL PROLOG OF THE *CANTERBURY TALES*

OVER A HUNDRED years ago Thomas Wright recorded his opinion that " the general introduction to the *Canterbury Tales* is one of the most perfect compositions in the English language." [1] In this chapter I will try to bring out some of those features of the general prolog which may have led Wright to his eminently sound conclusion. I begin at the beginning, with the passage in which Chaucer dates the pilgrimage:

> Whan that Aprille with his shoures sote
> The droghte of Marche hath perced to the rote
> And bathed every veyne in swich licour
> Of which vertu engendred is the flour;
> Whan Zephirus eek with his swete breeth
> Inspired hath in every holt and heeth
> The tendre croppes, and the yonge sonne
> Hath in the Ram his halfe cours yronne,
> And smale fowles maken melodye
> That slepen al the night with open ye
> (So priketh hem nature in hir corages):
> Than longen folk to goon on pilgrimages
> (And palmers for to seken straunge strondes)
> To ferne halwes, couthe in sondry londes;
> And specially, from every shires ende
> Of Engelond, to Caunterbury they wende,
> The holy blisful martir for to seke,
> That hem hath holpen whan that they were seke.

---

[1] *Percy Society* 24 (1847). xvi.

This elaborate period is done, for the most part, in the high style which Chaucer makes the host object to in his words to the clerk (E 16-20) :

> Your termes, your colours, and your figures,
> Kepe hem in stoor til so be ye endyte
> Heigh style, as whan that men to kinges wryte.
> Speketh so pleyn at this tyme, I yow preye,
> That we may understonde what ye seye.

The host would indeed have had trouble in understanding Chaucer's opening lines, where ordinary rainwater is called the liquor by virtue of which the flower is engendered, and where in general only a bookish man could follow with ease. But it is not my purpose to discuss Chaucer's high style as such. My revered master, John M. Manly, in his lecture on Chaucer and the rhetoricians, made it clear, nearly a quarter of a century ago, that in such passages the poet was writing in conformity to traditional literary precept and practice.[2] In the well-known passage of the nun's priest's tale, Chaucer parodies the high style of another Geoffrey, but he uses high style seriously when it suits his purpose, as it does here.

My own interest, however, lies less in the high style than in Chaucer's method of getting away from it. The style stays high for eleven lines. With the twelfth line it begins to come down:

> Than longen folk to goon on pilgrimages.

In this line the poet makes a statement plain and straightforward enough. But the fall must not be too swift; it must be cushioned, so to speak. A belly-landing would never do. The next two lines therefore, though not in high style, have a certain dignity and above all a remoteness from everyday life:

[2] *Proceedings of the British Academy* 12 (1926). 95-113.

> (And palmers for to seken straunge strondes)
> To ferne halwes, couthe in sondry londes.

The three lines that follow show more of the common touch, and bring the English reader or hearer home:

> And specially, from every shires ende
> Of Engelond, to Caunterbury they wende,
> The holy blisful martir for to seke,

And with the eighteenth line we hit bottom:

> That hem hath holpen whan that they were seke.

Nothing could be simpler and plainer than that.

We see then that Chaucer, in his capacity as a traditionalist, began his poem with an elaborate, conventional dating, done in high style. But by the end of the eighteen-line period the style has become familiar, and this without giving the reader any stylistic shocks. Having made an opening bow to traditional formality and artifice, Chaucer can now proceed in the informal style which he prefers.

Throughout the next passage, lines 19-42, the style is familiar. But in addition Chaucer makes it personal and even conversational by speaking of himself and by addressing his readers directly. I will dwell for a moment on the latter device. Once Chaucer has got everybody settled and comfortable at the inn, he says (lines 30-34),

> And shortly, whan the sonne was to reste,
> So hadde I spoken with hem everichon
> That I was of hir felawshipe anon,
> And made forward erly for to ryse
> To take our wey, ther as I yow devyse.

The *shortly* of this passage tempts one to a digression. It is a favorite stylistic trick of the poet to insist upon his own brevity. Others may string a story out, but he cuts it short. I must resist the temptation to go into this, however, and stick to my second person. The *yow* of line 34 obviously adds to the easy, chatty stylistic effect. But after all *ther as I yow devyse* is only a tag, one may say. So it is, but Chaucer makes of it a springboard from which he plunges into what amounts to a *tête-à-tête* with his readers. He takes time out, as it were, to talk to them about his plans:

> But natheles, whyl I have tyme and space,
> Er that I ferther in this tale pace,
> Me thinketh it acordaunt to resoun
> To telle yow al the condicioun
> Of ech of hem, so as it semed me,
> And whiche they weren, and of what degree,
> And eek in what array that they were inne.
> And at a knight than wol I first beginne.

In this passage of eight lines Chaucer uses *I* three times, *me* twice, and *yow* once. By the end of the passage the readers not only know what to expect but they feel at home with the author. He has taken them into his confidence, and a certain intimacy has already been established between him and them. But for the poet's use of the first and second persons here, no such effect would have been possible; at any rate, it would have been much harder to achieve.

Next come the descriptions of the pilgrims in lines 43-714. Here Chaucer has to use the third person, but he takes care to insert, from time to time, a construction with a pronoun of the first or second person. I have counted twenty-three of these constructions. Of the pronouns, *I* occurs fifteen times, *us* thrice, as follows:

I gesse 82, 117	I seyde 183	I undertake 288
I trowe 155, 524, 691	I telle 619	as I was war 157
I woot 389, 659	telle I 330	I durste swere 454
I noot 284	I seigh 193	us 363, 566, 623

The other pronouns of the first and second persons occur

once each: *me* 385, *my* 544, *our* 62, *ye* 642, *yow* 73. The occurrences are well distributed:

knight 2	prioress 2	clerk 1
squire 1	monk 2	man of law 1
yeoman 1	merchant 1	burgesses 1
cook 1	parson 1	reeve 1
shipman 1	Chaucer 1	summoner 3
wife of Bath 1	miller 1	pardoner 1

It is the stylistic function of these pronouns to emphasize the informal, conversational effect of the passages in which they occur.

At this point let me make a digression on the cook of London. This pilgrim is introduced with line 379, which reads

A cook they hadde with hem for the nones.

Since Chaucer regularly refers to the body of pilgrims in the first person (beginning with line 34, immediately after he has made himself one of them), the pronoun *they* of line 379 cannot have reference to the pilgrims as a whole and must refer to the group of burgesses described in the lines immediately preceding. In other words, this group of would-be aldermen took a cook along with them on the pilgrimage as a servant.[3] The only other pilgrim said to have a servant is the squire, whose yeoman Chaucer presumably intended us to think of as serving father as well as son.[4] Chaucer lays great stress on the wealth, dignity, and importance (or self-importance) of the little group of burgesses. The fact that they have a servant with

[3] But note Manly's cautious comment in his school edition of the *Canterbury Tales* (p. 522): "Here it is doubtful whether Chaucer represents the cook merely as being especially skilful or as being brought by the tradesmen for the express purpose of cooking their meals on the pilgrimage."

[4] The canon, like the squire, had a yeoman in his service, but the canon can hardly be reckoned one of the pilgrims, and he and his servant parted company almost as soon as they joined the pilgrims.

them emphasizes still more their high standing, or at any rate their pretensions, which our court poet evidently regards as amusing, burgess though he himself was in origin. Snobbishness did not fail to flourish even in Chaucer's day.

The long series of descriptions falls into two parts. The division is marked by the following passage (lines 542-544):

> Ther was also a Reve and a Millere,
> A Somnour and a Pardoner also,
> A Maunciple, and my self; ther were namo.

The passage serves as a special introduction to the five descriptions which end the series. By this simple and highly effective stylistic trick the reader is reassured. He has known from the start that the series would not be interminable: in line 24 the size of the group is specified at " wel nine and twenty." But by line 541 most readers have lost count, if they ever tried to keep count, and it is time for them to be told how much more of this kind of thing they may expect before the story proper is resumed.

Chaucer's division of the series of descriptions into two parts is decidedly unequal: Part One is about three times as long as Part Two. One might therefore expect to find more use made of subgrouping in Part One than in Part Two, and this is actually the case. We find five groups of pilgrims in the longer part, only one group in the shorter.

First comes a household group: knight, squire, and yeoman are father, son, and servant. Here the linkage is so perfectly natural that its stylistic motivation would escape notice but for the prying eye of the critic. The group that centers about the prioress might also be called a household group, though of another kind, without servants and without blood relationship. Here however the prioress herself gets all the attention, the others serving merely as her retinue. They are needed for the simple reason that a dignitary of the prioress's importance and sex could hardly be represented as traveling alone.

Our third group is better described as a pair of pilgrims: the man of law and the franklin. We are told only that they were traveling together. The burgesses and their servant the cook make a fourth group; the parson and his brother the plowman, a fifth. The other pilgrims of Part One travel without companions or followers: monk, friar, merchant, clerk, shipman, doctor, and wife of Bath. That the wife should be without male attendance may seem somewhat surprising, but Chaucer certainly represents her as well able to take care of herself.

In Part Two the summoner and pardoner appear not only as fellow-travelers but also as friends. The other pilgrims of this part travel alone: miller, manciple, reeve, and poet. One notes with interest the variety of these subgroups of pilgrims; no two of the groups are exactly alike in method of linkage.

The series of descriptions serves also as a list of the pilgrims. For this reason it includes the five pilgrims left undescribed. One of these is the poet himself; the other four (three priests and a nun) are traveling companions of the prioress. But the host, the canon, and the canon's yeoman, who join the group of pilgrims later, are of course neither listed nor described here.

We are given more descriptions at later points in the narrative. The description of the host comes a little further on in the general prolog itself; that of the canon and his yeoman, as part of the story of the ride to Canterbury. The host, when he calls on Chaucer to tell a tale, takes advantage of the occasion to give a brief and jocular description of the poet. The host and Chaucer combine to describe one of the three nun's priests just before and after this priest tells his tale. The other two nun's priests, however, are nowhere described; indeed, the *prestes three* of line 164 is the only evidence we have that more than one priest accompanied the prioress on the pilgrimage.

The nun who traveled with the prioress tells one of the tales, but is not described. Since the tale she tells has no headlink, one may indeed conjecture that if Chaucer had lived to write this link, he would have included in it a description of the nun, much as he actually provided a description of the nun's traveling companion, Sir John. But such a conjecture involves a very doubtful presumption: namely, that Chaucer would have provided for everything had he finished his masterpiece. Of some artists this may assuredly be said, but in my opinion it cannot rightly be said of Chaucer, who was quite capable of composing a headlink to the Life of St Cecilia without bothering to make it describe the nun who told the tale, even though this would leave us with no description of the nun at all. Chaucer was not the man to worry overmuch about loose ends, and he was not always careful to make things neat and tidy. This peculiarity goes well with his fondness for the informal style. One of the chief marks of this style is its irregularity, its carelessness, its intentional failure to provide for everything. Indeed, the easy, conversational effect aimed at in any informal style would infallibly be missed if everything was in order. The disorder need not be great, but some disorder there must be in every masterpiece of this style. And the *Canterbury Tales* is such a masterpiece.

Here we can do no more than glance at the descriptions themselves. There are twenty-two of them in the series, but they describe twenty-six pilgrims, since one of them deals with the five burgesses taken together. I have counted the lines and tabulated my results, as follows:

friar	62	knight	36	clerk	24	burgesses	18
parson	52	reeve	36	shipman	23	yeoman	17
pardoner	46	doctor	34	man of law	22	merchant	15
summoner	46	wife	32	miller	22	plowman	13
monk	45	franklin	30	squire	22	cook	9
prioress	45			manciple	20		

It will be seen that the seven representatives of the Church take 320 lines; the other nineteen pilgrims take 349 lines, a little more than half the total of 669 lines.[5]

The series of descriptions is carefully dovetailed at both ends into the story of the pilgrimage. The dovetailing passage which precedes the series has already been quoted (on page 147 above). The corresponding passage which follows the series I will now quote (lines 715-724):

> Now have I told yow shortly, in a clause,
> Th'estat, th'array, the nombre, and eek the cause
> Why that assembled was this companye
> In Southwerk, at this gentil hostelrye,
> That highte the Tabard, faste by the Belle.
> But now is tyme to yow for to telle
> How that we baren us that ilke night,
> Whan we were in that hostelrye alight,
> And after wol I telle of our viage,
> And al the remenaunt of our pilgrimage.

The two passages balance each other beautifully. Both are cast in the same form: direct address to the readers. Both are done in the same easy, friendly style. Both deal with the same matter: the course of the story and its interruption by the series of descriptions. The two differ only as one would expect them to differ in virtue of their respective places in the poem. The first passage tells the readers why the story of the pilgrimage is to be interrupted, and promises a series of descriptions of the pilgrims. The second passage proclaims the fulfilment of this promise

---

[5] This total of course does not include lines 163-164 and 542-544.

and goes on to make promises of its own about the narrative which is to follow.

But before Chaucer actually resumes the story he addresses his readers once more, this time to defend himself against prospective criticism. Needless to say, this apologetic passage was written with tongue in cheek. I will quote it first *in extenso,* as follows:

725 But first I pray yow, of your curteisye,
That ye n'arette it nat my vileinye
Thogh that I pleynly speke in this matere,
To telle yow hir wordes and hir chere;
Ne thogh I speke hir wordes properly.
730 For this ye knowen also wel as I,
Whoso shal telle a tale after a man,
He moot reherce, as ny as ever he can,
Everich a word, if it be in his charge,
Al speke he never so rudeliche and large;
735 Or elles he moot telle his tale untrewe,
Or feyne thing, of finde wordes newe.
He may nat spare, althogh he were his brother;
He moot as well seye o word as another.
Crist spak himself ful brode in holy writ,
740 And wel ye woot, no vileinye is it.
Eek Plato seith (whoso that can him rede),
The wordes mote be cosin to the dede.
Also I preye yow to foryeve it me
Al have I nat set folk in hir degree
745 Here in this tale, as that they sholde stonde;
My wit is short, ye may wel understonde.

The passage comes to 22 lines, and falls into two unequal parts. In the first part, of 18 lines, the poet apologizes for the fulness and the accuracy of his reporting. In the second part, only four lines long, he apologizes for his failure to present his characters in order of rank.

The latter fault the poet explains very simply and briefly indeed: " my wit is short." His true reason for not following a conventional and rigid order of presentation is easy to guess: such an order would cramp his style. But he says nothing about this, for it is far from his mind to discuss seriously his principles of literary composition. He touches upon his technic only to laugh it off. He mentions the matter because he wants his readers to know he is aware of what he is doing. Once he has mentioned it he is content to dismiss it with a joke at his own expense. The joke itself has a conventional basis: an author was supposed to be modest. But he makes his modesty extravagant and therefore humorous, a thing not to be taken seriously. We find like statements about Chaucer in various works of his. Thus, in *Troilus,* Book V, the author, speaking of the sufferings of the hero, says (lines 267-273):

> Who coude telle aright or ful discryve
> His wo, his pleynt, his langour, and his pyne?
> Naught alle the men that han or ben on lyve.
> Thow, redere, maist thiself ful wel devyne
> That swich a wo my wit kan nat diffyne.
> On ydel for to write it sholde I swynke,
> Whan that my wit is wery it to thynke.

Here the tone is serious, but Chaucer clearly represents his own wits as below par, and this gives a touch of humor to the passage. He does the same thing in the *Legend of Good Women*, lines 29-30:

> And as for me, though that my wit be lite,
> On bokes for to rede I me delyte.

In the same poem (F 547, Gg 537) the god of Love tells him

> Thy litel wit was thilke tyme aslepe,

and in the *House of Fame* the eagle points out to him that " in thy hed ful lyte is " (line 621) and that he is " a lewed man " (line 866). The man of law in his words to the host remarks that Chaucer " kan but lewedly " (B 47) when it comes to versifying, and Africanus in the *Parlia-*

ment of Fowls seems to be of the same mind, for he tells Chaucer (lines 167-168),

> And if thow haddest connyng for t'endite,
> I shal the shewe mater of to wryte.

All these slurs on the poet's intelligence and on his skill as a literary artist are meant to be funny.

Moreover, Chaucer is by no means so negligent of rank as he pretends to be. His descriptions of the pilgrims begin with the knight, the ranking member of the company, and he sees to it that the cut falls to the knight when the pilgrims draw cut. The sequence of the first three descriptions is one of rank; the yeoman comes before the prioress because he belongs to the household group made up of knight, squire, and yeoman. This arrangement shows that Chaucer in making his sequence took account of grouping as well as rank, but his choice of prioress and monk for fourth and fifth places in the sequence of descriptions shows that rank played an important part in determining the order: of all the company only the knight outranked these two pilgrims. From the point of view of rank the friar very properly follows the monk; the mendicant orders lacked the dignity and prestige of the older monastic orders, but their vows gave them a ranking higher than that of the secular priesthood.

The other descriptions of Part One come in the following order: merchant, clerk, man of law and franklin, burgesses and cook, shipman, physician, wife of Bath, parson and plowman. Within each of the three groups (man of law and franklin, burgesses and cook, parson and plowman) the descriptions are in order of rank. The group made up of parson and plowman ends Part One. Its final position marks it as a group of special interest to the author, if Schütte's Law applies here,[6] but one may also explain its

---

[6] According to the Danish folklorist Gudmund Schütte, first place in a

place at the end in terms of rank; of all the pilgrims the plowman ranked lowest. The high place given to the merchant may reflect the power and importance of the so-called Merchant Adventurers in fourteenth-century society. The clerk's position is too high, the physician's too low, in terms of rank. Chaucer may well have set the virtuous and unworldly student between merchant and man of law for the sake of contrast. Possibly the learned doctor of physic serves the same purpose in his place between the shipman and the wife of Bath.

Of the five pilgrims described in Part Two, only the pardoner could lay claim to anything better than a humble social status, and even he only *played* the part of " a noble ecclesiaste " (line 708). His bad character and degrading activities lost him the respect that was commonly shown to a man of the cloth. Chaucer may have put him in last place to symbolize his low opinion of pardoners in general and this pardoner in particular.[7] The summoner and the pardoner make a group, as we saw a few minutes ago, and if the pardoner got last place the summoner would have to be put next to last. It is not easy to explain the order in which the other three descriptions appear, but that of the manciple makes a good contrast with those of the miller and the reeve and therefore seems appropriate between them. It is worthy of note that the order of descriptions in Part Two does not agree with the order in which the corresponding pilgrims are named in lines 542-544 (but the summoner precedes the pardoner in both places).

From the point of view of rank the pilgrims named in the general prolog are reasonably well ordered. We do

traditional list goes to the person or group to which greatest honor or respect is due; last place, to the person or group in which the maker of the list has the greatest interest.

[7] But the pardoner's final position may exemplify Schütte's law. See note 6 above.

not find a uniform descent from highest to lowest, but most departures from this pattern find their explanation in the groupings and in the division of the series of descriptions into two parts. When Chaucer apologized for not having " set folk in their degree . . . as they should stand '" (lines 744-745), he did so not because an apology was really needed but because he wished to make clear to his readers that he knew what he had done. But the apology had a further purpose: it gave the poet an opening for a characteristic joke.

Chaucer's apology for the fulness and accuracy of his reporting (lines 725-742) likewise has a humorous purpose. Here the poet is talking about what is to come, as line 731 reveals. In telling what the pilgrims said he must repeat every word, so far as that is humanly possible, no matter how objectionable or even offensive some of the words may be. If a reporter allows himself to add anything, leave anything out, or tone anything down, he thereby falsifies the facts. The truth, the whole truth, and nothing but the truth must be his only concern. He must not pick and choose between words, taking one but omitting or changing another; all the words actually uttered must be equally sacred to him. In setting up these principles Chaucer, on the face of it, is defending himself in advance against a prospective accusation of vulgarity (*vileinye*, line 726), with his smutty tales particularly in mind. But since author and reader alike know perfectly well that the pilgrimage is a fiction and that every word spoken by every pilgrim was put in his mouth by Chaucer himself, the poet's defense cannot be taken seriously and was not meant to be so taken. It makes part of a little game that Chaucer constantly plays with his readers: he poses as a historian. The pose itself is conventional enough, but Chaucer upon occasion turns it to humorous purposes, as here.

To this day novelists, poets, and other writers often find it useful to pretend that they are telling their readers about something that actually happened. Works of the imagination may still be cast in a form ostensibly historical. And though history always deals with the past, that past need not be remote. The thing told of may be said to have happened only " this other night," as in the *Book of the Duchess* (line 45). The pseudo-historical form is one so familiar in works of literary art that it hardly needs comment or discussion. In the present passage Chaucer plays the part of historian in order to disclaim responsibility for what the pilgrims said. He gains a humorous effect by insisting that he must repeat their *ipsissima verba* in the interests of historical truth. In the same way the nun's priest disclaims responsibility for the cock's words (B 4455-4456):

> Thise been the cokkes wordes, and nat myne;
> I kan noon harm of no womman divyne.

The same device for raising a laugh appears elsewhere in the *Canterbury Tales*, as the diligent reader will readily find for himself.

With line 747 the story of the pilgrimage is resumed. But the poet does not take up exactly where he left off. There is a bit of overlapping; or perhaps it would be better to say that the poet repeats, with variation and expansion, what he had said in lines 28-34. There is no repetition of that part of the earlier narrative which concerns the poet personally: " to make a long story short, by sunset I had spoken with every one of them in such a way that I was of their company at once " (lines 30-32). The narrative is resumed with a new treatment of the hospitality told of in lines 28-29:

> The chambres and the stables weren wyde,
> And wel we weren esed atte beste.

Here we have a very general statement indeed, a summary account [8] which Chaucer returns to in lines 747-750 in order to make it more specific and more personal:

> Greet chiere made oure hoost us everichon,
> And to the soper sette he us anon.
> He served us with vitaille at the beste;
> Strong was the wyn, and wel to drynke us leste.

The details here given, and above all the introduction of the host, make a vivid and lively picture denied us in the earlier treatment of the theme of hospitality. The solicitous host of the lines just quoted dominates the action from this point on, though he soon stops being solicitous to become domineering.

Since the host is to play so vital a part in the story, we need a description of him, and Chaucer gives it to us at this point. It is only seven lines long, however (two lines shorter than the shortest of the descriptions of the pilgrims), and one gets the impression that the poet wants to go on with his story and rather skimps the description of his most important character. The seventh line, which tells us that the host was a merry man, belongs not only to the description but also to the narrative, and serves to dovetail the one into the other:

> 757   Eek therto he was right a myrie man,
> And after soper pleyen he bigan,
> And spak of myrthe amonges othere thynges,
> Whan that we hadde maad our rekenynges.

The speech that follows begins with a host beautifully solicitous; he bids his customers welcome and pays them compliments in his best innkeeping style. But by the end of the speech he has become the domineering Harry Bailly we know so well, the lord of all he surveys.

---

[8] Be it noted that the *we* of line 29 means not the company of pilgrims but that company plus Chaucer; at this point in the narrative the poet had not yet made himself one of their number.

Up to this point in the story we have found no conflict between the summary account given in lines 28-34 and the fuller version which we are now looking at. We have noted differences but no inconsistencies. But the *forward* (i. e. agreement) which Chaucer tells of in line 33 does not answer to the one of which the host speaks in line 829. The couplet

33   And made forward erly for to ryse
      To take oure wey ther as I yow devyse

gives us no hint of the host and his scheme. It looks as if Chaucer, when he wrote this couplet, had no such scheme in mind. His happy idea of putting the host in charge of the pilgrimage may not have come to him until he had done his descriptions of the pilgrims. The picture of our poet starting to work on a poem before he had mapped it out need not shock us. Chaucer never showed any fondness for making or following cut-and-dried schemes. He did not scorn system, but he felt free to do as he pleased, within reasonable limits. The French formalists from whom he drew so much would have been shocked indeed if they had known how he treated their compositions; luckily they had no English and never found out. We may safely presume that Chaucer began to write the general prolog with a frame-story in mind. He expected to insert into his story of the pilgrimage tales told by the pilgrims. But he may perfectly well have begun the process of composition without knowing just how he would make these insertions. In artistic creation the important thing is to get started. The artist of course must have some idea of what he wants to do before he begins, but his idea may be, and usually is, pretty vague. As he proceeds, he warms up, and if things go well the course which he must follow comes to him in a series of inspirations, some of which he thinks over and casts aside, while others he takes and uses. In my opinion this was Chaucer's way of making his *Canterbury Tales*.

The scheme which the host proposes and which the pilgrims accept is simple enough. The host will join the company of pilgrims and become their leader. On the journey to Canterbury and back each pilgrim will tell four tales: two going and two coming. The pilgrim who tells the best tale will get a prize, to be paid for by the rest of the company: a supper at the Tabard, when the pilgrims have come back from Canterbury. From the wording one gathers that the host himself will not compete for the prize. He is to be " of our tales juge and reportour " (814) and he is to " sette a soper at a certeyn prys " (815); that is, he will decide who gets the prize and determine how good (or how dear) the prize supper shall be. To speak more generally, the host is given autocratic power over the pilgrimage from first to last, a power which makes him lord of the pilgrims indeed. The whole situation is intentionally comic, as we shall see in Chapter X below.

Once the scheme of the host has been proposed and accepted, the action of the story moves on at high speed:

A 819   And therupon the wyn was fet anon;
          We dronken, and to reste wente echon,
          Withouten any lenger taryinge.
          Amorwe, whan that day bigan to sprynge,
          Up roos oure hoost, and was our aller cok,
          And gadrede us togidre alle in a flok,
          And forth we riden a litel moore than paas
          Unto the wateryng of Seint Thomas.

Here Chaucer in eight lines puts the pilgrims to bed, gives them a night's rest, and gets them started on the road to Canterbury, with the host very conspicuously in command. There follows the scene in which the host has the pilgrims " draw cut " to see who shall tell the first tale. This method of choosing a speaker is never used again. Thenceforth the host chooses the speaker, though now and then circumstances make him change his decision. This departure from a pattern of procedure duly set up is characteristic of Chaucer. A few minutes ago we had another instance of it, when Chaucer named the pilgrims to be described in Part Two of his series and then proceeded to describe them in an order different from that in which he named them. Such irregularities make Chaucer akin to the Baroque artists of the sixteenth and seventeenth centuries, artists who delight in breaking patterns. A fondness for irregularity goes well, of course, with a fondness for the colloquial style. We have noted time and again the colloquial character of Chaucer's most characteristic passages and most successful effects. The longer one studies his art the more clearly one sees that what he did hangs together, is of a piece.

CHAPTER IX

THE CANTERBURY PILGRIMS

THE CANTERBURY pilgrims have been with us now for nearly 600 years. Until the nineteenth century, people were content to enjoy them, but with the rise of Anglistic scholarship the men of learning, if not the general reading public, began to pick them to pieces. They are still at it. Their studies have flooded us with good things, and in the process we professional students, at least, run the risk of drowning. The ordinary reader is willing enough to skip a footnote, and it does not bother him much if he misses the exact point of this or that detail. Not so the scholar, who is unhappy if anything escapes him, and feels ashamed if he misunderstands anything, however insignificant it may be. His passion for full and accurate knowledge, like any other compulsion of the human mind, has both a good and a bad side. The great danger is that we may become so absorbed in our study of the parts that we lose sight of the whole. This danger is ever present in any kind of exact scholarship. It threatens us here and now. But if we bear it constantly in mind, we may hope to reduce the hazards of our undertaking and reach a better understanding and appreciation of Chaucer's literary art than would otherwise be possible.

Let us begin by looking at the Canterbury pilgrims as a whole. What have they in common, other than their status as pilgrims to the shrine of Thomas Becket? Three things, as far as I can make out. First, they are

                              in a companye,
A 25   Of sondry folk, by aventure yfalle
        In felawshipe,

but still a company. This fellowship of theirs is the most
important thing about them. On it all else depends.
Secondly, they are English. In the fourteenth century the
Canterbury pilgrimage was made by many not of English
nationality, but Chaucer's pilgrims have no foreigners
among them. Thirdly, they are commoners. They vary
much in social status, but not one of them belongs to the
nobility.

How does Chaucer treat the pilgrims in the general
prolog? Most of them (21, to be exact) he describes
individually. Five of them, the burgesses, he describes as
a group. And four of them (or five, if you count Chaucer
himself) he mentions but does not describe. The following
of the prioress, as you will remember, consists of a nun
and three priests. These four pilgrims are not described
in the general prolog, and we hear no more of them anywhere in the text, except for Sir John, the teller of the
nun's priest's tale, who is described, and identified as the
nun's priest, in the headlink of his tale, and described again
in the endlink. The legend of Saint Cecily is given to the
second nun (that is, to the nun who accompanies the
prioress) in the rubrics that go with the tale, but in the
prolog of the tale itself the narrator calls himself a *son*
of Eve, and it seems evident that Chaucer wrote this tale
originally for a man. The five burgesses are not described
as individuals at all, but we have a delightful group description of them (A 361-378):

                An haberdassher and a carpenter,
                A webbe, a dyere, and a tapicer
                Were with us eek, clothed in o liveree,
                Of a solempne and greet fraternitee.
                Ful fresh and newe hir gere apyked was;

Hir knyves were ychaped noght with bras,
But al with silver, wroght full clene and weel,
Hir girdles and hir pouches every deel.
Wel semed ech of hem a fair burgeys
To sitten in a yeldhalle on a deys.
Everich, for the wisdom that he can,
Was shaply for to been an alderman,
For catel hadde they ynogh and rente,
And eek hir wyves wolde it wel assente;
And elles certein were they to blame.
It is ful fair to been yclept ' *ma dame*,'
And goon to vigilyes al bifore,
And have a mantel royalliche ybore.

This is the first and the last we hear of the burgesses. Their servant the cook tells a tale (or begins one) , and otherwise plays a part in the story of the pilgrimage, but his five masters are never once mentioned again.

It is worth noting that though the burgesses are described as a group, no two of them follow the same trade. The same principle holds for the 21 pilgrims who get individual descriptions: among them we find only one knight, only one miller, only one cook, etc. In the little group of five made up of the prioress and her attendants, however, things are markedly different: this group consists of two nuns and three priests. One may argue, it is true, that the two nuns differ a good deal in status, since one of them has the exalted position of prioress. The threeness of the priests cannot be explained away so readily, but it remains true that only one of them appears elsewhere and he is there spoken of, not as one of the nun's priests but simply as the nun's priest. Finally, the group of burgesses includes a carpenter, and since the reeve likewise is a carpenter by trade it would be hard to deny that two of Chaucer's pilgrims are carpenters. Here again one may get out of the difficulty, after a fashion, by arguing that the reeve has risen in the world and that his work as a

carpenter belongs to the days of his youth. But the reeve
himself, in his quarrel with the miller, makes so much of
his trade that we are forced to agree with him and call
him a carpenter. Be it noted, too, that the canon's yeoman is added to the squire's in the course of the pilgrimage.

What does all this come to? We conclude that Chaucer's
general scheme forbade duplication, much less triplication,
but that he felt free to depart from this scheme now and
then if he found such a departure convenient. In other
words, Chaucer refused to be hampered by what the
Germans call *systemzwang*. He was willing to be reasonably systematic, but not rigorously so. We shall find this
easygoing technic characteristic of Chaucer's art.

If in general a given profession, calling, trade, or occupation is represented by one pilgrim only, what is that
pilgrim's relation to his fellow-practitioners? Is he meant
to be truly representative or typical of his calling? For
instance, is the plowman to be taken as a typical peasant?
Let us see what Chaucer has to say about the plowman:

A 529 With him ther was a plowman, was his brother,
        That hadde ylad of dong ful many a fother.
        A trewe swinker and a good was he,
        Livinge in pees and parfit charitee.
        God loved he best with al his hole herte
        At alle tymes, thogh him gamed or smerte,
        And thanne his neighebour right as himselve.
        He wolde thresshe, and therto dyke and delve,
        For Cristes sake, for every povre wight,
        Withouten hyre, if it lay in his might.
        His tythes payed he ful faire and wel,
        Bothe of his propre swink and his catel.
        In a tabard he rood upon a mere.

Obviously the plowman is no ordinary peasant. He is the
best of all possible peasants, a superlatively good man in
that station of life to which it has pleased God to call
him. He is a faithful and competent worker, a pious and

conscientious Christian, a self-sacrificing neighbor, a man
admirable in every respect. The other pilgrims are equally
superlative, though most of them lack the moral perfection
of the plowman. Kittredge in his first Johns Hopkins
lecture of 1914 [1] explains these characterizations thus:

> Chaucer had an immense enthusiasm for life in this world; . . . What-
> ever was good of its kind was a delight to him. And he had such
> stupendous luck in always meeting nonpareils! There was no better
> priest than the Parson anywhere; no such Pardoner from one end of
> England to the other; never so great a purchaser as the Man of Law.
> If you sought from Hull to Carthage, you couldn't find a mariner
> to match the Shipman. The Wife of Bath was so excellent a cloth-
> maker that she actually beat the Dutch. The Sumner's bass voice
> was more than twice as loud as a trumpet. The Friar was the best
> beggar in his convent. . . . [p. 32].

The superlative quality of Chaucer's pilgrims is beautifully brought out in the passage which I have just quoted.
The explanation given is less satisfying. When Kittredge
speaks of Chaucer's stupendous luck he is only jesting, of
course; the luck was of Chaucer's own making, as Kittredge knew perfectly well. But it is not enough to explain
Chaucer's characterizations as an outgrowth of his enthusi-
asm for life, and his delight in whatever was good of its
kind. The pilgrims are actually superlative for *literary*
reasons. From time immemorial it has been the custom
in story-telling to make the characters heroic, larger than
life, extraordinary rather than ordinary people. The hero
is commonly stronger and nobler than other men; the
villain is a devil incarnate. The stories current in Chaucer's
own day regularly conform to this model. Nobody in the
fourteenth century would have thought of doing otherwise.
Chaucer conformed with the rest. His pilgrims, if they
were to be of interest to the reading public, had to be

---

[1] These lectures were published in 1915 under the title *Chaucer and his
Poetry*. My quotations from them refer to this book.

unusual, striking, remarkable in every possible way, and so they are.

Before leaving the point it may be well to take another illustration, and for this I choose the description of the knight:

> A 43 A knight ther was, and that a worthy man,
> That fro the tyme that he first bigan
> To ryden out, he loved chivalrye,
> Trouthe and honour, fredom and curteisye.
> Ful worthy was he in his lordes werre,
> And therto hadde he riden (no man ferre)
> As wel in Christendom as hethenesse,
> And ever honoured for his worthinesse.

His campaigns in Christendom are mentioned but not specified or dwelt upon, for Chaucer wishes to make of him a great champion of Christianity against the heathen. The tale of his campaigns in *hethenesse* runs thus:

> A 51 At Alisaundre he was, whan it was wonne;
> Ful ofte tyme he hadde the bord bigonne
> Aboven alle naciouns in Pruce.
> In Lettow hadde he reysed and in Ruce,
> No Cristen man so ofte of his degree.
> In Gernade at the sege eek hadde he be
> Of Algezir, and riden in Belmarye.
> At Lyeys was he, and at Satalye,
> Whan they were wonne; and in the Grete See
> At many a noble armeë hadde he be.
> At mortal batailles hadde he been fiftene,
> And foughten for our feith at Tramissene
> In listes thryes, and ay slayn his fo.
> This ilke worthy knight had been also
> Somtyme with the lord of Palatye,
> Ageyn another hethen in Turkye:
> And evermore he hadde a sovereyn prys.

His fighting for the faith had taken him to the frontiers of Christendom and beyond, in Europe, Asia, and Africa. Such a record as this is surely unexampled and makes of our knight a Christian hero indeed, a man worthy of all admiration. But the glory which he had gained in warfare did not go to his head:

A 68　And though that he were worthy, he was wys,
　　　And of his port as meke as is a mayde.
　　　He never yet no vileinye ne sayde
　　　In al his lyf, unto no maner wight.
　　　He was a verray parfit gentil knight.

Chaucer not only makes his knight perfect, he calls him perfect in so many words.

Yet human perfection has its limits, and the knight fails on one occasion to live up to Chaucer's description of him. Or it would be better to say that Chaucer here, as often, finds it convenient to depart from the rigors of consistency. The knight, it appears, is not perfect after all. Even though

　　　He never yet no vileinye ne sayde
　　　In al his lyf unto no maner wight,

he breaks the habits of a lifetime to stint the monk of his tale.

B 3957　Ho! quod the knight, good sir, namore of this!
　　　That ye han seyd is right ynough, ywis,
　　　And mochel more!

This piece of rudeness does not go without defense, of course. The knight justifies himself by presenting his views on story-telling, views which, in his opinion, are not peculiar to himself but are widely held. He says,

　　　　　　　　　　For litel hevinesse
　　　Is right ynough to mochel folk, I gesse.
　　　I seye for me, it is a greet disese
　　　Wheras men han ben in greet welthe and ese
　　　To heren of hir sodeyn fal, allas!
　　　And the contrarie is joie and greet solas,
　　　As whan a man hath been in povre estaat,
　　　And clymbeth up, and wexeth fortunat,

> And ther abydeth in prosperitee:
> Swich thing is gladsom, as it thinketh me,
> And of swich thing were goodly for to telle.

Here we get what amounts to a new characterization of the knight in terms of his literary taste, a characterization put in the knight's own mouth and therefore highly authoritative — who could know better than he himself does what it is that he likes and dislikes? And we discover that our military hero has the taste of a child, or at any rate of a thoroughly unsophisticated person, when it comes to works of literary art. Tragedy he cannot abide. A story must end happily, or he will have none of it. He feels so strongly about this (or so Chaucer would have us think) that his feelings overcome his gentility and make him commit a gross breach of good manners.

There are various ways of looking at this incident in the story of the pilgrimage. One may say that Chaucer has made the knight more human by making him less perfect, and this is undoubtedly true, but it seems altogether likely that the change in characterization is no more than a by-product of the action. But if the interruption itself is the important thing, what was Chaucer's reason for having such a thing happen? Interruption of a speaker in the midst of his speech may be looked upon as a dramatic device which amuses the audience and enlivens the action. The speaker is the victim (the butt) of a jest, and his discomfiture makes you laugh. Chaucer cast himself in the part of such a victim or butt when he had the host interrupt him in the midst of the tale of Sir Thopas. The host stints Chaucer of his tale because he finds it not to his taste. He denounces it in the most vigorous terms:

> B 2109   No more of this, for goddes dignitee,
> Quod oure hoste, for thou makest me
> So wery of thy verray lewednesse
> That, also wisly god my soule blesse,

Myn eres aken of thy drasty speche;
Now swiche a rym the devel I biteche!
This may wel be rym dogerel, quod he.
Why so? quod I, why wiltow lette me
More of my tale than another man,
Sin that it is the beste rym I can?
By God, quod he, for pleynly, at a word,
Thy drasty ryming is nat worth a tord;
Thou doost nought elles but despendest tyme.
Sir, at o word, thou shalt no lenger ryme.
Lat see wher thou canst tellen aught in geste,
Or telle in prose somwhat at the leste
In which ther be som mirthe or som doctryne.

We have here a pattern of stinting which Chaucer found so effective that he repeated it, with variations, later on, using the knight, instead of the host, to do the dirty work, and making the monk the victim or butt of the jest. That the knight and the monk are the two men of highest rank and greatest distinction among the pilgrims only adds to the comic effect.

But the device has another purpose besides, the most important purpose of all, I think. Chaucer's rime of Sir Thopas is indeed a literary gem, one of the most delightful and successful parodies in the English language. But Chaucer did not care to finish it. He had done what he wanted to do to his full satisfaction, and to keep on doing it to the length of a whole metrical romance seemed to him needless. Why labor a parody, once you have made your points? The device of stinting came in handy here. By using it, Chaucer could leave his parody unfinished and put the blame for its unfinished state on the host. This was a little hard on the host, no doubt, who had to be represented as disliking a very choice specimen of literary art. But the host's shoulders were broad, and Chaucer had no scruples.

The device of stinting was used a second time for a like

reason. Chaucer had composed for the monk's mouth as many tragedies as he wanted to do. The general theme, *de casibus virorum illustrium,* is endless; history and story alike afford a plentiful supply of men in great place who fall. An easy and amusing way of ending the series of falls is to have it broken off. Chaucer makes the knight do the stinting partly for variety's sake and partly because he thereby heightens the dramatic effect. To have so gentle a person as the knight do so rude a thing makes the stinting far more dramatic than it could possibly be if put in the hands of the host, from whom politeness was not to be expected.

Kittredge in the fifth of his Johns Hopkins lectures gives another explanation. He says,

The Monk belonged to the " gentles," and the Host was not so ready to interrupt him as in the case of Chaucer, who was a somewhat ambiguous personality, even to the omniscient Bailly. Not altogether because Harry was considerate. He stood in no awe of Dan Piers; the preliminaries demonstrate that. He was simply at his wit's end. . . . the situation was just a trifle beyond his control; and so the natural leader [i. e. the knight] asserted himself, as many a time on the perilous edge of battle when it raged. [p. 164].

This view illustrates a mistake into which literary critics fall all too often: the mistake of treating the characters in a work of literary art as if they were actual human beings instead of creatures of the artist's fancy. The host failed to stint the monk, not because the situation was beyond his control, but because Chaucer, when he used for the second time the narrative device of interruption, used it (for artistic reasons) with variation instead of repeating it mechanically.

After the knight spoke up, the host had a good deal to say, in his usual impudent style, but his literary opinions need not be taken any more seriously here than in the case of Sir Thopas. His comments on both tales are meant to be funny. They are not meant to be literary criticism. Actually the monk's tale is not tedious. The knight objects to it for another reason, as we have seen. The knight's views, unlike the host's, *are* meant to be literary criticism of a sort. The knight expresses in all seriousness the attitude of the general unsophisticated public toward literary art. His esthetic naiveté gives us the right to smile, and that is probably what Chaucer wanted us to do.

There is something else about the knight's perfection that needs a word or two, if not extended comment. Chaucer calls him a perfect knight, not a perfect man, and the distinction is important. His perfections are those of knighthood. For that very reason his weakness in the literary realm does not matter much; we do not expect a soldier to have a keen and discriminating appreciation of the niceties of literature. The perfections of the other pilgrims likewise do not range far afield; they stay within, or not far without, the orbit of their respective occupations. The miller's talents as a wrestler, and as an opener of doors, have no direct connection, it is true, with his thumb of gold, but they befit this calling, and his station in life, well enough, whereas in the knight such talents would be out of place. In real life, of course, misfits abound; many people follow a trade or profession which they dislike and to which they are ill suited. Not so in Chaucer. His pilgrims thoroughly enjoy what they do and they do it supremely well. In that sense they *are* typical; it would be hard to imagine the knight, for instance, as anything but a knight. His characteristics are determined by the ideals of his specific profession.

But what of pilgrims like the monk, the friar, and the pardoner? Are they not misfits in their clerical profession? From one point of view, yes. But Chaucer, it would seem, did not find the monastic or the mendicant life sympathetic, much less the sale of indulgences. Upon these departments (so to speak) of the Church he looked with a cold and realistic eye. He saw them as they were in the fourteenth century, of course, and what he saw was not edifying. Chaucer took the standards of conduct then prevalent as he found them, and made his monk, his friar, and his pardoner to fit. All three are eminently successful men. They have all gone far in their respective professions.

The monk is described in the general prolog as

> a fair for the maistrye,

And Chaucer quickly makes this description more specific: the monk is

A 167   A manly man, to been an abbot able.

He has already risen high, though not yet an abbot. He is an outrider (that is, an inspector), and the keeper of a cell (that is, the head of a dependent monastery). Chaucer goes so far as to call him a lord, a title usually given only to abbots and bishops among the clergy. In short, our monk is no common soldier in the ranks. He has made good (to use a bit of modern business slang) and has risen almost to the top. His success goes to show that he has chosen the right career for himself. He is by no means a misfit; on the contrary, he is a perfect fit.

The perfection of his fit comes out in another way. He is happy in his profession. He enjoys being a monk. If he were a misfit he could hardly get such satisfaction out of monastic life. His way of being a monk was not the old-fashioned way, one must admit, but

A 175   This ilke monk leet olde thinges pace,
         And held after the newe world the space.

He saw no reason to stick to his cloister and follow the dull routine of prayer, study, fasting, and manual labor fixed by the old rule:

A 184   What sholde he studie, and make himselven wood,
        Upon a book in cloistre alwey to poure,
        Or swinken with his handes, and laboure,
        As Austin bit? How shal the world be served?
        Lat Austin have his swink to him reserved.

And in fact the monk did no swinking. Instead, he went hunting, and he gratified his taste for fine clothes, choice food, blooded horses, and the like. In sum, he lived like a lord (or perhaps it would be better, these days, to say he lived as lords used to live), and the effects of this good living were manifest in his person. As Chaucer puts it,

A 200   He was a lord ful fat and in good point.

The host describes him to much the same effect:

B 3122   I vow to god, thou hast a ful fair skin.
        It is a gentil pasture ther thou goost;
        Thou art nat lyk a penaunt or a goost.
        Upon my feith, thou art som officer,
        Som worthy sexteyn or som celerer,
        For by my fader soule, as to my doom,
        Thou art a maister whan thou art at hoom,
        No povre cloisterer ne no novys,
        But a governour, wyly and wys,
        And therwithal of brawnes and of bones
        A welfaring persone for the nones.

Here is a perfect picture of a successful man, if ever there was one. Be it noted in passing that the monk, when he comes to tell a tale, changes character. The man who scorns to stick his nose in a book turns exceedingly bookish. His story smells strongly of the lamp, and we get not so much as one whiff of the hunting field. Here again Chaucer chooses to be inconsistent.

The monk is worldly but not wicked. The friar is just as worldly as the monk and wicked besides. The difference between them answers to the difference between their orders. The monk represents a religious aristocracy. He lives on the income from inherited wealth, and his style of living, irreligious though it be, has a certain dignity about it, a distinction characteristic of institutions and individuals whose possessions have been in the family for a long time. The rents are not used as the pious givers of the capital endowments intended, but time has dulled the edge of memory and custom has lent a kind of warrant to the misuse of the funds. The monks, like the secular landed proprietors, do not have to work for a living and can devote themselves to activities congenial to their tastes and suited to their capacities. And their inheritance brings with it something more than mere wealth: a measure of sophistication and cultivation which enables them to live graciously as well as pleasantly.

The friar, on the other hand, belongs to a mendicant order, an order which, in theory at least, derives its income not from endowments but from begging. Our friar accordingly spends his working hours currying favor with people who he hopes will give him something. His practice of the mendicant art does not bring him any store of heavenly treasure; certainly he does not have the virtue of humility. But he reaps substantial earthly gains, and the life he leads suits him to perfection. He has mastered the art of begging. It is his profession and he knows all the tricks. To quote,

A 221   Ful swetely herde he confessioun,
         And plesaunt was his absolucioun;
         He was an esy man to yeve penaunce
         Ther as he wiste to han a good pitaunce;
         For unto a povre ordre for to yive
         Is signe that man is wel yshrive.
         For if he yaf, he dorste make avaunt
         He wiste that a man was repentaunt.
         For many a man so hard is of his herte
         He may nat wepe althogh him sore smerte;
         Therfore, in stede of weping and preyeres,
         Men moot yeve silver to the povre freres. . . .

249   And overal, ther as profit sholde aryse,
      Curteys he was, and lowly of servyse;
      Ther nas no man nowher so vertuous.
      He was the beste beggere in his hous;
      For thogh a widwe hadde noght a sho,
      So plesaunt was his *in principio*
      Yet wolde he have a ferthing er he wente.
      His purchas was wel bettre than his rente.

And the friar's powers of persuasion are not restricted to monetary matters. He is an expert seducer of young women, for one thing. He also knows how to get into the good graces of important people. Indeed, he is such a tremendous success in his profession that he has become an important person himself. In Chaucer's words, " he was like a master or a pope." And he associated by preference with other important people, neglecting the work with the poor to which a friar was supposed to devote himself.

The pardoner was the worst of the lot, as his profession was the most contemptible. Chaucer pictures him, too, as a tremendous success, a salesman supremely good at his task because perfectly suited to it. He is the ideal pardoner, if one may speak of ideals in such a connection. He was also admirably equipped with the tools of his trade. His wallet was brim-full of pardons " come from Rome all hot," and he also had a choice collection of relics, among them a pillow-case

A 695   Which that, he seyde, was our lady veyl.
      He seyde he hadde a gobet of the seyl
      That seynt Peter hadde, whan that he wente
      Upon the see, til Jesu Crist him hente.
      He hadde a croys of latoun, ful of stones,
      And in a glas he hadde pigges bones.
      But with thise relikes, whan that he fond
      A povre person dwelling upon lond,
      Upon a day he gat him more moneye
      Than that the person gat in monthes tweye.

> And thus, with feyned flaterye and japes,
> He made the person and the peple his apes.
> But trewely to tellen, atte laste,
> He was in chirche a noble ecclesiaste.
> Wel coude he rede a lessoun or a storie,
> But alderbest he song an offertorie,
> For wel he wiste, whan that song was songe,
> He moste preche, and wel affyle his tonge,
> To winne silver, as he ful wel coude;
> Therfore he song so meriely and loude.

Chaucer's own characterization of the pardoner in the general prolog is supplemented by an extraordinarily frank and elaborate piece of self-characterization, the prolog of the pardoner's tale. By putting this devastating description in the pardoner's own mouth Chaucer gains an effect dramatic in the extreme, though at the expense of verisimilitude. Kittredge, it is true, denies that there is any sacrifice of verisimilitude here. In the last of his Johns Hopkins lectures he argues that the pardoner

is simply forestalling the reflections of his fellow-pilgrims. " I know I am a rascal," he says in effect, " and you know it; and I wish to show you that I know you know it." Like many another of us poor mortals, the Pardoner is willing to pass for a knave, but objects to being taken for a fool. To deceive mankind is his business, but this time no deception is possible, and he scorns the role of the futile hypocrite. [p. 214].

This argument does not lack ingenuity, but it has a modern ring. The truth of the matter is, Chaucer does not much concern himself with verisimilitude as we understand the term. He makes no serious effort to be true to life, when he characterizes his pilgrims. One and all, they are too good to be true. Such remarkable specimens of humanity as they are simply cannot be found in actual life. Chaucer's pilgrims belong to literature, and in presenting them Chaucer follows the conventions of literature, the conventions of his own day.

One of these conventions is that of self-characterization. This particular convention goes back to the very beginnings of English literature. We find it in *Beowulf,* for instance. In later times it belonged especially to the drama. By way of illustration I may mention Belial's characterization of himself in the *Castle of Perseverance.* Such a self-characterization commonly appears as the first speech, or the first important speech, of the character, a speech which serves to make clear to the audience just who the character is and what kind of character he is. Chaucer follows this procedure: when the pardoner takes the center of the stage, in response to the host's request that he tell a tale, he begins by telling the pilgrims about himself. He does a very thorough job of self-description; by the time he has finished his prolog we know him through and through. Of course the readers of the general prolog are well informed about him already, but Chaucer is taking no chances: some may have skipped or missed the earlier passage and some may have forgotten it by this time.

The pardoner's exposure of himself does not stand isolated in the *Canterbury Tales.* Parallel to it is the long and extremely frank prolog of the wife of Bath's tale, where the wife gives us what is perhaps the most elaborate piece of self-characterization in the English language. Another striking case is that of the reeve, which has a quality all its own:

A 3864 So thee'k, quod he, ful wel coude I yow quyte
    With blering of a proud milleres ye,
    If that me liste speke of ribaudye.
    But ik am old, me list not play for age;
    Gras-tyme is doon, my fodder is now forage,
    This whyte top wryteth myne olde yeres,
    Myn herte is also mowled as myne heres,
    But-if I fare as dooth an open-ers;
    That ilke fruit is ever leng the wers,
    Til it be roten in mullok or in stree.

We olde men, I drede, so fare we;
Til we be roten can we nat be rype;
We hoppen ay, whyl that the world wol pype.
For in oure wil ther stiketh ever a nayl,
To have an hoor heed and a grene tayl,
As hath a leek; for thogh our might be goon,
Our wil desireth folie ever in oon,
For whan we may nat doon, than wol we speke.
Yet in our asshen olde is fyr yreke:
Foure gledes han we, whiche I shal devyse,
Avaunting, lying, anger, coveityse;
Thise foure sparkles longen unto elde.
Our olde lemes mowe wel been unwelde,
But wil ne shal nat faillen, that is sooth,
And yet ik have alwey a coltes tooth,
As many a yeer as it is passed henne
Sin that my tappe of lyf bigan to renne.
For sikerly, whan I was bore, anon
Deeth drogh the tappe of lyf and leet it gon;
And ever sith hath so the tappe yronne
Til that almost al empty is the tonne.
The streem of lyf now droppeth on the chimbe;
The sely tonge may wel ringe and chimbe
Of wrecchednesse that passed is ful yore;
With olde folk, save dotage, is namore.

Here what begins as self-characterization turns into a characterization of old people generally. The passage brings these no comfort, but it ends with a metaphor so beautiful that one almost forgets how hideous the picture is meant to be.

We have looked at three representatives of the Church: the monk, the friar, and the pardoner. With them goes the summoner, who though not in holy orders belongs to the Church group, since he is a functionary of the ecclesiastical courts. The summoner is presented as the pardoner's friend and traveling companion, and the association is appropriate, since the two are equally unscrupulous. But Chaucer includes among his pilgrims several others who have devoted themselves to the service of the Church, and four of these are described: the prioress, the parson, the clerk, and the nun's priest. The rest of the present chapter will deal with these four pilgrims.

The prioress is the female counterpart of the monk, but since her worldliness is that of a woman, it takes a shape very different from his. She is interested above all in elegance and refinement of manners, with the royal court as her model. One might describe her as the most ladylike of all ladylike ladies. Chaucer's description of her is the most delicately, daintily humorous passage in the *Canterbury Tales*. He takes her lightly, but he does not do anything so gross as poking open fun at her would be. The name he gives her, Eglentyne, has no religious associations, so far as I know; it goes back to the *chansons de geste*, and fits the lady to perfection.

It is noteworthy that religion hardly enters into Chaucer's description of the prioress. In this respect the description differs radically from what is said about the other pilgrims who follow the religious life. In so far as Chaucer touches on religion at all in his words about the prioress, he gives it a worldly twist. Thus, in the familiar lines,

> A 122 Ful wel she song the service divine,
>   Entuned in hir nose ful semely,

the devotional act has been turned into a performance, with propriety as its central feature. The prolog of the prioress's *tale*, however, is devotional enough. One is reminded of the contrast between the monk of the general prolog, scornful of books, and the monk who, in the prolog of his tale, defines tragedy with the utmost learning.

But if Chaucer in describing the prioress says nothing about her religious feeling he does make much of her tenderheartedness, or *conscience*, as he calls it:

A 142   But, for to speken of hir conscience,
        She was so charitable and so pitous,
        She wolde wepe if that she sawe a mous
        Caught in a trappe, if it were deed or bledde.
        Of smale houndes had she, that she fedde
        With rosted flesh, or milk and wastel-breed,
        But sore weep she if oon of hem were deed
        Or if men smoot it with a yerde smerte;
        And al was conscience and tendre herte.

Here the superlative quality which we find in all Chaucer's pilgrims is beautifully exemplified. The prioress is not only tenderhearted; she carries this tenderness of feeling to its uttermost limits when she weeps at the sight of a dead mouse in a trap. One is inevitably reminded of eighteenth-century sentimentalism. Kittredge, in his fifth Johns Hopkins lecture, links the tenderheartedness of the prioress with frustration. He says (p. 178),

What can the prioress know of a mother's feelings? Everything, though she is never to have children, having chosen, so she thought, the better part. But her heart goes out, in yearnings which she does not comprehend or try to analyze, to little dogs, and little boys at school. Nowhere is the poignant trait of thwarted motherhood so affecting as in this character of the prioress.

No doubt this is an excellent piece of modern psychological analysis, though one finds it rather risky to put back into the fourteenth century such an interpretation of the nun's behavior. But Kittredge goes even further. He says of the prioress, " Her little dogs went with her on the journey, and she watched over them with anxious affection " (p. 177). But there is no statement to that effect in the text, and in the absence of such a statement we have no right to presume that the puppies as well as their mistress took part in the pilgrimage. The prioress exists as a character of fiction only, and her actions should be strictly confined to those recorded in the text; they should not be augmented by hypothetical biographical details.

The nun's priest is not described in the general prolog, but the host, when he calls upon him to tell a tale, gives us a brief description of him:

> B 4000   Com neer, thou preest, com hider, thou sir John,
>   Tel us swich thing as may our hertes glade,
>   Be blythe, though thou ryde upon a jade.
>   What though thyn hors be bothe foul and lene,
>   If he wol serve thee, rekke nat a bene;
>   Look that thyn herte be mery evermo.

Here the host, with his usual impudence, brings out the fact that the nun's priest has a miserably poor mount, and this is only another way of saying that the priest has no great store of this world's goods. Evidently, however, sir John takes his poverty in good part:

>   Yis, sir, quod he, yis, host, so mote I go,
>   But I be mery, ywis, I wol be blamed.
>   And right anon his tale he hath attamed,
>   And thus he seyde unto us everichon,
>   This swete preest, this goodly man, sir John.

The prolog of the nun's priest's tale thus ends with a single line in which Chaucer himself describes sir John as a sweet-spirited priest and an excellent man. In the epilog of the tale the host adds a little to the picture:

>   See, whiche braunes hath this gentil preest,
>   So greet a nekke and swich a large breest!
>   He loketh as a sperhauk with his yen.
>   Him nedeth nat his colour for to dyen
>   With brasil, ne with grayn of Portingale.
>   Now sire, faire falle yow for youre tale!

From this we learn more about the priest's physique than about his character, but what is said of his character is highly favorable.

The other two clerics, the parson and the clerk, both appear in the general prolog, where they are praised in the highest terms. The parson is presented as an ideal parish priest; the clerk, as an ideal man of learning. The description of the parson begins thus (A 477 ff.) :

> A good man was ther of religioun,
> And was a povre persoun of a town,
> But riche he was of holy thoughte and werk.
> He was also a lerned man, a clerk,
> That Cristes gospel trewely wolde preche;
> His parisshens devoutly wolde he teche.

It will be noted that the ideal includes learning as well as poverty, piety, and devotion to duty. Other notable features of the description are its length (no less than 52 lines) and its consistently serious tone. The clerk, on the other hand, is disposed of in 24 lines, livened with touches of humor. The description of the clerk begins as follows (A 285 ff.) :

> A clerk ther was of Oxenford also,
> That unto logik hadde long ygo.
> As lene was his hors as is a rake,
> And he was nat right fat, I undertake,
> But loked holwe, and therto soberly.
> Ful thredbar was his overest courtepy,
> For he had geten him yet no benefyce,
> Ne was so worldly for to have offyce.
> For him was lever have at his beddes heed
> Twenty bokes, clad in blak and reed,
> Of Aristotle and his philosophye,
> Than robes riche or fithele or gay sautrye.

His poverty, like that of the nun's priest, is marked by the leanness of his horse, but for the clerk Chaucer is not content with this touch; he goes on to speak of the hollow look and the threadbare coat of the man of learning, features particularly appropriate in one who had devoted himself to scholarship and the academic life.

It is a matter of no little interest that Chaucer's good

clerics, truly religious men, are all poor, whereas the bad clerics, and the worldlings, all live in comfort or even in luxury. Chaucer seems to have taken poverty for an outward sign of holiness. The loathly lady in the wife of Bath's tale, be it noted, points out to her husband that

D 1178   The hye god, on whom that we bileve,
              In wilful povert chees to live his lyf.

The man of law, however, in the prolog of his tale, pictures poverty as an unmitigated evil. One could hardly imagine him choosing to be poor, but then he was a man of law, not a man of God. For the creature comforts, pets, fine clothes, gold ornaments and the like of the two world-lings (the monk and the prioress) there is less excuse, since they had taken the vow of poverty, but one might plead that technically speaking they had not broken this vow, since, in theory at least, they had no possessions, though the orders to which they belonged were wealthy enough to provide them with luxuries as well as the necessities of life. Moreover, Chaucer does not accuse the worldlings of avarice, and he treats their worldliness with a kind of amused tolerance. The friar and the pardoner belong to a very different category, that of wicked, vicious clerics. They make money hand over fist, by fraud, deceit, and trickery of the basest and most despicable kind. For them there is no excuse, no saving grace. Their gains are ill gotten indeed.

CHAPTER X

THE CANTERBURY PILGRIMS (CONTINUED)

IN MY STUDY of the *Canterbury Tales* I have proceeded throughout on the presumption that Chaucer's pilgrims are fictitious, that they owe their existence to the workings of a great poet's imagination, and that they have no reality apart from the poem in which they appear. Modern researches into the background of Chaucer's life and writings, however, have unearthed various persons of flesh and blood who can be connected, more or less plausibly, with specific pilgrims in Chaucer's poem, and such connections have actually been made, notably by my revered master, the late John M. Manly, in his Lowell Institute lectures of 1924, later published in book form under the title *Some New Light on Chaucer*. What of these connections, and what bearing have they on our study of Chaucer's art? It will be convenient to approach this problem by a look at the host, a pilgrim who almost certainly had a counterpart in real life.

Chaucer gives the host special treatment in various ways which we need not go into here. For one thing, he tells us his full name. We have no such information about anybody else on the pilgrimage, apart from Chaucer himself. In the course of the narrative we learn the Christian names of eight other pilgrims, it is true. In the descriptions of the general prolog two such names are given: the prioress is called Eglentyne; the friar, Hubert. Later on, six other names appear: the miller is called Robin; the reeve, Oswald; the cook, Roger or Hodge; the monk, Piers; the nun's priest, John; and the wife of Bath, Alison or Alice. The remaining pilgrims go without names altogether; they are referred to exclusively as the knight, the squire, the man of law, and so on. The host's name, Harry Bailly, comes out in his quarrel with the cook; elsewhere he is called simply the host.

Now the records of the time show that there *was* an innkeeper of Southwark named Henry Bailly or Baillif. They do not tell us the name of the inn he kept, but the inference that he was the innkeeper of the Tabard seems plausible enough, and is generally made. Manly concludes (*op. cit.*, p. 83) that " the Host of the *Canterbury Tales* was modeled upon " the Henry Bailly that we know of from the historical records.

Even if this conclusion were correct it would not follow that the two Harry Baillies are to be identified. A work of art is one thing; its model in real life, something else again. The strictest of imitations does not reproduce the thing imitated. A copy always differs from its original. (These truisms Manly would of course agree with.) But evidence is wholly wanting that Chaucer's Harry Bailly had anything in common with the Harry Bailly of flesh and blood other than name, habitat, and occupation, three features not without importance but essentially external. Chaucer's characterization of the host reads thus:

A 751 A semely man our hoste was withalle
For to han been a marshal in an halle.
A large man he was, with eyen stepe,
A fairer burgeys is ther noon in Chepe:
Bold of his speche and wys and wel ytaught,
And of manhood him lakkede right naught.
Eek therto he was right a mery man.

The superlative quality which we find in all the pilgrims appears again here, quite as one would expect, though the perfections of the host (as Chaucer is careful to tell us) befit not so much an innkeeper as a marshal. Such a host belongs to literature rather than to life, and in particular such a host belongs to the *Canterbury Tales*, where he fits well enough into the pattern of characterization regularly followed.

Nevertheless one cannot deny the possibility that the Harry Bailly of actual life was himself just such a person, however unlikely this may seem. Have we any evidence of Chaucer's intention in the matter? If he was intent on making a true portrait of a living model, if, as Edith Rickert puts it, he " had the habit of drawing his figures from the life " (*Chaucer's World*, p. 192), he would surely stick to the truth about his model, so far as he could. Now as it happens we know that the Harry Bailly of flesh and blood had a wife named Christian. In Chaucer, however, the host calls his wife not Christian but Godelief. Manly points this out and adds (*op. cit.*, p. 81),

What are we to say? It is possible, but hardly probable, that Godelief was Latinized in the record as Christian or that the English Godelief was used as a sort of bye-form of Christian. It is possible, of course, that the Christian of 1380 had died and that Harry Bailly had taken another wife by the time Chaucer had the Canterbury Tales in hand. And finally it is of course possible that Christian was still living but that Chaucer—although he calls her husband by his right name—preferred, for reasons best known to himself, not to use the right name of the wife.

Manly does not mention another possibility: that Chaucer, in giving to the host's wife the name Godelief, intended to distinguish his Harry Bailly from the Harry Bailly of actual life. But even this does not exhaust the possibilities. It seems to me quite possible that Chaucer did not know the actual Harry Bailly except by name, or that at any rate he did not know him well enough to know what his wife's name was. If so, the picture of the wedded pair, as well as the name of the wife, in the *Canterbury Tales*

becomes essentially fictitious or imaginative, not a repro-
duction of the actual innkeeper of Southwark and his wife.
The passage in which the host's wife is characterized has
a special interest, not only for its own sake but also because
it gives us a clue to Chaucer's choice of a name for the
woman:

B 3079 Whan ended was my tale of Melibee,
         And of Prudence and hir benignitee,
         Our hoste seyde, as I am faithful man,
         And by the precious corpus Madrian,
         I hadde lever than a barel ale
         That Godelief my wyf had herd this tale!
         For she nis nothing of swich patience
         As was this Melibeus wyf Prudence.
         By goddes bones! whan I bete my knaves,
         She bringth me forth the grete clobbed staves,
         And cryeth, slee the dogges everichon,
         And brek hem, bothe bak and every boon.
         And if that any neighebor of myne
         Wol nat in chirche to my wyf enclyne,
         Or be so hardy to hir to trespace,
         Whan she comth hoom she rampeth in my face
         And cryeth, false coward, wrek thy wyf!
         By corpus bones! I wol have thy knyf,
         And thou shalt have my distaf and go spinne!
         Fro day to night right thus she wol beginne:
         Allas! she seith, that ever I was shape
         To wedde a milksop or a coward ape,
         That wol be overlad with every wight!
         Thou darst nat stonden by thy wyves right!
         This is my lyf, but-if that I wol fighte;
         And out at dore anoon I mote me dighte
         Or elles I am but lost, but-if that I
         Be lyk a wilde leoun fool-hardy.
         I woot wel she wol do me slee som day
         Som neighebor, and thanne go my wey.
         For I am perilous with knyf in honde,
         Al be it that I dar nat hir withstonde,
         For she is big in armes, by my feith;

That shal he finde, that hir misdooth or seith.
But lat us passe away fro this matere.

The host is here presented as a hen-pecked husband, a figure of fun, a comic character of ancient vintage, perennially amusing. His wife likewise is a character of broad comedy or farce: domineering, muscular, formidable beyond words, highly irascible, easily affronted, always looking for trouble and always making trouble for her unfortunate spouse. The name she bears, Godelief, that is, good and dear, is grotesquely at variance with her character, and thus adds to the comic or farcical effect.

The host has more to say about his wife in the epilog of the merchant's tale:

E 2426   But doutelees, as trewe as any steel
          I have a wyf, though that she povre be;
          But of hir tonge a labbing shrewe is she,
          And yet she hath an heep of vyces mo;
          Therof no fors, lat alle swiche thinges go.
          But, wite ye what? in conseil be it seyd,
          Me reweth sore I am unto hir teyd.
          For, and I sholde rekenen every vyce
          Which that she hath, ywis, I were to nyce,
          And cause why? it sholde reported be
          And told to hir of somme of this meynee;
          Of whom, it nedeth nat for to declare,
          Sin wommen connen outen swich chaffare;
          And eek my wit suffyseth nat therto
          To tellen al; wherfor my tale is do.

Here the host flatters himself that *his* wife is faithful to him, by way of contrast with the wife in the merchant's tale, who deceives *her* husband grossly. But fidelity seems to be the only virtue which the host's wife has. In this speech the host plays once again the part of the hen-pecked husband. He says he is afraid to make a clean breast of his domestic troubles, for fear some of the female pilgrims may tell his wife about it and bring another

domestic storm down on his devoted head. But he has
another reason for not going on with his sad story. His
wife has so many vices that he can never hope to do
justice to the subject; it would take a wit far greater than
his to carry through so gigantic a task.

It will be seen that the host's wife, even though she is
not one of the pilgrims, is characterized at some length,
and in the usual superlatives. Chaucer puts the characterization in the husband's mouth, presumably for comic
effect. The husband's confidence that his wife is faithful
to him, whatever her faults may be, is doubtless meant to
be funny, coming as it does immediately after May has
convinced January of *her* fidelity in spite of the evidence
of his own eyes. Certainly the rest of the host's speech
about his wife is there to make us laugh. To me it seems
wholly unlikely that Chaucer is giving us a true portrait
of the wife of the actual Harry Bailly. The character of
Godelief comes out of stock; every detail is conventional,
and hoary with age. Godelief is a literary wife, not a wife
of flesh and blood. And she is all the funnier for that.

As with the wife, so with the husband, even though he
has his name in common with an actual innkeeper of
Southwark. The host at every turn shows himself to be
a character of fiction. His salient characteristic in the
frame story is impudence, or " rude speech and bold," as
Chaucer calls it. Such impudence as his belongs to broad
comedy, in which servants habitually insult their masters
and the masters take it with the utmost meekness. No
such impudence befits an innkeeper in real life. The
successful host in a tavern is commonly respectful to
everybody, and particularly so to his betters. But *our*
host plays a comic part, almost from the beginning. He
bullies the pilgrims into taking him for guide and master
of ceremonies; he brooks no opposition; he makes a point
of being rude; he is high-handed at every turn. All this

is meant to be funny. There is no realism about it; it is remote from the actualities of everyday existence.

One example of the host's behavior must suffice. The franklin is much impressed by the squire's tale, and by the personality of the squire, and he says so. He then goes on to speak of his own son, who has been a great disappointment to him:

> F 688   I have my sone snibbed, and yet shal,
> For he to vertu listeth nat entende;
> But for to pleye at dees, and to despende,
> And lese al that he hath, is his usage.
> And he hath lever talken with a page
> Than to comune with any gentil wight
> Ther he mighte lerne gentilesse aright.

At this point the host interrupts the franklin with the utmost rudeness:

> Straw for your gentilesse, quod our host;
> What, frankeleyn? pardee, sir, wel thou wost
> That eche of you mot tellen atte leste
> A tale or two, or breken his beheste.
> That knowe I wel, sir, quod the frankeleyn;
> I preye yow, haveth me nat in desdeyn
> Though to this man I speke a word or two.
> Telle on thy tale withouten wordes mo.
> Gladly, sir host, quod he, I wol obeye
> Unto your wil; now herkneth what I seye.
> I wol yow nat contrarien in no wyse
> As fer as that my wittes wol suffyse;
> I prey to god that it may plesen yow,
> Than woot I wel that it is good ynow.

Here the discourtesy of the host and the humble submission of the franklin are equally obvious and equally untrue to life. Note in particular the host's use of the lordly *thou*, and the franklin's response with the respectful *ye*. On an actual pilgrimage in fourteenth-century England this give and take would have been impossible: no innkeeper would have dreamt of behaving in this way towards a gentleman, and if he did so behave no gentleman would have put up with it. But in literature, and on the stage, the normal relationships of life may be, and often are, turned topsy-turvy for humorous purposes. The technic here used is that of broad comedy, with a deliberate and complete disregard for the realities of social intercourse.

The device which makes it possible for the host to behave as he does is explained in detail in the general prolog. Chaucer's account is humorous from start to finish, the host telling the pilgrims what to do and the pilgrims obeying his orders in comic reversal of the customary relationship between an innkeeper and his guests. The host begins by using a little flattery before bringing forward his proposal:

A 761   Now, lordinges, trewely,
      Ye been to me right welcome hertely:
      For by my trouthe, if that I shal nat lye,
      I ne saugh this yeer so mery a companye
      At ones in this herberwe as is now.
      Fain wolde I doon yow mirthe, wiste I how.

Having opened the way by these words, he makes his proposal, presenting it as an inspiration which has just come to him:

      And of a mirthe I am right now bithought,
      To doon yow ese, and it shal coste noght.
      Ye goon to Caunterbury; god yow spede,
      The blisful martir quyte yow your mede.
      And wel I woot, as ye goon by the weye,
      Ye shapen yow to talen and to pleye;
      For trewely, confort ne mirthe is noon
      To ryde by the weye doumb as a stoon;
      And therfore wol I maken yow disport,
      As I seyde erst, and doon yow som confort.

This is the proposal. You will note that the host does not

say what his scheme is. He merely assures the pilgrims
that it will give them pleasure. And now he asks them to
take a vote on it:

> And if yow lyketh alle, by oon assent,
> Now for to stonden at my jugement,
> And for to werken as I shal yow seye,
> To-morwe, whan ye ryden by the weye,
> Now, by my fader soule, that is deed,
> But ye be merye, I wol yeve yow myn heed.
> Hold up your hond, withouten more speche.

What are they to vote for? Not for any particular scheme,
since no scheme has been laid before them. In effect, they
are asked to sign a blank cheque. They must agree to do
what the host tells them to do. And the agreement must
be unanimous. Moreover, this action must be taken at
once, and without any discussion whatsoever. Such a
proposal seems a bit unreasonable, but the pilgrims accept
it without demur, as they well might on an imaginary
pilgrimage done in comic style, though hardly on a pilgrimage in real life:

> Our counseil was not longe for to seche;
> Us thoughte it was nought worth to make it wys,
> And graunted him withouten more avys,
> And bad him seye his verdit as him leste.

The host now outlines his scheme for keeping the pilgrims
occupied on the way to Canterbury and back:

> A 791   That ech of yow, to shorte with your weye,
> In this viage, shal telle tales tweye,
> To Caunterbury-ward, I mene it so,
> And hom-ward he shal tellen other two,
> Of aventures that whylom han bifalle.
> And whiche of yow that bereth him best of alle,
> That is to seyn, that telleth in this cas
> Tales of best sentence and most solas,
> Shal have a soper at our aller cost

> Here in this place, sitting by this post,
> Whan that we come agayn fro Caunterbury.
> And for to make yow the more mery,
> I wol myselven gladly with yow ryde,
> Right at myn owne cost, and be your gyde.
> And who-so wol my jugement withseye
> Shal paye al that we spenden by the weye.
> And if ye vouche-sauf that it be so,
> Tel me anon, withouten wordes mo,
> And I wol erly shape me therfore.

The scheme is obviously preposterous. Picture in your mind's eye thirty-odd pilgrims on horseback, strung out for a quarter of a mile on the Canterbury road, trying to listen to one of their number who is telling a tale as they ride along. How well could they hear him? Those nearest to the teller of the tale might hear much of it, though even they would miss a good deal. The rest of the pilgrims (by far the greatest number) would hear nothing, or, at most, would hear the speaker's voice without being able to make out the words. But did any of the pilgrims point out this practical difficulty, when the host made his proposal? Not at all; they took it without a murmur. They also accepted the host as their guide and governor, and made no objection to the huge fine which anyone who withstood him was to pay:

> Shal paye al that we spenden by the weye.

In sum, the pilgrims took the host and his nonsensical scheme without hesitation and on his own terms:

> 814 This thing was graunted, and our othes swore
> With ful glad herte, and preyden him also
> That he wolde vouche-sauf for to do so,
> And that he wolde been our governour,
> And of our tales juge and reportour,
> And sette a soper at a certein prys;
> And we wold reuled been at his devys
> In heigh and lowe; and thus, by oon assent,
> We been accorded to his jugement.

Thenceforth the host ruled the company of pilgrims; his word was law, and his decisions prevailed. And he did not hesitate to assert his authority. As Chaucer puts it,

A 3900   He gan to speke as lordly as a king.

This lordliness of his is of course meant to be funny. A lordly innkeeper in the nature of the case is a comic figure.

The idea of putting an innkeeper at the head of the group of pilgrims was one of Chaucer's best inspirations. It gave rise to a long series of amusing incidents in the course of the pilgrimage, incidents which could not have been staged had the knight or one of the other " gentils " been put in command. The further idea of having the host *seize* the leadership was also a very happy one. The host took command in a highly amusing way, rushing the thing through so fast that the pilgrims had no time to consider what they were doing. One might say that the host used a kind of *blitz* technic in taking command. The absurdity of his program makes its adoption by the pilgrims much funnier than the adoption of a sensible program could possibly have been. And throughout the frame story the fun keeps up. The host proves a very fountain of merriment, one of the great comic characters of English literature. Besides, he is the link between the individual tales and the story of the pilgrimage. He makes the wheels go round. Through him a collection of tales becomes a unified work of art. Chaucer did not find such a character ready-made. The host is Chaucer's own creation, a figure of fiction, not a portrait of the actual innkeeper of Southwark.

But one may ask why Chaucer did not provide the host with a more reasonable scheme of story-telling than is the one which we find in the text. I have already tried to answer this question by pointing out that for Chaucer, bent on fun-making as he habitually was, the very absurdity of the program made it the right program, the one which had for him an irresistible appeal. This was the all-important consideration, but two things more may be said with some confidence. First and foremost, as we have already seen, Chaucer was not deeply concerned with plausibility or verisimilitude, whether in plot or in characterization. Secondly, when he decided to use the Canterbury pilgrimage for a frame he committed himself to a short journey and therefore had to use all his time for story-telling. Had the pilgrimage been one to Rome, say, he could have restricted the story-telling to overnight stops on the way, with the rout gathered about the speaker in conventional audience, but this procedure was not possible for a journey that lasted only three days. But what made him choose the Canterbury pilgrimage? Or, more precisely, what made him think of this pilgrimage? One can only guess that he had actually made the Canterbury pilgrimage himself and that his experiences as a pilgrim gave him the idea of using this pilgrimage as a frame. Certainly the Canterbury pilgrimage was deeply rooted in English life and this fact would surely have meant much to a man like Chaucer. But we have clearly got away from our proper subject.

The host is not the only character among the Canterbury pilgrims whose counterpart has been sought in real life. Manly in his third Lowell Institute lecture takes up also the case of the reeve. Certain details in Chaucer's description of the reeve made Manly think

that Chaucer had in mind a definite person. One was the statement that the Reeve came from Norfolk, beside a town called Baldeswelle; the second was the description of his house as situated on a heath and well shaded by green trees; the third was the specific statement that he had had charge of the manor since his lord was twenty years of age (*op. cit.*, p. 85).

Such details undoubtedly have a realistic effect; that is,

they give the illusion of actuality. But the use of realistic
detail is one of the characteristic features of Chaucer's
style, and we need not presume that Chaucer's description
of the reeve is a portrait of an actual reeve who lived on a
heath near Baldeswelle, though one cannot deny the possibility that such a reeve existed and served Chaucer as a
model. Much the same may be said of the other pilgrams
for whom models have been sought in the historical
records.

It will be instructive to examine some of the realistic
passages in Chaucer's descriptions of the pilgrims. I begin
with the knight:

A 73   But for to tellen yow of his array,
        His hors were gode, but he was nat gay.
        Of fustian he wered a gipoun,
        Al bismotered with his habergeoun,
        For he was late ycome from his viage,
        And wente for to doon his pilgrimage.

From this passage we learn a number of details: that the
knight had with him a spare mount; that both his horses
were of good quality; that he had on a coarse tunic decidedly the worse for wear; that his clothes were on the
sober side; and that he was making the pilgrimage in
fulfilment of a vow, after coming back from a campaign
(or journey) safe and sound. The spots on his tunic bear
witness to his campaigns, since they came from the constant rubbing of the tunic against his hauberk. The
description indicates that the knight was rather indifferent
to smartness in personal appearance, a feature of the
characterization which may have been put in for the sake
of contrast with the knight's son, the " embrouded " squire.

The earlier parts of the description of the knight likewise
have realistic details; thus, that he fought thrice in the lists
at Tramissene and slew his foe each time. The catalog of
his campaigns, however, though made up of items each

of which might be thought of as a realistic detail, gives a total effect superlative rather than realistic in kind. Through this catalog Chaucer tries to make us think of the knight as heroic in stature, a fighting-man bigger than life. The like may be said of many other items in the description. The idealization is particularly obvious, of course, in the famous summing up of the knight's character:

> He was a verray parfit gentil knight.

We may say, then, that the description of the knight is made up of two different kinds of statements: on the one hand, statements which sing his praises and make of him a heroic or ideal exemplar of knighthood; on the other hand, statements which give him idiosyncracies or marks of individuality and make him come alive as a character. Some of the items in the text, let me hasten to add, serve both these purposes at once; thus, the statement that he was as meek as a maid in his bearing. But the distinction between the two kinds of statements is important, and worthy of careful and detailed study.

The description of the miller abounds in realistic detail:

A 545   The Miller was a stout carl, for the nones,
        Ful big he was of braun, and eek of bones;
        That proved wel, for overal ther he cam,
        At wrastling he wolde have alwey the ram.
        He was short-sholdred, brood, a thikke knarre,
        Ther nas no dore that he nolde heve of harre,
        Or breke it, at a renning, with his heed.
        His berd as any sowe or fox was reed,
        And therto brood, as though it were a spade.
        Upon the cop right of his nose he hade
        A werte, and theron stood a tuft of heres,
        Reed as the bristles of a sowes eres;
        His nose-thirles blake were and wyde.
        A swerd and bokeler bar he by his syde;
        His mouth as greet was as a greet forneys.

He was a jangler and a goliardeys,
And that was most of sinne and harlotryes.
Wel coude he stelen corn and tollen thryes;
And yet he hadde a thombe of gold, pardee.
A whyt cote and a blew hood wered he.
A baggepype wel coude he blow and sowne,
And therwithal he broghte us out of towne.

Chaucer begins his account of the miller by saying that he was a strong man, very big of brawn and bone, and so good at wrestling that he always took the prize. These details are realistic enough but they also have a superlative quality. This quality is more than maintained as we proceed.

The next talent of the miller which Chaucer mentions has to do with his methods of getting a door open: he would either lift it from its hinges or break it down by butting it with his head. But the miller was a man of varied interests. He cultivated the fine arts: he was fond of telling stories, usually of a shady kind, and he played the bagpipe well. His talents reached their height, however, in his practice of his trade. The miller did well in his trade because he was a superlatively good thief: he knew how to get three times as much as he was entitled to for his services in grinding corn. An ability to overcharge to that extent and get away with it is really phenomenal, and marks a talent for theft not far removed from genius. He did well in his trade for another reason, besides. He had a thumb of gold; that is to say, he was an expert in grinding corn and the meal that came from his mill had just the right degree of fineness. In other words, our miller regularly stole from his customers but he gave them meal of such good quality that he kept them satisfied. Few if any modern millers do as well.

Chaucer also gives us a good idea of what the miller looked like. After telling us at the beginning that he was strong and big, he goes on with a series of particulars: the miller was short-shouldered, broad, thick-set, with a beard as red as a sow or a fox and shaped like a spade. There was a wart right on the tip of the miller's nose, and on the wart stood a tuft of hairs, red as the bristles of a sow's ears. The miller's nostrils were black (that is to say, dirty) and wide. His mouth was as big as a big furnace. Here Chaucer is thinking of the miller with his mouth open. The cavernous recesses thereby revealed are of course red and remind the poet of a huge open furnace with its red flames and live coals. The comparison is extravagant, no doubt, but fits in well with Chaucer's usual superlatives. The miller wore a white coat and a blue hood. He went on the pilgrimage armed with sword and buckler. He also had his bagpipe with him and played it when the pilgrims were leaving Southwark to start their journey to Canterbury. As Chaucer puts it, " he brought us out of town " with the bagpipe.

These details are realistic enough, and give us a vivid picture of the man. The most striking details belong unmistakably to caricature, a feature which fits in beautifully with the exaggeration or extravagance so characteristic of Chaucer's descriptions in general. Taken as a whole, the description emphasizes the grossness and the dynamic force of the miller's personality. But the miller is not meant to be repulsive to us. He is no villain, but a comic character. This function of his comes out clearly in the description, which is marked by lightness of touch throughout. The tone which Chaucer here uses prepares us for the comic scene after the knight has told his tale.

The miller's white coat is a mark of his trade. He wears it on the pilgrimage (something he would never do in real life) because the poet's pattern of description includes clothes appropriate for the pilgrims in their everyday activities. If he had put them in conventional pilgrim garb he would have gained in realism but lost much in variety, and he would have sacrificed an outward sign very useful if not indeed essential to him in making their looks fit their respective occupations or characters. A survey of the descriptions with this point in mind may prove worth while.

The knight wore a " gipoun," that is, a tunic or vest. Soldiers commonly wore this garment under the hauberk, and the knight's tunic had suffered accordingly; it was all besmuttered by constant contact with the coat-of-mail. In other words, the sad state of the tunic marked its wearer as a fighting-man. We are not told, be it noted, that the knight wore a hauberk on the pilgrimage, and we may infer that he did not wear one, since in such case the tunic would not have been visible. The squire wore a short gown with long and wide sleeves, a garment then in the height of fashion for young gentlemen. It was presumably ornamented with elaborate embroidery, for Chaucer describes the squire as " embrouded." The yeoman was clad in coat and hood of green, a mark of his occupation as a forester.

The dress of the prioress is not described but taken for granted; she was presumably in regular monastic garb. We are told that her wimple was in perfect order and that her cloak was very elegant. In the same way, the monk's garb is not described, but we get a couple of characteristic details: the sleeves of his gown were trimmed with fur of the finest quality, and his boots were supple. Of the friar we learn only that his cloak was short and made of double worsted; that is, the cloak was of the best quality. All three of these pilgrims were worldlings, and their worldliness comes out in the description of their clothes.

The merchant was dressed in motley; he wore an imported beaver hat and a pair of boots with handsome and elegant clasps. His clothes were in every way appropriate to his calling and station in life. The clerk wore a coat " full threadbare," indicative of the poverty which became him as a man of learning. The man of law is said to have ridden " but hoomly," that is, in ordinary clothes. Chaucer describes his coat as a woolen garment made of cloth of different shades. He also wore a striped silk belt. The franklin's clothes are not described, but we are told that a silk purse, white as morning milk, hung at his girdle. This purse was an article of luxury and was a very suitable thing for a rich man like the franklin to have, though not at all appropriate for a pilgrimage.

The burgesses were all dressed in the livery of their brotherhood; they wore knives, girdles, and pouches of the best quality, indicative of their ample incomes. The cook's clothes are not described. The shipman wore a short gown of coarse cloth, suitable enough for a man of his station when off duty. The physician was dressed very handsomely, in the garb usual for prosperous members of his profession:

> A 439   In sangwin and in pers he clad was al,
>   Lyned with taffata and with sendal.

The wife of Bath dressed in such a way as to get the most striking effects possible. She wore red stockings, fine new shoes, kerchiefs of the best quality, an attractive wimple, and a hat " as broad as is a buckler or a shield." The kerchiefs she wore to church on Sunday weighed no less than ten pounds, but we are not told that she wore so elaborate a kerchief as that on the pilgrimage. She also wore a foot-mantle to shield her clothes against the mud cast by the horses' hoofs as they rode along, and she was equipped with a pair of spurs.

The parson's clothes are not described. His brother the plowman wore a tabard; that is, a loose sleeveless coat then worn by the lower classes. We are not told what the

manciple wore. The reeve had on a long surcoat made of
blue cloth. The summoner's clothes are not mentioned, but
we are told that he had set a huge garland on his head,
presumably in festive spirit. His friend the pardoner wore
a cap; he also had a hood, which he had put away in his
wallet; otherwise nothing is said about his clothes.

In most of these descriptions the clothes contribute to
the characterization. They are played up particularly in
the description of the wife of Bath. In one other description, that of the canon, much depends on the clothes. The
passage reads thus:

> G 554   Whan ended was the lyf of seint Cecyle,
>   Er we had riden fully fyve myle,
>   At Boghton under Blee us gan atake
>   A man, that clothed was in clothes blake,
>   And undernethe he hadde a whyt surplys.
>   His hakeney, that was al pomely grys,
>   So swatte, that it wonder was to see;
>   It semed he had priked myles three. . . .
>   566   A male tweyfold on his croper lay,
>   It semed that he caried lyte aray.
>   Al light for somer rood this worthy man,
>   And in myn herte wondren I began
>   What that he was, til that I understood
>   How that his cloke was sowed to his hood;
>   For which, when I had long avysed me,
>   I demed him som chanon for to be.
>   His hat heng at his bak down by a laas,
>   For he had riden more than trot or paas;
>   He had ay priked lyk as he were wood.
>   A clote-leef he hadde under his hood
>   For swoot, and for to kepe his heed from hete.
>   But it was joye for to seen him swete!

Later on, the host and the canon's yeoman fall into talk,
and the yeoman claims that his master could pave the road
to Canterbury " al of silver and of gold." The host replies,

629 This thing is wonder merveillous to me,
   Sin that thy lord is of so heigh prudence,
   Bycause of which men sholde him reverence,
   That of his worship rekketh he so lyte;
   His oversloppe nis nat worth a myte,
   As in effect, to him, so mote I go!
   It is al baudy and to-tore also.
   Why is thy lord so sluttish, I thee preye,
   And is of power better cloth to beye,
   If that his deed accorde with thy speche?
   Telle me that, and that I thee biseche.

Here Chaucer recognizes that the man is a canon by the
fact that his cloak is sowed to his hood, and the host is
skeptical of the yeoman's claims for the canon because he
has noticed that the canon's garment (overslop) is all
dirty and ragged. These and other realistic details makes
the episode of the canon and his yeoman come alive with
a vividness rarely equaled and never surpassed.

Another detail in the description of the miller has to do
with his weapons:

A swerd and bokeler bar he by his syde.

The miller is very much of a civilian, and one would not
expect him to bear weapons, particularly on a pilgrimage.
This item I take to be an element in the characterization.
The miller had an aggressive personality; the sword and
buckler may symbolize this part of his character. But in
Chaucer one does well to be always on the lookout for
humorous effects, and the picture of the miller dressed in
his workaday white coat but armed with sword and buckler
may be intended to make us laugh. In this connection it
is interesting to note that neither the knight nor his son
the squire bears arms on the pilgrimage, though their
servant the yeoman is armed to the teeth: he bears a
sword, a buckler, a dagger, a bow, and a sheaf of arrows.
The yeoman's own weapon is the bow, of course, and

perhaps we are to understand that his other weapons are for the use of his masters in case of need. The only other pilgrims that bear arms are the shipman with his dagger and the reeve with his rusty blade. The hunting-knife of the franklin and the knives of the burgesses are hardly weapons (though they could be used as such) but were taken on the journey for peaceable purposes. We still carry knives in our pockets, though ours are much smaller and less formidable than were those of fourteenth-century pilgrims.

The yeoman not only bore ordinary weapons; he also had with him a silver image of St Christopher for luck. The prioress had a gold brooch, with the Latin motto *Amor vincit omnia* on it; she wore it attached to her rosary. The monk had a gold pin, the head of which made a love-knot. He used the pin to fasten his hood with. None of the other pilgrims are said to have any ornaments or jewelry, not even the wife of Bath. The brass cross which the pardoner owns can hardly be classified as an ornament; it it is rather one of his spurious relics. The prioress's brooch and the monk's pin both serve as outward signs of worldliness.

The descriptions of the general prolog are supplemented, as the story of the pilgrimage proceeds, by other passages of characterization, passages usually put in the mouth of the host. The first of these comes when the pilgrims leave Southwark the morning after they have put themselves in the hands of the host:

A 822   Amorwe, whan that day bigan to springe,
       Up roos our host, and was our aller cok,
       And gadrede us togider, alle in a flok,
       And forth we riden, a litel more than pas,
       Unto the watering of seint Thomas.
       And ther our host bigan his hors areste,
       And seyde, lordings, herkneth, if yow leste.
       Ye woot your forward, and I it yow recorde.

> If evensong and morwesong acorde,
> Lat see now who shal telle the firste tale.
> As ever mote I drinke wyn or ale,
> Whoso be rebel to my jugement
> Shal paye for al that by the weye is spent.
> Now draweth cut, er that we ferrer twinne;
> He which that hath the shortest shal beginne.
> Sir knight, quod he, my maister and my lord,
> Now draweth cut, for that is myn acord.
> Comth neer, quod he, my lady prioresse;
> And ye, sir clerk, lat be your shamfastnesse,
> Ne studieth noght; ley hond to, every man.

The host begins his speech by reminding the pilgrims of
their decision of the night before, and after reasserting his
authority he calls on the pilgrims to draw cut. He then
turns to three particular pilgrims in succession. His words
to the knight are very respectful indeed:

> Sir knight, quod he, my maister and my lord,
> Now draweth cut, for that is myn acord.

He does not fail in respect when it comes to the prioress,
either, though he has less to say:

> Comth neer, quod he, my lady prioresse.

When he addresses the clerk, however, his impudent ways
reassert themselves:

> And ye, sir clerk, lat be your shamfastnesse,
> Ne studieth noght.

This speech serves, of course, to characterize not only the
speaker but also the person spoken to. Chaucer himself
in his description of the clerk had said,

> Of studie took he most cure and most hede.
> Noght o word spak he more than was nede.

That is one way of looking at it. The host gives us a
different point of view. He explains the clerk's seriousness

and silence as bashfulness and absence of mind. We get the same characterization when the host calls on the clerk for a tale:

E 1 Sir clerk of Oxenford, our hoste seyde,
   Ye ryde as coy and stille as doth a mayde,
   Were newe spoused, sitting at the bord;
   This day ne herde I of your tonge a word.
   I trowe ye studie aboute som sophyme,
   But Salomon seith, every thing hath tyme.
   For goddes sake, as beth of bettre chere,
   It is no tyme for to studien here.

But the host has other reservations about the clerk. He fears that the man of learning will be dull, or severe, or hard to understand:

   Telle us som mery tale, by your fey;
   For what man that is entred in a play
   He nedes moot unto the pley assente.
   But precheth nat, as freres doon in Lente,
   To make us for our olde sinnes wepe,
   Ne that thy tale make us nat to slepe.
   Telle us som mery thing of aventures.
   Your termes, your colours, and your figures,
   Kepe hem in stoor til so be ye endyte
   Heigh style, as whan that men to kinges wryte.
   Speketh so pleyn at this tyme, I yow preye,
   That we may understonde what ye seye.

The host's words to the clerk, as to many others, need not be taken too seriously. His explanations and characterizations are meant to be funny. Not that there is no truth in what he says; but he exaggerates (that is, Chaucer has him exaggerate) to amuse the reader. Thus, the comparison of the clerk to a modest young bride, overcome with shame and not able to say a word, is there to make us laugh, not to make us believe that the man of learning actually behaves like a bride, or that his silence is really due to shyness or bashfulness. The host is baiting the clerk.

in a mild way, when he accuses him of *shamfastnesse*. He does not use such tactics, of course, with everybody. His respectful attitude toward the knight is more than matched by his elaborate courtesy when he calls on the prioress to tell a tale:

B 1637   My lady prioresse, by your leve,
         So that I wiste I sholde yow nat greve,
         I wolde demen that ye tellen sholde
         A tale next, if so were that ye wolde.
         Now wol ye vouche-sauf, my lady dere?

Nobody can be more polite than the host when Chaucer wants him to be. It is well enough for him to poke fun at the clerk but not at the prioress; that would be going too far, and Chaucer usually knows very well indeed when to jest and when to be serious.

CHAPTER XI

THE CANTERBURY PILGRIMS (CONCLUDED)

THE *CANTERBURY TALES*, as the name implies, is
a collection of tales, held together by a frame story,
the story of a pilgrimage to Canterbury during which
various pilgrims tell tales for the edification and entertainment of the company. The frame story takes 3180
lines, somewhat less than a sixth of the whole. This
figure includes the 858 lines of the general prolog and the
828 lines of the wife of Bath's prolog. These two prologs,
taken together, make more than half the frame story.
Both of them, though including a certain amount of
narration, are chiefly concerned with other matters. The
general prolog gives us descriptions of individual pilgrims,
and the wife of Bath's prolog is primarily a piece of self-
characterization, the most famous and most elaborate
example of this device to be found in the *Canterbury Tales*.

It is the contention of some scholars that the tales which
the pilgrims tell are also examples of self-characterization,
in that the personality and point of view of a given
narrator come out in his choice of a tale and in the way
he tells the tale of his choice. Kittredge in his fifth Johns
Hopkins lecture formulated this theory in the following
dictum (*Chaucer and his Poetry*, p. 155):

Structurally regarded, the stories are merely long speeches expressing,
directly or indirectly, the characters of the several persons. They are
more or less comparable, in this regard, to the soliloquies of Hamlet
or Iago or Macbeth. But they are not mere monologues, for each is
addressed to all the other personages, and evokes reply and comment,
being thus, in a real sense, a part of the conversation.

210

If this dictum is right, it follows that the stories in the Canterbury collection are not there for their own sakes, so to speak, but for use in characterizing the persons who tell them. They are a mere device to give us more information about the characters of the frame story, namely, the Canterbury pilgrims. Kittredge accepts this consequence of his dictum when he says, " the Pilgrims do not exist for the sake of the stories, but *vice versa* " (p. 155) .

If this was actually Chaucer's intention, one can only say that he failed to carry it out. Very few of the tales in the collection have much value for the characterization of their tellers. Chaucer shows, it is true, a due sense of propriety in assigning tales to pilgrims; thus, the gentry tell stories befitting their social respectability, and the smutty stories are put in the mouth of the common herd. But it would be a great mistake to interpret a given story as serving primarily to characterize its teller as an individual. Indeed, some of the tales seem quite unsuitable to their tellers as we find them described in the general prolog. In the following pages I will take up the various tales in terms of their function as pieces of self-characterization, beginning with the only tale in the collection which the author expressly marks as such: the pardoner's tale.

The pardoner's tale not only befits the teller but also makes an integral part of his characterization of himself. The integration is clearly marked as such in the text itself, and one can be in no possible doubt of the author's intentions. The doctor of physic has just told the sad story of Virginius and Virginia, and the host, at the end of his comments on teller and tale, complains that the fate of poor Virginia has almost broken his heart. He considers three remedies for his heartburn, or *cardiacle*, as he calls it: a dose of medicine, a draft of ale, and a merry story. He chooses the third of these remedies and calls on the pardoner to administer it:

C 318   Thou bel amy, thou pardoner, he seyde,
         Tel us som mirthe or japes right anon.
         It shal be doon, quod he, by seint Ronyon.
         But first, quod he, heer at this ale-stake
         I wol both drinke and eten of a cake.
         But right anon thise gentils gonne to crye,
         Nay, lat him telle us of no ribaudye;
         Tel us som moral thing, that we may lere
         Som wit, and thanne wol we gladly here.
         I graunt, ywis, quod he, but I mot thinke
         Upon som honest thing whyl that I drinke.

The pardoner is perfectly willing to tell a merry tale, but
the gentils of the company object, because they fear that
his mirth will be ribaldry. They ask for a moral tale
instead. The host says nothing; in other words, Chaucer,
having got a comic effect with the host's heartburn and the
remedies proposed for it, has no further use for the device
and drops it, and the host with it.

As for the pardoner, he yields. " All right," he says,
" but surely I may be allowed to think of something proper
while I drink." When he begins, he prefaces his tale with
the long piece of self-characterization which I discussed
in Chapter IX above. He ends this preface or prolog as
follows:

C 454   But herkneth, lordings, in conclusioun:
         Your lyking is that I shal telle a tale;
         Now have I dronke a draughte of corny ale,
         By god, I hope I shal yow telle a thing
         That shal, by resoun, been at your lyking.
         For though myself be a ful vicious man
         A moral tale yet I yow telle can,
         Which I am wont to preche, for to winne.
         Now hold your pees, my tale I wol beginne.

Next comes the tale, a sermon which, as the pardoner has
been careful to explain beforehand, he is " wont to preach,
for to win." The sermon ends with its practical applica-

tion: the preacher exhorts his congregation to beware of
the sin of avarice, and, more particularly, to come forward
with their money or other possessions, in return for which
he will absolve them from all their sins:

C 913   I yow assoile, by myn heigh power,
         Yow that wol offre, as clene and eek as clere
         As ye were born; and, lo, sirs, thus I preche.

With the words, " and lo, sirs, thus I preach," the scene
suddenly shifts from the church and its congregation, with
the pardoner in the pulpit, to the Canterbury road and the
company of pilgrims. We are back in the frame story.
And the pardoner's statement that that is how he preaches
marks his tale unmistakably as a picture of him at work,
a demonstration of how he uses his powers to fill his
pockets. Strictly speaking, the tale throws no new light
on the character of the pardoner; we knew what his
methods were already. But a demonstration brings things
home to us as nothing else can do. The sermon, one of
the most powerful in all the range of English literature,
puts us for the time being under the spell of the pardoner,
and we see, as nothing else could make us see, what
manner of man he is and how he preaches for to win.

One other Canterbury pilgrim, the parson, preaches a
sermon as his contribution to the *sentence* and *solas* of the
company. It is of course appropriate that a parson for his
tale should choose a sermon, and this particular sermon undoubtedly supports Chaucer's characterization of the parson in the general prolog, confirming as it does Chaucer's
statement that the parish priest is a learned man, a clerk.
The sermon deals with penitence; incorporated into it is
what amounts to another sermon on the seven deadly sins.
For the purposes of this chapter I recently read the
parson's tale from beginning to end at one sitting; my
reading time was three hours and 21 minutes. If the

parson's tale adds anything to Chaucer's characterization of the parson in the general prolog, it does so by revealing that the worthy priest was long-winded.

But it would be a gross error to think of the parson's tale as told primarily to bring out the character of the teller. Here as everywhere we must be guided by our text, and the prime function of the tale is explained in its prolog, explained so clearly that the author's intention cannot be doubtful. The host says,

> I 16   Now lakketh us no tales mo than oon. . . .
> Almost fulfild is al myn ordinaunce;
> I prey to god, so yeve him right good chaunce
> That telleth this tale to us lustily.
> Sir preest, quod he, artow a vicary?
> Or art a person? Sey sooth, by thy fey!
> Be what thou be, ne breke thou nat our pley;
> For every man, save thou, hath told his tale
> Unbokel, and shewe us what is in thy male;
> For trewely, me thinketh, by thy chere,
> Thou sholdest knitte up wel a greet matere. . . .

Chaucer has saved the parson to the last. He is to bring the Tales of Canterbury to an end. And this end must be devotional, pious, edifying rather than entertaining. The parson answers the host accordingly:

> I 31   Thou getest fable noon ytold for me; . . .
> Why sholde I sowen draf out of my fest
> Whan I may sowen whete, if that me lest?
> For which I seye, if that yow list to here
> Moralitee and vertuous matere,
> And thanne that ye wol yeve me audience,
> I wol ful fayn, at Cristes reverence,
> Do yow plesaunce leefful, as I can. . . .
> And therfor, if yow list, I wol nat glose.
> I wol yow telle a mery tale in prose
> To knitte up al this feeste, and make an ende. . . .

All the pilgrims agreed that this was a good way to end the pilgrimage:

I 61 Upon this word we han assented sone,
For, as us semed, it was for to done,
To enden in som vertuous sentence,
And for to yeve him space and audience;
And bede our host he sholde to him seye
That alle we to telle his tale him preye.

This action of theirs, otherwise unexampled in the story
of the pilgrimage, has the artistic function of emphasizing
the chief feature of the concluding tale of the collection:
its *vertuous sentence*. Chaucer brings the action about by
having the priest snub the host rather sharply [1] and then
turn to the company as a whole, saying that he would
consent to speak of " morality and virtuous matter " if
they cared to hear such a tale and would listen to what
he had to tell. The host takes all this meekly enough and
does what he is told to do:

Our hoste had the wordes for us alle:
Sir preest, quod he, now faire yow bifalle!
Sey what yow list, and we wol gladly here. . . .

And now the parson tells his tale, to knit up a great matter.
And from a medieval point of view the matter was indeed
knit up well.

From the parson we shift over to the wife of Bath. In
her prolog the wife gives her views on wedded woe and
wedded bliss. Here I will say nothing about the woe, and
not much about the bliss. It will be enough to point out
that the wife and her fifth husband actually achieve
wedded bliss in the end, after the husband duly submits to
her authority. In her tale the wife tells the pilgrims about
another wedded pair who have the same experience. In
this case, however, the husband yields to argument or

---

[1] " Thou wilt get no fable told through me . . ." The host had laid himself open to this rough answer by using the oath " for cokkes bones " (line
29) in addressing the priest. Compare lines B 1165 ff., where a like oath
moved the priest to rebuke the host expressly.

persuasion; in other words, his wife uses methods very different from those of the wife of Bath, though it all comes out the same in the end. Our notions of the wife of Bath are based on the prolog of her tale, naturally and properly enough, for there she characterizes herself expressly and we must believe what she says. When we come to the tale as distinct from its prolog, we get into a different world, the world of Arthurian romance, with a royal court, a knight for hero, and a heroine who proves to be a shape-shifter and miracle-worker from fairyland. Here the wife of Bath is not at home, and if it was Chaucer's intention to have the wife tell a tale as well suited to her as the pardoner's and parson's tales are to them, his choice of a tale for her was not altogether happy. Moreover, that part of the tale most sympathetic to the wife of Bath as we find her in her prolog takes a course strangely at variance with her own practice, as I have already pointed out. The long speech which the loathly lady makes to her husband, the speech which turns him from a rebellious into an obedient mate, is marked by a sweet reasonableness and a gentle persuasiveness alien to the character of our Alice, who reports it indeed, but only as the mouthpiece of the author, not in her own right.

We conclude that Chaucer gave this Arthurian romance to the wife of Bath, not because it was just the tale to bring out her characteristic qualities, but because its theme and particularly its ending could be linked with her views on marriage and her final achievement of wedded bliss. These features of the story kept it from being a complete misfit and enabled Chaucer to end the tale with a passage in the wife's best vein:

> D 1257 And thus they live, unto hir lyves ende,
> In parfit joye; and Jesu Crist us sende
> Housbondes meke, yonge, and fresh abedde,
> And grace t'overbyde hem that we wedde.

And eek I preye Jesu shorte hir lyves
That wol nat be governed by hir wyves;
And olde and angry nigardes of dispence,
God sende hem sone verray pestilence.

Be it noted, however, that this passage, except for the first line and a half, belongs to the frame story, the transition to which is marked by the word " us " (that is to say, women, of whom the wife here makes herself the spokesman) .

Two other passages in the tale likewise give us the full flavor of the wife's personality: the opening passage of 25 lines, in which the wife manages to attack her fellow-pilgrim the friar, who has offended her by his comments on her prolog; and the long passage about the various things that women love most (D 925-982) . One may say that although Chaucer did not fully integrate prolog and tale, he did what he could to make the tale fit the prolog. But this way of putting the matter would hardly do him justice or make clear his actual procedure. For him the tale, not the teller, came first, in spite of Kittredge and his followers. The wife of Bath's tale is told for its own sake. The wife tells it in her own characteristic style wherever this style serves well to bring out points inherent in the narrative or readily added to it. But wherever the economy of the tale as such is best served by a style or tone different from that characteristic of the teller, Chaucer without hesitation, and almost without thought, adopts that style or tone, turning the teller into a mere mouthpiece of the author's. For Chaucer the tale is the thing.

Chaucer seems to have changed his mind about the tale to be given to the wife of Bath. Certainly he wrote the shipman's tale for a woman, and that woman was surely the wife of Bath, since we have no other serious contenders for the honor, and since various things in the tale go well with the wife's prolog. But though the woman of the tale gets the better of her husband, she does so thanks to a rascally monk who gets the better of her, and this fly in her ointment may have moved Chaucer to give the wife of Bath another tale, a tale in which the triumph of womanhood was complete. This done, he gave the wife's old tale to the shipman, but without making the needful revision of the text. No doubt he would have made this revision had he lived to finish his undertaking, but the transfer of this tale from the wife of Bath to the shipman shows clearly enough that for Chaucer the tale was there for its own sake, not for the sake of the teller. In the same way, Chaucer wrote the tale of St Cecilia for a man, but afterwards he assigned it, without revision, to the second nun, if one may go by the rubrics in the manuscripts. Such treatment of a tale cannot be reconciled with the dictum of Kittredge quoted at the beginning of this chapter.

The only other woman on the pilgrimage was the prioress. She told the tale of the little boy who was killed by the Jews because he sang a song in honor of the Virgin as he passed through the Jewish quarter on his way to and from school. Although his throat is cut, the Virgin by a miracle keeps him alive and allows him to sing again and thus to lead his mother to his body. The story belongs to a very large and popular group of tales then current, tales of miracles wrought by the Virgin. Such a tale is very appropriately told by a nun, and, as Kittredge has pointed out, the tenderheartedness of the prioress makes a tale about a child especially suitable for her. On the other hand, this tenderheartedness of hers does not go very well with the story of a murder, much less the murder of an innocent child. A woman who weeps at the sight of a dead mouse is hardly the right person to tell a tale of throat-cutting and torture. Moreover, the devotional quality which marks the prioress's tale is not what one would expect after reading the description of the worldly lady in the general prolog. A courtly tale would be more consistent with Chaucer's characterization of the prioress. But, as I have said before, Chaucer is not deeply concerned with consistency. The story of the little clergeon is told for its own sake, and it is given to the prioress because a nun seems a suitable person to tell it. The earlier characterization of the prioress as a tenderhearted worldling is simply dropped. It is several thousand lines away, and the reader or hearer has probably forgotten it by this time.

Even more drastic is the treatment given to the monk, though Manly surely overstates the case when he says (*New Light*, p. 261),

Chaucer completely threw over the one described in the *Prologue* and substituted for him a gloomy and uninteresting person, who retains nothing of the original brilliant figure except the horse with its jingling bells.

Here Manly overlooks the description of the monk which the host gives when he calls on him to tell a tale, a description wholly consistent with the one in the general prolog. But when the monk himself begins to speak, two characteristics appear which are not found in the earlier passages: loquacity and erudition. First let us look at the evidence for the monk's loquacity:

B 3155 This worthy monk took al in patience,
And seyde, I wol doon al my diligence
As fer as souneth unto honestee
To telle yow a tale, or two, or three.

This readiness to tell " a tale, or two, or three " seems a little too much of a good thing, and one has the feeling that here is a man who likes to talk interminably. Our impression becomes a conviction when we read the next four lines:

> And if yow list to herkne hiderward,
> I wol yow seyn the lyf of seint Edward;
> Or elles first tragedies wol I telle,
> Of whiche I have an hundred in my celle.

The monk does not actually say that he will first tell 100 tragedies and then the life of St Edward; but his words make it evident that he has a very large stock of story and is perfectly willing to give the pilgrims the full benefit of it.

In this passage so much is made of the monk's loquacity that one is surprised when nothing comes of it later on. Most of the seventeen tragedies that the monk actually tells are extremely short, and when the knight stints him he does so because they are tragedies, not because they are long. The host then takes charge and, after performing in his usual impudent way for a while, calls on the monk to tell another story:

> B 3995   Sir, sey somwhat of hunting, I yow preye.

This proposal takes us back to the monk of the general prolog, who, as you will remember, is described as first and foremost a hunting man. And since the host asks the monk to keep on talking, one would expect a second monk's tale. When Chaucer was stinted of his first he told a second; why not the loquacious monk? But no. The monk proves to be not so loquacious after all:

> Nay, quod this monk, I have no lust to pleye;
> Now let another telle, as I have told.

Indeed, the monk is the only pilgrim in the whole story who declines to tell a tale when the host asks him to tell one. We must conclude that Chaucer made the monk loquacious for comic effect and then decided not to have him exhibit his loquacity — a very wise decision, no doubt.

The monk's erudition is another matter. It comes out in the lines I have already quoted, and grows steadily more impressive as the monk's prolog and tale proceed. The worthy prelate, having mentioned the tragedies which he has on file, goes on to define the word *tragedy* for the benefit of the pilgrims, few of whom had ever heard of such a thing before if they were like the host:

B 3163 Tragedie is to seyn a certain storie,
As olde bokes maken us memorie,
Of him that stood in greet prosperitee
And is yfallen out of heigh degree
Into miserie, and endeth wrecchedly.
And they ben versifyed comunly
Of six feet, which men clepe *exametron.*
In prose eek been endyted many oon,
And eek in metre, in many a sondry wyse.
Lo! this declaring oughte enough suffyse.

He follows up this admirable medieval definition with an apology for the order in which he tells his tragedies, an apology strongly reminiscent of Chaucer's apology in lines 743-746 of the general prolog. The tragedies themselves are preceded by an introductory stanza which reads thus:

B 1381 I wol bewayle in maner of tragedie
The harm of hem that stode in heigh degree,
And fillen so that ther nas no remedie
To bringe hem out of hir adversitee;
For certein, whan that fortune list to flee,
Ther may no man the cours of hir withholde;
Lat no man truste on blind prosperitee;
Be war by thise ensamples trewe and olde.

The learned character of this stanza, and of the monk's tale in general, is manifest, and the erudition of the monk stands in sharp opposition to what Chaucer says of him in the general prolog. There is no need to labor the point. Chaucer assigned this tale to the monk because monks are supposed to be learned, and the monk's tale is undoubtedly a suitable one for a monk to tell. But it does not suit at all the hunting man and scorner of books of the general prolog, and its assignment to him nevertheless shows with perfect clarity that the tale is there for its own sake, not as a device for the characterization of its teller.

The tale of the canon's yeoman, on the other hand, is rooted in the teller's own experiences, as servant to an alchemist. The integration is so complete that it has affected the manuscript record, which labels the yeoman's account of his own master, and his story about another alchemical canon, as parts one and two of a single tale. Nevertheless the character of the yeoman remains throughout a matter of incidental interest only. The words put in the yeoman's mouth have for their whole point and purpose the exposure of alchemy for what it is: a fraud and a delusion. Of this tale least of all can one say, with Kittredge, that it exists for the sake of the teller.

The clerk's tale of patient Griselda is one which fits the teller so perfectly that it seems needless to comment on the matter, beyond exclaiming over the inspiration that brought the two together in Chaucer's mind. But the author chose to add to the tale two stanzas and an envoy markedly inconsistent with the character of the clerk as we find him described in the general prolog. The clerk of Chaucer's description is still speaking when, after he has told the tale, he points out the moral lesson to be drawn from it:

E 1142 This storie is seyd, nat for that wyves sholde
     Folwen Grisilde as in humilitee,
     For it were importable, though they wolde;
     But for that every wight, in his degree,
     Sholde be constant in adversitee
     As was Grisilde; therfor Petrark wryteth
     This storie, which with heigh style he endyteth.

     For, sith a womman was so pacient

> Unto a mortal man, wel more us oghte
> Receyven al in gree that god us sent,
> For greet skile is, he preve that he wroghte. . . .

In other words, Griselda represents not the ideal wife but the ideal Christian. Her humility makes her accept her troubles in the faith that God knows best. She is so conscious of her own unworthiness that she takes for true what her husband tells her and does what he says without repining, however much it makes her suffer, and when she learns the truth she takes her new-found happiness not as her just deserts but as something that has come to her by grace:

> E 1093 O tendre, o dere, o yonge children myne,
> Your woful mooder wende stedfastly
> That cruel houndes or som foul vermyne
> Had eten yow; but god, of his mercy,
> And your benigne fader tenderly
> Hath doon yow kept.

Walter does not deserve such praise, of course, but Griselda in her humility looks to others for virtue, not to herself.

The clerk's tale, then, has nothing to say, at bottom, on the subject of marriage. Still less does it deal with the question of whether the husband or the wife should rule. The tale originally ended without any reference whatever to the wife of Bath and her views about marriage. But Chaucer was never the man to resist making fun, and he changed the tale by adding a second ending, an ending meant to be funny. Here it is:

> E 1163 But o word, lordinges, herkneth er I go:
> It were ful hard to finde nowadayes
> In al a toun Grisildes three or two;
> For, if that they were put to swich assayes,
> The gold of hem hath now so bad alayes
> With bras, that thogh the coin be fair at ye,
> It wolde rather breste atwo than plye.

For which heer, for the wyves love of Bathe,
Whos lyf and al hir secte god maytene
In heigh maistrye, and elles were it scathe,
I wol with lusty herte fresshe and grene
Seyn yow a song to glade yow, I wene,
And lat us stinte of ernestful matere—
Herkneth my song, that seith in this manere.

Grisilde is deed, and eek hir pacience,
And bothe atones buried in Itaille;
For which I crye in open audience,
No wedded man so hardy be t'assaille
His wyves pacience, in hope to finde
Grisildes, for in certein he shal faille.

O noble wyves, ful of heigh prudence,
Lat noon humilitee your tonge naille,
Ne lat no clerk have cause or diligence
To wryte of yow a storie of swich mervaille
As of Grisildis pacient and kinde,
Lest Chichevache yow swelwe in hir entraille.

Folweth Ekko, that holdeth no silence,
But evere answereth at the countretaille;
Beth nat bidaffed for your innocence,
But sharply tak on yow the governaille.
Emprinteth wel this lesson in your minde
For comune profit, sith it may availle.

Ye archewyves, stondeth at defence,
Sin ye be stronge as is a greet camaille;
Ne suffreth nat that men yow doon offence.
And sclendre wyves, feble as in bataille,
Beth egre as is a tygre yond in Inde;
Ay clappeth as a mille, I yow consaille.

Ne dreed hem nat, do hem no reverence;
For though thyn housbonde armed be in maille,
The arwes of thy crabbed eloquence
Shal perce his brest and eek his aventaille;
In jalousie I rede eek thow him binde,
And thou shalt make him couch as doth a quaille.

If thou be fair, ther folk been in presence
Shew thou thy visage and thyn apparaille;

> If thou be foul, be free of thy dispence,
> To gete thee freendes ay do thy travaille;
> Be ay of chere as light as leef on linde,
> And lat him care and wepe and wringe and waille.

The brilliance of this new ending is such that nearly all students of the *Canterbury Tales* are swept off their feet. But luckily for our understanding of the tale, the old ending was not canceled. The two endings stand together, and can be compared by anyone who feels so inclined. A little study, I think, is enough to convince any reasonable person that the old ending goes with the tale and belongs to it, whereas the new ending has no real pertinence to the theme of the tale and actually clashes with the effect which the tale as a whole was intended to produce. Moreover, as I have already said, the new ending does not fit the character of the clerk, into whose mouth it is put. In the general prolog the clerk is thus described:

> A 303   Of studie took he most cure and most hede.
> Noght o word spak he more than was nede,
> And that was seyd in forme and reverence,
> And short and quik, and ful of hy sentence.
> Souning in moral vertu was his speche,
> And gladly wolde he lerne, and gladly teche.

There is no trace of *reverence*, of *hy sentence*, or of *moral vertu* in the second ending of the clerk's tale. This ending is Chaucer pure and simple, naked and unashamed. Its rubric in the manuscripts, *Lenvoy de Chaucer*, shows how people felt about it in Chaucer's own day. When Chaucer added the new ending to the tale he showed that fun-making meant more to him than consistency of tone and a unified effect.

The satirical passage on wives which Chaucer added to the clerk's tale leads directly to the prolog of the merchant's tale, the first line of which echoes the last line of the envoy:

E 1213   Weping and wayling, care, and other sorwe
          I know ynogh, on even and amorwe,
          Quod the marchant, and so don othere mo
          That wedded been, I trowe that it be so.
          For, wel I woot, it fareth so with me.
          I have a wyf, the worste that may be;
          For though the feend to hir ycoupled were,
          She wolde him overmacche, I dar wel swere.
          What sholde I yow reherce in special
          Hir hye malice? she is a shrewe at al.
          Ther is a long and large difference
          Bitwix Grisildis grete pacience
          And of my wyf the passing crueltee.
          Were I unbounden, also moot I thee,
          I wolde never eft comen in the snare.
          We wedded men live in sorwe and care;
          Assaye whoso wol, and he shal finde
          I seye sooth, by seint Thomas of Inde,
          As for the more part, I sey nat alle.
          God shilde that it sholde so bifalle!
          A! good sir hoost! I have ywedded be
          Thise monthes two, and more nat, pardee;
          And yet, I trowe, he that al his lyve
          Wyflees hath been, though that men wolde him ryve
          Unto the herte, ne coude in no manere
          Tellen so muchel sorwe as I now here
          Coude tellen of my wyves cursednesse.

The merchant's wedded woes are of course meant to be funny. In general, husbands whose wives are too much for them get no sympathy but become figures of fun. Certainly that is what happens to them in our older literature, however it may be in actual life. For the purposes of this prolog, the merchant loses all the dignity and self-importance ascribed to him in the general prolog; he lays bare to the host and the other pilgrims his most private sorrows with a frankness familiar in stage comedy but less often found in ordinary public gatherings. The conversation of the merchant is described in the general prolog as follows:

His resons he spak ful solempnely,
Souning alway th'encrees of his winning.

How differently he talks in his own prolog! But this very
difference makes his speech funnier than it could otherwise
be. When this distinguished importer and banker, when
this eminent man of business, when this discreet person who
knows how to hold his tongue, when this merchant tells
the pilgrims what an awful wife he has, and what a mistake
he made in getting married, the comic effect is far more
striking than it would be if an ordinary man had so un-
burdened himself. The greater the departure from normal
and proper conduct (that is, from the realities of ordinary
life), the greater the comic effect.

The merchant's prolog is closely parallel to the words of
the host after Chaucer's tale of Melibeus. In both cases a
husband unbosoms himself about his wife, and in both
cases the disclosure is tied to the preceding tale, a tale
which in both cases deals with a wife notable for patience.
The host and the merchant each contrasts his own wife
with the patient and altogether admirable heroine of the
tale that has just been told. In this way an exceedingly
serious and edifying story is followed by a comic passage,
giving an effect which students of the drama call comic
relief.

In the general prolog, the merchant is a dignified and
important person; in his own prolog, he is somebody to be
laughed at; when he tells his tale, he is a savage satirist.
For subject he takes the marriage of old January and
young May and what comes of it, truly a subject fit for
satire, and one to which the merchant does full justice.
Here as always in such stories the husband gets no
sympathy, but the merchant attacks poor January with
a ferocity hard to parallel in such tales. The bitterness and
cynicism of the merchant's tale have no counterparts
elsewhere in Chaucer's writings. It will hardly do, how-

ever, to say that Chaucer used the tale as a device to characterize its teller. Even Kittredge admits that the merchant is " the last man from whom so furious an outburst would be expected " (*op. cit.*, p. 202). Here Kittredge is thinking of the character which Chaucer gives the merchant in the general prolog. If we set this characterization aside and look only at the merchant as he appears in his own prolog, we find him consumed with hatred of his wife, whom he describes as a complete shrew. His tale, to agree with this characterization, ought to center its attack on a shrewish wife. But in the actual tale young May is anything but a shrew and gets off lightly; the merchant concentrates his fire on her dotard of a husband. We conclude that the merchant's tale is told for its own sake, and that the merchant when he tells his tale is speaking, not in character, but as the author's mouthpiece.

Four of the tales are motivated by quarrels among the pilgrims. The miller starts the pattern by getting drunk and telling a story in which a carpenter serves as victim or butt. The reeve, who is a carpenter by trade, takes offense and pays the miller back by telling a tale in which a miller is put to shame. Later on, the friar and the summoner have it out in like manner. The motivation for both quarrels is slight. We have to do with a quarrel *device*, suitable for comic effects, but not meant as serious characterization of the pilgrims who do the quarreling. In broad comedy no true motivation is needed or expected for anything that happens. The flimsiest excuse is enough to set going an uproariously funny series of actions, and no reader or hearer can reasonably ask for more plausibility than the comic conventions require. Likewise, the four stories which the quarrelers tell are not properly taken for four monologs serving as self-characterizations of the respective pilgrims.

The miller and the reeve tell tales dealing with student

life, the miller choosing Oxford, the reeve Cambridge. But Chaucer does not mean to imply that these two churls, as he calls them, the miller and the reeve, were at home in the academic settings which they so admirably recapture in their stories. They serve as the author's mouthpieces, and their status as churls gives him an excuse for putting smutty stories in their mouths. His apology for including such stories is first made in the general prolog and is then repeated in the prolog of the miller's tale:

A 3167   What sholde I more seyn, but this millere
         He nolde his wordes for no man forbere,
         But tolde his cherles tale in his manere.
         M'athinketh that I shal reherce it here.
         For goddes love, demeth nat that I seye
         Of evel entente, but that I moot reherce
         Hir tales alle, be they bettre or werse,
         Or elles falsen som of my matere.
         And therfore, whoso list it nat yhere,
         Turne over the leef, and chese another tale; . . .
         Blameth nat me if that ye chese amis.
         The miller is a cherl, ye knowe wel this;
         So was the reve, and othere many mo,
         And harlotrye they tolden bothe two.
         Avyseth yow and put me out of blame;
         And eek men shal nat make ernest of game.

The last line of this apology is Chaucer's true defense of what he is doing: one must not take entertainment or amusement seriously. The rest of the passage is comedy. When Chaucer said that he was very sorry indeed that he had to tell this smutty story, but in the interests of scientific accuracy he could do no other — when he said that, he did not expect his readers to take him at his word; he expected them to laugh. Again, when Chaucer said the miller was a churl and told a churl's tale (that is, a smutty tale), he did not expect this excuse to be taken at its face value. No doubt churls tell smutty stories, but people of higher rank do too. In fact, Chaucer himself must have liked the smutty stories he included in the *Canterbury Tales*; if he did not like them, why did he include them? The tales which the four quarrelers tell befit them well enough, in some ways, but far from perfectly. Thus, apart from the smut, there is little about the miller's tale particularly characteristic of the miller and there is much not at all characteristic of him. These four tales are all told for their own sakes, not to bring out the characters of their tellers. So far as they have any characterizing function, this function is incidental, a mere by-product of the tale-telling.

The cook's tale gives every indication of befitting the teller exceptionally well, but Chaucer left it unfinished; indeed, he barely began it. The other unfinished tale, that of the squire, goes well enough with the squire's characterization as a lover in the general prolog. The host when he calls on the squire for a tale harks back to this characterization:

> F 1   Squier, com neer, if it your wille be,
>   And sey somwhat of love, for certes, ye
>   Connen theron as muche as any man.

The squire responds with a love story, as requested. It is worthy of note, however, that the squire in the course of his tale disclaims any true knowledge of love. He says,

> F 275   This noble king is set up in his trone,
>   This strange knight is fet to him ful sone,
>   And on the daunce he gooth with Canacee.
>   Heer is the revel and the jolitee
>   That is nat able a dul man to devyse.
>   He moste han knowen love and his servyse,
>   And been a festlich man as fresh as May,
>   That sholde yow devysen swich array.
>   Who coude telle yow the forme of daunces,
>   So uncouthe and so freshe countenaunces,

Swich subtil loking and dissimulinges
For drede of jalous mens aperceivinges?
No man but Launcelot, and he is deed.
Therfor I passe of al this lustiheed.

Here the squire calls himself a dull man, ignorant of love and love's service, in direct contradiction to Chaucer's and to the host's characterization of him. Line 281 in particular gives one pause when compared with line 92 of the general prolog:

He was as fresh as is the month of May.

Can it be that in lines F 279 ff. Chaucer had himself in mind, forgetful of the fact that the young squire is supposed to be telling the tale? If the lines really describe Chaucer, the squire here serves indeed as the author's mouthpiece. Like characterizations of the poet have been assembled in Chapter VI above.

The squire's father, the knight, since he was a great champion of Christendom against pagan foes, might well have told a tale that dealt with one of his campaigns or with the crusades of others. Instead, he too tells a love story, and the action of his story is put in remote pagan times. It seems evident that Chaucer paid little heed to his characterization of the knight when he gave him a tale to tell. On the other hand, a knight would serve admirably as mouthpiece for a tale of chivalry, and this the story of Palamon and Arcite undoubtedly is, in spite of its classical setting. Again, the knight as the ranking member of the company of pilgrims was the logical man to tell the longest and most impressive tale that Chaucer had on hand; namely, the poet's reworking of Boccaccio's *Teseide*. We conclude that the knight was given this particular tale in virtue of his knighthood, his characteristics as an individual playing only a minor part in the selection of a tale for him.

The tales given to the manciple and the physician both have a vague appropriateness, but hardly more. The cunning manciple tells a story dealing with duplicity, and the learned physician draws from learned sources. But if the manciple had told the physician's tale one could still say that he told a story dealing with duplicity, and if the physician had told the manciple's tale one could still speak of his tale as more or less learned in character. One can find no compelling reason for the assignment to these two pilgrims of the particular tales they told.

Four tale-telling pilgrims remain: the nun's priest, the franklin, the man of law, and Chaucer himself. The characterization of the nun's priest is very brief, and restricted to the headlink and endlink of his tale. The tale itself is so very Chaucerian that one is inclined to call the priest Chaucer's deputy and let it go at that. The franklin's tale is very suitable for one of the gentils among the pilgrims, dealing as it does with courtly love, honor, gentility, and a threefold rivalry in generosity. I see no special link with the franklin as an individual, however, and find it reasonable to believe that the tale was given to him because of his station in society. In other words, he serves as the author's mouthpiece, and the tale he tells throws light on his social milieu rather than on his personality.

The case of the man of law makes serious difficulties. When the host calls on him for a story, he replies,

B 39   Hoste, quod he, depardieux ich assente,
        To breke forward is not myn entente.
        Biheste is dette, and I wol holde fayn
        Al my biheste; I can no better seyn.
        For swich lawe as man yeveth another wight,
        He sholde himselven usen it by right;
        Thus wol our text; but natheles certeyn
        I can right now no thrifty tale seyn.

From these words one would conclude that the man of law,

although he recognizes his obligation to tell a story, is
not ready to tell one at the moment. He continues,

> But Chaucer, though he can but lewedly
> On metres and on ryming craftily,
> Hath seyd hem in swich English as he can
> Of olde tyme, as knoweth many a man.

After this one expects the man of law to propose that
Chaucer tell the next tale instead of himself. But actually
this proposal is never made. The man of law goes on,
instead, to give a list of Chaucer's works, and he follows
that up by naming some stories that Chaucer did *not* tell!
He gets back to himself by adding that he too refuses to
tell such stories. This brings him once more to the point,
and he says,

> B 90 But of my tale how shal I doon this day?
> Me were looth be lykned, doutelees,
> To Muses that men clepe Pierides . . .
> But nathelees, I recche noght a bene
> Though I come after him with hawe-bake;
> I speke in prose and lat him rymes make.

On the face of it these lines indicate that Chaucer has just
told a tale in verse and that the man of law is about to
come after him with a tale in prose. Actually Chaucer
does not tell a tale at this point, and the tale that the man
of law tells is in verse. It has been conjectured that
Chaucer when he wrote the man of law's prolog intended
to have him tell the tale of Melibeus. We have no way of
knowing the truth of the matter, but the conjecture seems
plausible. In any case the tale finally assigned to the man
of law, the story of Constance, is a pious legend in no way
connected with the character of the teller as described in
the general prolog. The story is surely told for its own
sake, not as a means of throwing light on the man of law.
  Of all the pilgrims who told tales on the way, only

Chaucer himself now remains. Our text does not provide a set description of him, but we get a few touches here and there. He tells us at the start something of significance about himself:

> A 30   And shortly, whan the sonne was to reste,
> So hadde I spoken with hem everichon
> That I was of hir felawship anon.

We gather that he was a friendly, sociable man. The host, however, gives him another character later on:

> B 1893   He semeth elvish by his contenaunce,
> For unto no wight dooth he daliaunce.

How seriously we are to take this I cannot say, but when Chaucer tells us " My wit is short " (A 746) we may be sure the item is there to raise a laugh, not to give us a piece of serious characterization. See my discussion in Chapter VIII above.

But what of the two tales that Chaucer himself tells? It seems highly unlikely that he put either tale in his own mouth as a device for giving his readers further insight into his personality. On the contrary, both tales are surely there for their value as entertainment (Thopas) or instruction (Melibeus) as the case may be. They throw light, of course, on Chaucer's tastes and interests (as do the other tales of the collection) , but this is a mere by-product, not their point and purpose.

We have come to the end of our survey of tales and tellers. Our conclusion cannot be doubtful. The dictum of Kittredge cannot be maintained. In one case, that of the pardoner, the story, though told primarily for its value as such, also serves as part of the teller's characterization of himself. In no other case does the story have this function, and though a couple of the tales befit their tellers so well that one is tempted to turn them into pieces of indirect self-characterization the temptation must be resisted. It will not do to read medieval works of art in modern terms. More precisely, Chaucer's methods of characterization must be determined by objective study of his text, in the light of the customs that governed story-telling in his day. In the last three chapters of this book I have tried to make such a study. It is obviously incomplete, but I hope the reader will find it of service in his own study of one of the world's greatest story-tellers.

INDEX OF PROPER NAMES AND PILGRIMS